WORTH A DETOUR

NEW ZEALAND'S UNUSUAL ATTRACTIONS AND HIDDEN PLACES

Peter Janssen

Hodder Moa

For Shaun and Fiona.

National Library of New Zealand Cataloguing-in-Publication Data
Janssen, Peter (Peter Leon)
Worth a detour : New Zealand's unusual attractions and hidden places /
by Peter Janssen.
Includes index.
ISBN 978-1-86971-134-4
1. New Zealand–Description and travel. 2. New Zealand Guidebooks.
3. New Zealand–Miscellanea. I. Title.
919.304–dc 22

A Hodder Moa Book
Published in 2008 by Hachette Livre NZ Ltd
4 Whetu Place, Mairangi Bay
Auckland, New Zealand

Reprinted 2010

Typeset by Jazz Graphics, Nelson
Printed by Everbest Printing Co. Ltd, China

Front cover photographs: trees at Slope Point (top), British Car Museum's Morris
Minor Collection (left), Katiki Point lighthouse (centre), Riff Raff statue (right).
Back cover photographs: Elvis Presley Memorial Record Room (top left), Tokoroa's
Talking Poles (bottom left), ruins at Bendigo goldfields (centre), Museum of Fashion
(top right), the Bearded Mining Company (bottom right).

Contents

Acknowledgements

Many thanks to all those people throughout the country who have taken the time to share their experiences, pet projects and passions with me. As always a special thanks to the patient editors, Mike Wagg and Jane Hingston, who fashioned some pretty rough material into a book I hope is worth reading.

Introduction

Over the past few years, while researching a number of guide books, I have travelled just about every road and visited every town and hamlet in New Zealand. While well-known attractions have their appeal (that is why they are well known in the first place) I have enjoyed finding the more offbeat attractions, the quirky places bypassed by most travellers and the eccentric characters that have great stories to tell. Some of the places in the book are well known to locals, but visitors have often never heard of them or are short on time and go straight for the 'must see'. Even our bigger cities have corners and places that remain unexplored by most. This book is a varied collection of the places throughout the country that I think are worth a small detour. There is something for everyone, from the collection of Morris Minors and homemade baking, rural pubs to old time wineries through to empty beaches and hair-raising backcountry roads.

Of course by its very nature a book of this type comes down to personal choice but I trust, through experience, that the choices are good ones. Perpetually nosy, I am more than ready to hear about other places I might have missed.

Peter Janssen
May, 2008

Kaitaia

① Whangarei

⑫

①

Auckland

Coromandel

①

Hamilton

Tauranga

② Whakatane

① ⑤

Rotorua

⑤

③ Taupo

Gisborne

New Plymouth

⑤

④ ①

②

③

Napier

③ Hastings

Wanganui

Palmerston North

② Masterton

① ②

WELLINGTON

NORTH ISLAND

NORTHLAND

NORTHLAND

Far North

◀◀ Gumdiggers Park

Located on an actual gumfield, this park offers a fascinating insight into an industry unique to Northland. Kauri gum had a wide range of uses, including high-quality varnishes, but it was hard won by men working in extremely difficult conditions. The footwear used in the extraction of the gum gave rise to the very Kiwi word 'gumboot', and workers on this field included Dalmatians from the Croatia coast who first arrived in Northland in 1885 and by 1900 numbered nearly 5000. Many of these men worked hard, saved their money and returned to their homeland, while others moved south to Auckland and became particularly influential in the wine, construction, and fishing industries.

This gumfield was based on two extinct kauri forests: the first may have declined owing to climate change 150,000 years ago, while the second is believed to have been subjected to a more severe event such as a tsunami about 45,000 years ago. Information boards and reconstructions detail both the kauri gum industry and life on the gumfield, and the trees in this park are said to be the oldest preserved timber in the world.

In addition to the old gum workings, Gumdiggers Park has a small viewing platform so visitors can look out over the tops of the trees, and also breeds the Northland Green Gecko (*Naultinus grayii*), that can be viewed in the Gecko House.

> 171 Heath Road, signposted from SH1, 25 km north of Kaitaia. Open
> daily 9 a.m. to 5.30 p.m., ph 09 406 7166, www.gumdiggerspark.co.nz;
> entry fee.

◀◀ Henderson Bay and Rarawa Beach

Among the many beautiful and often empty Northland beaches, what makes these two special is that while they are only a couple of kilometres apart, the sand on them is distinctly different. Henderson Bay is a magnificent long sweep of golden sand and with its rolling breakers is very popular with surfers. Just 2 km north, the sand at Rarawa Beach is a vivid white – the difference being the variation in the amount of silica in the sand.

11

The higher silica content at Rarawa and the beaches to the north gives them a dazzling whiteness that on a summer's day will make you reach for the sunnies – the contrast between the glare of the sun and the blue of the ocean is just stunning. If getting away from it all is what you are after, both these beaches fit the bill perfectly. Neither has any facilities, though there is accommodation nearby.

13 km north of Houhora to the Henderson Bay Road turnoff and 15 km to the Rarawa Beach turnoff. From each turnoff, it is 6 km to either beach on an unsealed road.

◀◀ *St Jean Baptiste* Anchor, Far North Regional Museum, Kaitaia

While the voyages of Captain Cook are well documented, what is not so well known is that the French explorer Francis de Surville was exploring New Zealand at the same time. Considering that the country was virtually unknown to Europeans at that time, it seems incredible that at one stage both ships, Cook's *Endeavour* and de Surville's *St Jean Baptiste*, passed within a few kilometres of each other off North Cape in December 1769. At the time, bad weather obscured visibility so neither captain was aware that the other was sailing in the very same waters.

While sheltering in Doubtless Bay, de Surville was forced to cut both his anchors, and these were recovered in 1974 by diver and adventurer Kelly Tarlton. Rusted and a bit the worse for wear, but still impressive, one of these huge anchors is on display here at Kaitaia, while the other is in Te Papa, Wellington.

6 South Road (southern end of the shopping centre), Kaitaia.
Open Monday to Friday 10 a.m. to 4 p.m., weekends 1 p.m. to 4 p.m.,
ph 09 408 1403, www.farnorthmuseum.co.nz; entry fee.

◀◀ St Paul's Rock, Whangaroa Harbour

High above the small harbourside settlement of Whangaroa is an old volcanic plug known as St Paul's Rock. While the upper Whangaroa Harbour is tidal, the harbour towards the entrance is remarkably different, and from the top of this rock the true extent and beauty of Whangaroa is revealed. Bush-clad, the

almost enclosed harbour has fiord-like arms that stretch out to the narrow entrance and beyond to Stephenson/Mahinepua Island. The barren rock is an old pa site and the evidence of middens is everywhere – though why early Maori wanted to lug shellfish all the way up here when they could have eaten them down by the sea is a bit of a puzzle.

The track is a rough uphill climb, and the last section is a rocky scramble to the top, though chain handrails assist in the steepest places. Despite the signs warning of limited parking and turnaround space, there is in fact pretty good parking and easy turning just 50 metres beyond the beginning of the track at the end of the road.

Follow the road to Whangaroa off SH10 north of Kaeo. Take Old Hospital Road to the right, 500 metres past the Marlin Hotel and before the main wharf. The track begins at the top of this road.

Te Werahi Beach, Cape Reinga

In the middle of the summer Cape Reinga can be so packed with visitors that the magnificent scenery is often diminished by the crowds. Yet nearby and only a 45-minute walk away is Te Werahi Beach, where there is every chance you will find yourself alone. This wide sandy beach on the western side of the cape directly faces the wild Tasman Sea and is frequently exposed to strong westerly winds and rolling surf pounding in from the open ocean. In Maori tradition, it is along this coastline that the departing spirits of the dead journey to the underworld domain of Hine-nui-te-Po, the goddess of death. The twisted and gnarled vegetation along the coast represents where spirits have desperately attempted to cling to this life.

It is a wonderful wild place away from it all for the busloads of day trippers dawdling down to the lighthouse. Even better, the track down to the beach winds along spectacular coastal cliffs that drop hundreds of metres to the rocks below, and the salt-laden spray from the pounding waves produces bonsai-like manuka and diminutive pohutukawa.

The track to the beach begins to the left from the Cape Reinga lighthouse car park.

Bay of Islands

◀◀ Central Butchery, Kawakawa

While tourists in their thousands flock to the colourful Hundertwasser toilets in Kawakawa, right across from them is an iconic New Zealand butchery that is jam-packed with every type of meat product imaginable. Opening at 5 a.m., the shop is owned by the indefatigable Ray Taylor, a larger-than-life character who first began working as a butcher in 1960 and has been in this shop for nearly 30 years. He still cuts his meat on an ancient wooden butcher's block. Particularly famous for his smoked bacon and ham (all made on the premises), he also makes his own black puddings, smokes chickens, brings in fresh mussels from the Coromandel, catches and smokes his own fish (including mullet), and produces a tasty steamed hangi!

Ray is happy to hold forth to customers about the superiority of his shop. When a Scottish tourist dared to tell him that the Scots make the best black pudding in the world, Ray's reply was short and to the point: 'Your weather is s---, and so is your black pudding!'. The marvellous array of jerseys covering every spare bit of wall not devoted to what he sells is evidence of his other great love – rugby. Oh, and by the way, he also sells vegetables.

Gillies Street, Kawakawa (the main street), ph 09 404 0026.

◀◀ Collins Brothers Steam Sawmill

When setting up their sawmill in 1981, the Collins brothers, Dave and Mike, were faced with the expense of bringing in a power line from the nearest road. Already fans of steam technology, the brothers took an innovative approach and decided to drive their sawmill by steam. Utilising redundant plant from all around the country, the sawmill uses steam to generate electricity and is one of the very few commercial steam sawmills in the world.

What's more, the mill is self-sufficient in fuel as it generates a huge amount of wood offcuts and this by-product is used to fire the boilers. The old plant used in the mill comes from a variety of sources, including old hospital plant and scrapped vessels. Well worth a visit, the mill is not a museum but a business and is open to visitors during operational hours only.

Inlet Road, Kerikeri, signposted from Kerikeri Road. Open Monday to
Friday 8 a.m. to 4 p.m., closed public holidays, phone 09 407 9707,
www.steamsawmill.co.nz; entry fee.

Kawiti Glow-worm Caves

Located near the historic Kawiti marae, these caves combine history,
glow-worms and limestone formations. The caves were discovered in the
seventeenth century by Roku, the runaway wife of chief Haumoewarangi,
who successfully used them to hide from her husband and his family. Over
200 metres in length, up to 20 metres at their highest point and 12 metres
wide, the caves feature delicate stalactites and stalagmites and clusters of
glow-worms. Set in a limestone valley, they are surrounded by cliffs, boulders,
caverns and rock pillars. The famous fighting chief Kawiti, who held the
British at Ruapekapeka, is an ancestor of this marae. Entrance to the caves is
by guided tour only and includes a short bush walk.

5 km south of Kawakawa and 1 km off the main highway at Waiomio.
Open daily 9 a.m. to 5 p.m., guided tours only, ph 09 404 0583 or
09 404 1256; entry fee.

Hokianga and West Coast

Hokianga Harbour Entrance

Discovered by the legendary explorer Kupe, the full name of the harbour is
Hokianga-nui-a-Kupe, the Place of Kupe's Great Return. Narrow and long,
the harbour is an old drowned valley and winds surprisingly far inland to
Mangamuka Bridge on SH1 and was once an important transport link for
those travelling west to east. Both the north and south head of the Hokianga
Harbour are worth visiting.

On the north head are huge golden sand hills, and after millennia of
exposure to a combination of wind and rain the hard sand has been shaped
into deep gullies, wind-blasted cliffs and intriguing formations. This is a great
place to walk, though be aware that these sand hills are much larger close up
than they appear from a distance and walking on the sand can be a strain,

so don't be too ambitious. Devoid of any vegetation, they are also exposed to harsh winds, so make sure you take plenty of water in hot weather and thick clothing when it's cooler.

A short walk on the south head known as the Arai Te Uru Coastal Walkway meanders through wind-stunted manuka, flax and toetoe and has incredible views north over the giant golden sand hills on the northern shore, and west along the inland waterway of the harbour. Like the north head, the hard sandy soil has been shaped by persistent wind, and below the lookout is a lovely sandy cove, ideal for a swim on a hot day.

But like so many west coast harbours, Hokianga has a treacherous sandbar just offshore from the harbour mouth. Especially dangerous on a southwesterly swell, a pilot service and signal station were established here in 1832 by John Martin, the earliest such service in New Zealand and one which continued to operate until 1951. The signal station is still there, though the flagstaff was commandeered for other uses and now graces the Opononi RSA.

Access to the south head is via Signal Hill Road off SH12, 4 km east of Omapere; and for the north head, Hokianga Express Charters runs a water taxi from Opononi Wharf on the hour depending on demand.

◀◀ Horeke Hotel, Hokianga

One of the country's oldest European settlements, Horeke on the shores of the upper Hokianga Harbour was once a thriving settlement, but today is a quiet backwater bypassed by both progress and tourists. Just along from the Mangungu mission station is 'the Horeke' – not only the oldest pub building in New Zealand, but also one of the country's oldest European buildings. Although much altered over the years, the hip-gabled part of the hotel was in existence in 1833 to supply liquor to the workers at the local shipbuilder's yard, the first commercial shipbuilding operation in New Zealand. This part of the hotel still has pit-sawn kauri floors with some boards still attached by the original hand-made nails.

Horeke boasts several New Zealand firsts. Jackie Marmon, or 'Cannibal Jack', believed to be the first white person to settle in the Hokianga, helped build the hotel, and in 1837 Horeke was the site of New Zealand's first judicial execution when a Maori slave was shot on the small island in the front of the

hotel for his part in the murder of settler Harry Biddle. It was also at Horeke that the colourful Baron Charles de Thierry arrived to set up a personal fiefdom in the Hokianga after having met Hongi Hika in Britain in 1829 and (according to de Thierry) purchasing 40,000 acres from him for the price of 36 axes. In 1840 the hotel was the site of the country's first post office after a petition from the locals convinced Governor Hobson to set up a service between the Bay of Islands and Horeke. Though it had been operating for almost ten years, the Horeke wasn't actually licensed until 1842!

Today, as then, the Horeke Hotel sits right on the water, and with the wharf right out front is still accessible by boat. Only a little bit off the beaten track, at the Horeke the atmosphere is warm and friendly, the food tasty and the beds clean and comfortable, so expend the effort and make the trip.

2118 Horeke Road, Horeke, ph 09 401 9133

◀◀ Mangungu Mission House, Hokianga

Tucked away in the upper reaches of the harbour beyond Rawene is the Mangungu Mission House. Built on a hill with a great view down the harbour, the mission house itself has changed very little from the time it was first built in 1838, though most of the outbuildings have long gone. The house is stylish in its simplicity with a wide verandah running across the front of the building – an ideal spot to survey comings and goings on the harbour below.

The mission still houses the old table on which the third and largest signing of the Treaty of Waitangi took place at Mangungu on 12 February 1840, when a big contingent of Hokianga chiefs assembled to add their marks to the document. The following day, Governor Hobson provided a feast for those attending, quite possibly the first government-sponsored hui in the land.

Motukiore Road, 3 km from Horeke.
Limited summer opening hours, www.historic.org.nz; entry fee.

◀◀ Pouto Ki Rongomaraeroa, Dargaville Museum

Situated on a hill just west of the town with great views over the Northern Wairoa River, this museum is easily recognised by the two masts of the

Rainbow Warrior in front of the main building and holds one of this country's most intriguing and mysterious carvings.

Uncovered during a wild storm on the Kaipara Harbour near Poutu in 1991, a carving named Potou Ki Rongomaraeroa was found by a local woman. Nearly three metres tall, the kauri figure is that of a woman, but bears no resemblance to local carving styles – or for that matter any other Maori carving style. For some this is a clear link to the proposition that New Zealand was occupied much earlier by the mysterious Waitaha people, an ancient Polynesian culture allegedly overwhelmed by the much later immigration of Maori. For others the carving provides a connection to the Ainu people of Northern Japan who also created similar totem poles in the same style and who may have arrived in New Zealand during Chinese voyages of discovery in 1421 lead by Zhou Man.

The Maori section of the museum also holds the largest pre-European waka in the country at 16.2 metres long and carved by stone tools from a single totara trunk.

Harding Park, Mangawhare, Dargaville. Open daily 9 a.m. to 4 p.m., ph 09 439 7555, www.dargavillemuseum.co.nz; entry fee.

◀◀ Pouto Point, Kaipara Harbour

One of the largest harbours in the world, the Kaipara tends to be dismissed as a dirty, shallow expanse of water. With over 3200 km of shoreline and covering an expanse of 500 sq km, the Kaipara was once an important waterway giving access far inland via long tidal rivers and estuaries. Around AD 1350, after first landing at Kawhia, the waka *Tainui* voyaged north and entered Kaipara Harbour, beginning a long settlement of Maori in the area. In 1772 French explorer Marion du Fresne discovered the entrance, but did not enter the harbour, and it wasn't until 1836 that the first ships safely negotiated the bar.

The entrance to the harbour is wild, with constantly shifting sandbars and enormous shifts in water volume with each tide through the narrow entrance. Even with the building of the three-storey wooden lighthouse at Pouto in 1884 the harbour still claimed numerous ships, and at the entrance is an area known as 'the Graveyard', the location of 150 shipwrecks. While kauri was king, the Kaipara flourished, but after the timber was exhausted the harbour began its decline and in 1947 was closed as a port of entry.

Today the best place to experience the best of what the Kaipara has to offer is Pouto. The small seaside settlement is tucked inside the harbour entrance, protected from the worst of the westerly wind, but looking out over the channel near the entrance where the water is surprisingly clean and clear. From here it is possible to drive along the hard sand at low tide (if you know what you're doing) to the entrance itself, but its also a great place to go for a long, long walk in a wild and special place. It is a good 70 km from Dargaville, of which around 20 km is gravel, and facilities are limited (there is a camping ground). But if it's peace and solitude you're looking for, then Pouto is a great place to start.

⟨⟨ Tokatoka Peak

Tokatoka Peak, and its nearby neighbour Maungaraho, are both cores of old volcanoes that erupted millions of years ago and where, over eons, the outer volcanic material has eroded away. Tokatoka's distinctive shape is impossible to miss on the road from Ruawai to Dargaville, and from a distance the peak looks quite difficult to climb. However, the track through regenerating bush is not that hard and takes about 20 minutes one way, though it is rough in patches with a bit of a rocky scramble near the top. However, it is worth the effort as the views from up here are superb. Down below, the languid Wairoa River snakes through the flat landscape as it wends its way to the Kaipara Harbour to the south. To the east the views are inland to rugged bush-clad ranges.

Below the peak, sitting on a bluff alongside the river, is the distinct shape of an old pa site, ideally situated for both protection and to keep an eye on the comings and goings on the waterway. A pilot service also operated below the peak in the nineteenth century, and the pilot would climb the peak to scout the broad river for arriving vessels.

> At Tokatoka Tavern north of Ruawai turn right into Tokatoka Road. The track begins about 1.5 km on the left by the 'Scenic Reserve' sign.

◀◀ Trounson Kauri Park

Trounson Kauri Park is often bypassed in favour of the better known and more accessible Waipoua Forest, but this is a real gem and not at all difficult to get to. This forest remnant was set aside as a reserve by local landowner James Trounson, and now covers over 450 hectares of virgin kauri. The loop walk is through impressive groves of mature kauri with an understorey of nikau, fern and kiekie, and with fewer visitors the forest retains a quiet and primeval feel.

This forest is also a DoC 'mainland island' reserve where intense control of predators has seen a recovery of many species including kiwi and kereru. The walk through the forest is an easy loop that takes around 45 minutes and suits even very small children.

> Trounson Kauri Park can be accessed by a 15-km loop clearly marked off SH12 south of Waipoua.

Whangarei

◀◀ Clapham Clock Museum

With over 1200 clocks on display, this incredible collection is the largest in the southern hemisphere. Begun by local man Archibald Clapham in 1900 and gifted to the city of Whangarei in 1961, the huge variety of clocks includes everything from longcase and cuckoo clocks through to alarm clocks and even wristwatches.

Nineteenth-century clocks make up a significant portion of the collection and many of the clocks were brought to this country by early settlers, including the intriguing 1820 Ballet Clock. Not confined to clocks, the collection also encompasses clockwork devices such as a 200-year-old dulcimer music box. The oldest dated clock is from 1720, although a clock built by a blacksmith is thought to be much older but cannot be accurately dated.

Especially intriguing is the Speaker's Clock. Expressly made for the New Zealand Parliament, this simple clock had just one purpose and it wasn't to tell the time as such. The clock allowed the Speaker of the House to time parliamentary speeches, with one hour being the maximum. Consequently,

only the quarter, half, and three-quarter points were marked, and the clock was controlled by a switch next to the Speaker's chair.

> Town Basin, Whangarei. Open daily 9 a.m. to 5 p.m., ph 09 438 3993, www.claphamsclocks.com; entry fee.

Koanga Gardens

Kay Baxter is a passionate advocate of preserving old varieties of fruit and vegetables in the firm belief that not only does this produce taste better, but it also helps maintain a broad genetic base. Her collection of plants is incredible, as is her willingness to share her knowledge of them. The Koanga Gardens is the outlet for the Koanga Institute, which for the past 20 years has been collecting and saving heritage vegetables and fruit, although today the institute's mission has broadened to include a wide range of eco-friendly initiatives ranging from bee-keeping and bread-making through to New Zealand-made shoes.

Surrounding the shop that sells seeds and plants is a vegetable garden and small orchard open to the public and which varies considerably from season to season. For details of open days and workshops visit the website.

> 4 km north of Kaiwaka on SH1, on the left.
> Open daily 9 a.m. to 5 p.m., ph 09 431 2732, www.koanga.org.nz.

Mt Manaia

This distinctive mountain (460 m) is easily recognised by the numerous volcanic outcrops that define the peak. In Maori legend, the rocky peaks are the figures of the rangatira Manaia, his two daughters and his wife, pursued by the chief from whom Manaia stole his wife, and all turned to stone by Tawhaki, the god of thunder. The views from the top are spectacular in all directions, especially over Whangarei harbour, Bream Head and far to the south.

In the bush near the peak keep an eye out for the rare kaka parrots that you are more likely to hear before you spot them. The track is well formed and takes around two-and-a-half hours return. The historic school at the base of

the mountain was established in 1858 and the pupils were originally taught in Gaelic, a reflection of the strong Scottish background of the early settlers.

> From Whangarei, take Riverside Drive out towards the Whangarei Heads, and the beginning of the track is from the car park of the Mt Manaia Club, 30 km from the city.

Ruapekapeka Pa

Ruapekapeka pa, or the 'bat's nest', was the site of the final battle in the war of the north in 1845. The British, outnumbering the Maori three to one, were confounded by Kawiti's innovative defences. Realising that the traditional fortified pa offered little protection from modern weapons, at Ruapekapeka Kawiti built underground bunkers linked by tunnels, and foxholes to protect the defenders from cannon and musket fire. The pa only fell when the Maori, believing the British would not attack on a Sunday, were caught off guard and forced to abandon it.

The outline of the pa is very clear and complemented by good information boards. The pa site has great views over the surrounding countryside. Note that the car park is a little distance away, and the British position is not to be confused with the actual pa, the entrance of which is marked by a fine carved gateway.

> 35 km north of Whangarei on SH1, turn right at Towai into Ruapekapeka Road. The pa site is 4 km down this road, which is unsealed and narrow in places.

Smugglers Cove

Not just a fanciful name, Smugglers Cove was once a real smugglers' hideout. Imported liquor, then as now, was subject to duties and taxes. Wily Scots settlers, not terribly enthusiastic about paying the duty to Customs at Whangarei, rowed out to ships anchored offshore and smuggled crates of whisky, concealing them in the sand dunes to be recovered later. The ships then sailed on to dock at Whangarei Harbour with a somewhat lighter load.

This beautiful white sandy beach, overhung with pohutukawa, is only accessible via a 20-minute walk from Urquharts Bay – a journey just far enough to keep the beach uncrowded and often empty during the weekdays, even in summer. Overlooking the bay on Busby Head is an ancient pa site, and on the headland on the harbour side are the remains of a defensive gun emplacement built during the Second World War.

> The track to the cove begins at the car park at the very end of Urquharts Bay Road, Whangarei Heads.

Waipu Caves

This cave system, just a short walk from the road, features limestone formations, stalactites and stalagmites, and, deep within, glow-worms.

The larvae of the insect *Arachnocampa luminosa*, or the fungus gnat, glow-worms produce a light that attracts other insects on which they feed. In a particularly clever piece of evolutionary adaptation, the hungrier the larvae, the brighter the light. Not so clever though is that the adult insect has no mouth and doesn't get to eat at all, living only a few days.

A torch is essential as the caves are quite deep and it is necessary to wade through shallow water to see the glow-worms, which are about 100 metres to the left from the entrance.

> 13 km from SH1, clearly signposted at several points between Waipu and Whangarei. The last 5 km of the road is unsealed and narrow.

Whangarei Museum and Heritage Park

This large and rambling museum complex has some real gems and is well worth the 4-km drive out from the city. As well as the Clarke Homestead and the museum, there is a kiwi house, old railway stations, observatory, working vintage machinery, and a bush walk, but two unusual exhibits are as follows:

Oruaiti Chapel

This tiny church lays claims to a number of firsts. At just 6 metres in diameter, it is the smallest church in New Zealand and at most can hold fewer than 20 people. The church was built from a single kauri, and with a thatched roof, which was later replaced by kauri shingles. Built in 1859 and originally located at Oruaiti near Doubtless Bay, the chapel could only be reached by water. Another unusual feature is its octagonal shape, making the cramped internal space even more awkward. The reason behind this design is not known. The chapel's last claim to fame is that it is believed to be the smallest Methodist church in the world.

Woof Woof the Talking Tui

To the right of the museum building is the Native Bird Recovery Centre, where all injured birds, native or not, are cared for and 60 per cent achieve full recovery. As well as having an excellent information display, the centre houses a small aviary of permanently injured birds and this is where Woof Woof lives.

Wedged in a tree after falling from his nest, this tui permanently lost the use of his wings. Tui are well-known mimics, but this bird has a huge repertoire of phrases. While parrots have a parrot accent, Woof Woof's voice is very much a human one, sounding exactly like that of his rescuer Robert Webb. And the name Woof Woof? No one is quite sure where it came from, but in keeping with this bird's personality, it is one he chose for himself. Guaranteed to delight young and old, a visit to meet this bird is worth the trip alone.

4 km from SH1 on SH14 to Dargaville.
Open daily 10 a.m. to 4 p.m., www.whangareimuseum.co.nz,
ph 09 438 9630. The Recovery Centre is staffed by volunteers so has
variable opening hours; double-check on 09 438 1457.

AUCKLAND

North Auckland

◀◀ Dacre Cottage/Okura Bush Walkway

In 1848 retired sea captain Ranulf Dacre purchased the land around Karepiro Bay along the tidal Weiti River. Later, sometime in the early 1850s, his son Henry built a small cottage in the bay that is unusual in both style and construction. The house, consisting of just two rooms, was built of brick, a rare construction material at a time when wood – being both cheap and readily available – was the common choice of building material. The square floor plan and hipped roof also differs from the usual gable roof line and verandah style of most colonial cottages.

Restored in recent years, the cottage is only accessible on foot (or by water) along the attractive Okura Bush Walkway. The walk from Okura is about four hours return and is reasonably easy, though in patches it can be rough and muddy. The track initially passes through a magnificent stand of mature bush including an impressive grove of puriri trees that somehow survived the bush clearances of earlier times and then follows the shore of the Okura River where aquatic birds are common. The cottage is unfortunately closed due to continued vandalism, but the bay is a good spot for a picnic and the beach is swimmable at high tide.

> Drive north from the intersection of East Coast Road and Oteha Valley Road, North Shore. After 4.5 km, turn right into Haigh Access Road and the track begins at the end.

◀◀ The Fizgig, the Navy Museum, Devonport

The naval base at Devonport was established as early as 1841 and this small museum is crammed full of great stuff, and though a little hard to find, is well worth the effort. Just inside the door on the wall is a long fork known as a 'fizgig' and looking much like King Neptune's trident, but with five prongs instead of three. The word derives from fisga, or harpoon, and this fizgig was used to spear salted meat out of a barrel. Traditions die hard in the Navy and fizgigs were standard issue on New Zealand ships until 1956. A wooden rum barrel right next to the fizgig represents another naval tradition to die hard,

Auckland City

◀◀ All Saints Anglican Church, Howick

Today a suburb of Auckland, Howick was once a distant frontier settlement and the largest of the 'Fencible' towns. Fencibles were soldier/settlers encouraged by land grants to occupy areas on the margins of European settlement to protect the fledgling colony. One of Auckland's oldest churches, All Saints was Howick's first European building and held its opening service on 21 November 1847 when the structure consisted of only the walls and rafters with no roof.

Constructed under the instructions of Bishop Selwyn at the cost of £47 3s 9d, the church was designed by notable colonial architect Frederick Thatcher and it is said that the bishop himself helped on the actual building site. The handsome wooden building is enhanced by the stained-glass window presented by Robert McLean and dedicated on 20 December 1891; and a small but sad memorial to the children who died in the scarlet fever epidemic of 1851 can be found on the lych gate.

Corner Selwyn Road and Cook Street, Howick.

◀◀ Avondale Market

In recent years the inner-west suburbs of Auckland have become a melting pot for immigrants from around the world, and this very popular Sunday-morning market reflects, and caters for, the wide diversity of migrant cultures that now make up Auckland City. This is not a market of knick-knacks, but a serious affair where the locals come to do their weekly shopping. While strongly Asian and Polynesian in flavour, both the stallholders and shoppers encompass just about every nationality under the sun, and this is in turn reflected by the exotic food available, from live catfish to an amazing array of Asian vegetables and all at very good prices.

Avondale Racecourse, Ash Street, Avondale. Opens at 6 a.m. and runs through to noon.

《《 The Cocoa Tree, the Winter Gardens, Auckland Domain

Imagine your own chocolate tree. The elegant Winter Gardens comprises two large glasshouses linked by a formal courtyard and ornamental pond. Recently restored, the houses were completed in 1921, though lack of funds delayed the opening of the complex until 1928. The northern 'cool' house contains temperate plants and has a continual and stunning display of flowering plants, while the southern 'hot' house contains tropical varieties. Behind the pool is a deep hole, originally an old quarry and now the site of the Fernery, containing 100 different types of fern.

Incredibly, the 'hot' house contains 2000 specimens including a large cocoa tree, a plant normally found in the tropics. Within this warm environment this is the only cocoa tree in the country to actually produce fruit – though whether the gardeners use the beans to brew their own hot chocolate is not known!

《《 Eden Garden

Hidden away on the eastern side of Mt Eden is Eden Garden. This botanical haven was established in 1964 in a former quarry, and with a lot of hard work dedicated volunteers have transformed the dry barren quarry of scoria into a verdant tropical paradise. Covering over two hectares, plants include palms, camellias, rhododendrons, hibiscus, clivias, bromeliads, fuchsias and an extensive collection of natives. The garden has the largest and broadest collection of camellias in the country, and the rocky environment provides ideal conditions for the subtropical vireya rhododendrons.

> 24 Omana Ave, Epsom (off Mountain Road). Open daily 9 a.m. to
> 4.30 p.m., ph 09 638 8395, www.edengarden.co.nz; entrance fee.

《《 Melanesian Mission

In the heart of busy Mission Bay is one of Auckland's most historic buildings and one that is usually overlooked, for at a glance the simple yet attractive building just doesn't look that old. Founded by the Anglican Bishop of New Zealand George Selwyn, the short-lived Melanesian Mission began life in 1859 with the arrival of 38 Melanesian students on the ship *Southern Cross*

(these islands were at that time part of the bishop's diocese). The purpose of the mission was to train missionaries who would return to their homeland and spread the word of the Lord, though some also received medical and agricultural training.

Despite doing the Lord's work, disaster struck, and after an outbreak of dysentery that killed 14 students the mission at Auckland was closed and shifted to Norfolk Island in 1864. The mission buildings were either dismantled, or fell into disrepair and were demolished. With its volcanic stone walls and shingle roof, only the dining hall remains, now appropriately operating as a restaurant.

44 Tamaki Drive, Mission Bay.

◀◀ Onehunga Blockhouse

As the relationship between Maori and Pakeha deteriorated during the 1850s, a string of 10 protective forts, known as blockhouses, were built from Howick through Panmure, Otahuhu and Onehunga to Blockhouse Bay to protect the southern approaches to the city. Most were made of wood and all have long since disappeared, with the exception of the brick blockhouse built at Onehunga in 1860.

Situated on a strategic high point, then known as Green Hill, the Onehunga Blockhouse has a wide view to the south and across the Manukau, as an attack was considered most likely to come from that direction. However, that attack never eventuated and in the end it was the British who moved south into the Waikato and attacked the Maori. Subsequently the blockhouse was used as the Council Chambers and a school, and today the building is well preserved and a feature of the very pleasant Jellicoe Park. A careful inspection of the brick walls reveals a single vertical brick placed at regular spaces along the exterior. These were originally the loopholes from which the muskets were to be fired.

Two other buildings are now also on the site: Laishley House, built in 1856, was originally situated at 44 Princes Street, Onehunga; and a replica Fencible house, built in 1959, recognises Onehunga as a Fencible settlement.

Jellicoe Park, corner Quadrant Road and Grey Street, Onehunga.

◀◀ Parnell Pool

Originally a tidal swimming pool enclosed by a rock wall, the Parnell Pool is Auckland's only saltwater pool and a popular destination for both the serious swimmer and for family fun. Most patrons would hardly notice the plaque on the wall indicating that the building was awarded a gold medal in 1957 by the New Zealand Institute of Architects. The pool was the work of Serbian-born Tibor Donner, the Auckland City architect, and was refurbished in the 'Lido' style in 1955.

The building is rather plain, but the outstanding feature is the huge, stylish, coloured-glass mosaic that graces the front. Designed by James Turkington, the mosaic is said to be inspired by Donner's visit to Mexico in 1956 as well as by the Matisse painting *The Swimming Pool*. For some unknown reason, the pool is 60 metres long, which doesn't match the usual swimming pool lengths of 25, 33 or 50 metres.

Judges Bay Road, Parnell.

◀◀ Savage Memorial Park

Just where *is* Michael Joseph Savage? Elected in 1935, New Zealand's first Labour government introduced many key aspects of the welfare state and for many decades its leader himself was regarded as the hero of the New Zealand working class. In fact, it was not unusual for a photograph of Savage to hold pride of place above the living-room mantelpiece of many New Zealand homes. At the time of his death in 1940, over 200,000 Aucklanders lined the streets to watch the funeral procession make its way to his burial site on a bluff called Takaparawha above Tamaki Drive. The grand memorial consists of an obelisk, formal gardens and a reflecting pool with an outlook over the city and harbour.

However, the whereabouts of his remains is a mystery. In the room under the obelisk is the original tomb, but recently this was found to be empty. Further investigation has revealed another coffin beneath this tomb. It is not yet known if this in fact contains the remains of Michael Joseph Savage. The question of why he was buried in the coffin below the tomb or whether the body in the coffin even is the remains of New Zealand's most beloved prime minister still awaits an answer.

31

West Auckland

◀◀ Mazuran's Vineyards

Lincoln Road, Henderson was once the stronghold of West Auckland vineyards, but urban sprawl has made the land too expensive to grow grapes and today Mazuran's Vineyards is the lone survivor. Producing mainly sherries and ports from a small vineyard behind the house, Mazuran's is typical of the mainly Croatian (better known as Dalmatian or 'Dally') wineries that flourished in this area from around 1900. George Mazuran arrived from Croatia in 1926, established the winery in 1938, and like most winemakers of the time produced sherries and ports for the unsophisticated New Zealand palate.

Over the years, Mazuran's became best known for its quality port and today has on sale a port for every year since 1942, produced under a label largely unchanged for decades. Mazuran's also claims to be the first New Zealand winery to send wine to an international competition, in 1956. Not resting on yesteryear glory, however, in 2005 Mazuran Port was the only port in the world to take a double gold medal in the prestigious San Francisco International Wine Fair (which included entries from Portugal, the original home of port). A Mazuran Port took home another double gold from San Francisco in 2007. The small shop, once the family garage, is lined with old barrels full of maturing wine and Mazuran's wines are only available from this outlet.

255 Lincoln Road, Henderson. Monday to Saturday 9 a.m. to 6 pm, Sunday 9 a.m. to 5 p.m., ph 09 838 6945, www.mazurans.com.

◀◀ Sapich Brothers Winery, West Auckland

Being confronted by the astounding range of wines from this vineyard is like stepping back in a time machine, but in the very best possible way. Sapich Brothers has an incredible array of fortified wines that have long since disappeared elsewhere: cream sherries, ports of every kind, ginger wine, Blackberry Nip, apricot and cherry brandies, and an especially delicious Old Cream Liqueur that has been matured in totara barrels for no less than 25 years. This winery also produces the infamous Purple Death, a red wine concoction in production since 1966 and which proudly claims on the label:

'an unusual rough-as-guts aperitif that has the distinctive bouquet of horse shit and old tram tickets'. If none of this range is to your taste then the winery also produces more modern-style red and white wines.

Established in 1933 and covering 30 hectares, three generations of the Sapich family, originally from Dalmatia (modern Croatia) currently work at the winery, and in the tradition of old West Auckland it will always be a family member who serves the visitors in their small shop. This is a friendly place, the shop-cum-tasting area is worn and cosy with the atmosphere of an old bar, and you are even welcome here in your gumboots! For those wanting a genuine 'Westie' experience of hospitable Dally winemaking, you can't go past Sapich Brothers.

150 Forrest Hill Road, Henderson. Open Monday to Thursday noon to 6 p.m., Friday and Saturday 10 a.m. to 6 p.m., Sunday 1 p.m. to 4 p.m., ph: 09 814 9902, www.sapich.co.nz.

Waikumete Cemetery

At over 100 hectares, Waikumete is the largest cemetery in New Zealand and has been the main Auckland cemetery since 1908, though it was used for local burials as early as 1886. A vast rolling area of both new and old gravesites, it has some historic sections notable in their own right. Unidentified passengers from the 1979 Air New Zealand Erebus crash are buried in a site near the main entrance marked by a memorial etched with both the names of those buried here and those not recovered from Antarctica. Another memorial, in the form of a granite slab, remembers the Holocaust and is located next to the Hebrew Prayer House. Buried at the base of the memorial is an urn of ashes taken from the Auschwitz concentration camp.

Mausoleums are uncommon in New Zealand cemeteries, but Waikumete contains a large number, mainly for Dalmatian families from West Auckland, including two fine examples belonging to the Corban and Nobilo winemaking dynasties. In marked contrast to these elaborate edifices is the large grave of the victims of influenza who collectively have one granite memorial. During the 1918 influenza epidemic over 1600 people died and the bodies were transported from the city to Waikumete by train for mass burial.

Great North Road, Glen Eden. Gates are opened at 7.30 a.m. and closed at 6 p.m. (winter) and 8.30 p.m. (summer).

◀◀ Whatipu

Standing on the broad windswept sands of the North Head of the Manukau harbour, it is hard to believe that it is less than an hour's drive to downtown Auckland. The rugged, bush-covered volcanic northern shore is markedly different to the barren sand country to the south. The crashing surf of the wild and treacherous Manukau Bar is in direct contrast to the sheltered bays just inside the harbour entrance. On 7 February 1863 the HMS *Orpheus* struck the Manukau Bar while trying to enter the harbour. Of the 259 men aboard only 70 survived, and this is still New Zealand's worst maritime disaster. The small lighthouse on Nine Pin Rock now guides ships safely in.

Whatipu was once the terminal for a tramway that ran along the coast used in the extraction of kauri from the bush inland that was then shipped to Onehunga. Below the cliffs are several large sea caves and a small camping area. Shaped by years of wave action, the caves are now a considerable distance from the sea as the marshy area between the cliffs and the ocean has built up since 1940. The largest of the caves was once used for dances, though sand has now raised its floor level 5 metres. Although substantial, torches are not necessary.

The stark rock Paritutu on the harbour may look easy to climb, but be warned, it is very difficult to get back down again. A popular fishing spot, Whatipu is also the beginning of the Gibbons Track, a six-hour loop walk along the cliff tops and returning along the beach.

> Take the road through Titirangi to Huia on the northern side of the Manukau Harbour and continue along a narrow unsealed road to Whatipu.

South Auckland

◀◀ Awhitu Regional Park

Once easily accessible by boat from Onehunga, today the Awhitu Peninsula on the western side of the Manukau Harbour is a bit of a haul from central Auckland. Nestled on the sheltered eastern side of the peninsula, this attractive park is a lovely combination of natural and human history. At its heart is the nineteenth-century Brook homestead, typical of the comfortable

farm villas of the day and set among fine old trees on a rise above the beach. However, just in front of the homestead is a small, roughly built and very modest cottage that initially housed the family until sufficient money was available to build a more substantial home.

The area is very tidal and is honestly more attractive closer to high tide, though the tidal flats provide an important feeding ground for birds. Within the park are substantial wetlands, home to shy and elusive fernbirds, bitterns and banded rail.

> From Waiuku, drive north along the Awhitu Peninsula to Matakawau, and 2 km past Matakawau turn right into Brook Road to the park.

◀◀ Duders Regional Park

Duders Regional Park occupies the Whakakaiwhara Peninsula and is currently almost entirely farmed with just a few tiny patches of bush remaining. The peninsula has long Maori associations dating back to AD 1300 when the waka *Tainui* anchored at its very end while sheltering from a storm, and is remembered in the place name *Te Tauranga o Tainui*. Whakakaiwhara pa was strategically located at the very tip of the peninsula, and terraces, kumara pits and defensive ditches are still visible today.

The Duder family purchased the land in 1866, and continued to farm it up to 1994 when it was sold to the Auckland Regional Council. The park is not large but the views are marvellous, out over the Firth of Thames, the Gulf islands of Waiheke, Ponui, Browns and Rangitoto, and east to the blue-tinged Coromandel. To get there from the Southern Motorway is a bit tortuous, but it's a great place for a peaceful walk for an hour or two.

> From SH1, travel towards Whitford and on to Maraetai, then follow the coast south to Umupuia Beach. From the southern end of Umupuia turn right into North Road, and the entrance to the park is on the right a short distance down.

Mangere Mountain

While tourists pack the peaks of Mt Eden and One Tree Hill, the largest and least modified of Auckland's volcanoes is a quiet haven. Auckland City is built on a volcanic field scattered with over 50 extinct cones and craters. The newest volcano is the iconic Rangitoto Island, which last erupted less than 400 years ago and is now also extinct. While Auckland's population of over one million doesn't give it much thought, the volcanic system is still very active and a new volcano could pop up anywhere on the isthmus.

At Mangere, the rich volcanic soils sustained a large Maori population in pre-European times, growing kumara and taro, with easy access to seafood in the Manukau Harbour. Maori land boundaries indicated by low stone walls fan out from the base of the mountain, and kumara pits and whare sites are clearly visible inside the crater. Nearby, good examples of lava flows can be seen in Kiwi Esplanade and lava caves in Ambury Park.

The main entrance is at the end of Domain Road off Coronation Road, Mangere Bridge.

Tawhitokino Bay

It is hard to believe that in a city of over one million people this little-known bay on the Firth of Thames coast remains relatively obscure. Safe for swimming in all tides, this long sandy beach is fringed by large spreading pohutukawa trees and has an uninterrupted view of the Coromandel Peninsula across the firth. Possibly the 45-minute walk from the car park to the beach via the equally pretty Tuturau Bay is just enough to put people off, but on a lovely summer's day or a bright clear winter's afternoon this bay is a genuine treat.

From Kawakawa Bay, follow the coast road for 4 km to the car park at Waiti Bay and walk around the rocks and over a headland to the beach.

HAURAKI GULF

◀◀ Great Barrier Island/Aotea

The largest and most distant island of the Gulf, Great Barrier, or Aotea in Maori, is believed to be the original landing point of the first Polynesian explorers, who named the whole country Aotearoa, or land of the long white cloud, as from sea the first indication of land is the long low cloud.

Now considered remote, in early times when travel was by sea, Aotea was readily accessible and has a long history of both Maori and Pakeha occupation. While it is no untouched wilderness, having been ruthlessly stripped of its timber, the island, with a population of around a thousand people, has a relaxed lifestyle, beautiful beaches and some of the best fishing in the country. The western side has several excellent bush-clad harbours, while the east has great beaches. The main settlement is Tryphena in the south of the island (where the ferry terminal is), and while there is no public transport as such on the island, in typical island style getting around is easily arranged. Barrier Airlines, Mountain Air and Island Air all operate flights to the island, and Fullers (two-and-a-half hours one way) and SeaLink (four-and-a-half hours one way) operate regular ferry trips.

Medlands, the closest beach to Tryphena, is a beautiful stretch of white sand and has good surf, while Kaitoke is the longest beach on the island. Two other good beaches are Anawa Bay and, in the north, Whangapoua. At the end of Whangapoua Beach are the graves of some of the 130 souls who lost their lives when the SS *Wairarapa* struck rocks off Miners Head in October 1894.

While patches of kauri remain, the island was heavily logged from 1862 through to 1940 and the use of stringer dams to drive the huge logs down to the sea was common. On the island is the best-preserved kauri dam in the country. Built by George Murray in 1926, the dam is over 9 metres wide and 5 metres high. The walk to the dam takes about one and a half hours off Aotea Road, near Port Fitzroy or it can be added on to the Mt Hobson/Windy Canyon Track making it a full-day tramp.

Mt Hobson/Hirakimata is the highest point on the island at 627 metres and the spectacular walk through Windy Canyon to the summit traverses dramatic outcrops and rocky bluffs, evidence of the volcanic origins of the island. It takes around two hours return to the canyon, and four hours return to the top of the mountain but it is well worth the hike. From the summit the view of the Gulf is exceptional, though be aware that the peak is often shrouded in mist and cloud. The top of the mountain is, oddly enough, also the nesting ground of a rare seabird, the black petrel.

‹‹ Little Barrier Island/Hauturu

One of New Zealand's oldest wildlife reserves, Little Barrier was first protected in 1895, and ever since that time this island has played a pivotal role in the preservation of some of New Zealand's most endangered wildlife. With only a small portion ever cleared, the island is largely virgin bush and is now completely predator-free. The forest contains hard beech, a cooler-climate tree that usually occurs much further south, and the nikau palms are a subspecies with broader leaves than their mainland counterparts.

Rising to 722 metres, Hauturu (meaning 'resting place of the wind') is home to over 300 plant species, birds that are extinct or close to extinction on the mainland (including saddleback, stitchbird, kaka, kakariki, kiwi, black petrel, brown teal and kokako), 14 species of skink, gecko and tuatara, several species of weta, and both species of native bat.

It isn't easy to get to Little Barrier as access is restricted, often booked out well in advance, and landing on the island is by permit only. But it is certainly worth planning ahead and visiting at least once.

> To apply for a permit to visit Little Barrier, phone the Department of
> Conservation Warkworth area office on 09 425 7812.

‹‹ Motuihe

This small inner-Gulf island of only 179 hectares has a particularly colourful history and it is a pity that access to it isn't easier. Long settled by Maori, it was briefly farmed by John Logan Campbell in the early 1840s and then became the quarantine station for Auckland. A small cemetery on the island's northern end contains the graves of those who didn't make it through quarantine.

During the First World War it was a prisoner of war camp for Germans captured in Samoa, which was at the time a German colony. The island's most famous prisoner was the dashing Count Felix von Luckner, who engineered a daring escape in December 1917 and after a long sea chase was finally captured near the Kermadec Islands and imprisoned in Lyttelton Harbour.

A naval training base during the Second World War, some buildings remain from this period, and more recently the island has undergone reforestation and pest clearance for its latest role as a bird sanctuary.

Two fine sandy beaches, one facing west and the other east, together with short walks make this an ideal swimming and picnic spot in any weather. Unfortunately, there is no longer a ferry service to the island and the alternatives are not cheap.

> Reubens Water Taxis provides a service from downtown Auckland to Motuihe Island, freephone 0800 111 161.

COROMANDEL

Brian Boru Hotel

Like Brian Boru, the legendary king who led the Irish to victory over the Vikings at Clontarf in AD 1014, the Brian Boru Hotel has become a local Thames legend. Once Thames boasted 112 hotels, but today only a small handful remains, and even this hotel only narrowly escaped destruction in 1905, when fire was often the demise of many wooden hotels.

The Twohill family ran the hotel for 114 years until 1974, and it is said that the ghost of Florence Twohill, who with her sister Violet were the hotel's publicans in the 1920s, still lingers in the Brian Boru as she can't bear to leave. Built in 1868 by Ned Twohill, the hotel was originally called Reefers Arms, but after honeymooning in the Brian Boru Hotel in Greymouth, he returned to Thames and changed the name of his establishment to Brian Boru. It must have been some honeymoon!

Today it is hard to miss the two-storeyed Brian Boru with its magnificent Victorian facade and grand wraparound wooden verandahs. The main bar along Richmond Street is lined with historic photos of gold mining and timber milling, though a little battle-weary after 140 years of lively drinking. The dining room still has the old kauri floors, panelled walls and original ceilings, as well as a cheery open fire in winter to drive away the chills.

200 Richmond Street, Thames, ph 07 868 6523,
email: brian.boru@xtra.co.nz.

Broken Hills

Gold was first discovered here in 1893 and, as was typical of goldfields, a small town sprang up overnight. In the 1930s the gold ran out and today Broken Hills is a maze of short walks that lead to fascinating collections of ruins. Not far from the car park are the substantial remains of the battery built in 1899 to service the gold workings. Nearby is a small gloomy cave that very effectively served as the local jail – a popular spot for children.

A longer track follows the old water race that supplied the battery and this walk entails ducking through a number of short tunnels. Further up the hill are old mine shafts and the impressive Collins Drive. This tunnel, over 500 metres long, was dug not to find gold, but as a short cut through some particularly steep and difficult terrain. A torch is necessary for the Collins

Drive and there are some great lookout points from this track as well. There is also a great DoC camping ground beside the river.

> Take Morrison Road opposite the Pauanui turn off on SH25 and after 1 km
> turn left into Puketui Road and drive 6 km to the car park just before the
> bridge.

◀◀ Butterfly and Orchid Garden

Over 400 butterflies from 15 to 25 species make their home in this garden of tropical shrubs and flowering plants. A butterfly has a lifespan of only two weeks and the garden has to continually breed up to 1000 replacement butterflies per month. The trick to enjoying the visit is to take your time, move slowly and sit for a while and wait for the butterflies to come to you. The relatively restricted opening hours coincide with the time the butterflies are most active, and the warm tropical temperature of the butterfly house makes a visit here especially appealing in winter.

> 3.5 km north of Thames on SH25.
> Open daily 10 a.m. to 4 p.m. (to 3 p.m. in winter), ph 07 868 8080
> www.butterfly.co.nz; entrance fee.

Coromandel Beaches

For many, Coromandel is epitomised by visions of an azure sea breaking on the sparkling white sand of a lonely beach backed by huge shady pohutukawa. The reality, however, is that Coromandel is a popular holiday destination for both New Zealand and international visitors and is often crowded and busy. Well-known beaches such as Cathedral Cove and Hot Water Beach can be just as packed as Takapuna Beach or Oriental Parade in the height of summer. The good news is that it only takes a short walk to reach some very idyllic spots, and while you may not have the beach all to yourself, you will be far away from noisy crowds.

These five beaches, all on the eastern side of the Coromandel Peninsula, are easy-to-get-to beauty spots that won't disappoint. A word of warning, though – isolation has its price, and most of these beaches are without any

facilities including toilets and none are patrolled by lifeguards in summer. The eastern side of the peninsula is often exposed to heavy swells directly off the open ocean and can be dangerous for swimming. The beaches are listed north to south.

New Chums Beach

A 20-minute walk from the northern end of Whangapoua Beach is a long stretch of white sandy shore lapped by clear water. The beach is backed by handsome native bush and overhung with old pohutukawa trees that provide plenty of shade on a hot summer's day.

Otama Beach

In comparison with tree-shaded New Chums, Otama Beach is totally open and backed by high sand dunes covered in grasses. With only a few houses at the southern end, the dunes are now a nature reserve protecting the whole length of the beach from further development. The beach looks out over the Mercury Islands and the best access is from the northern end at the bottom of the Black Jack Hill. There is a basic camping ground at Otama with water, but no toilets.

To reach Otama from Kuaotunu take the Black Jack Road for 5 km. The road is narrow, unsealed and winding.

Opoutere Beach

While this beach is just a 10-minute walk from the road, that seems to be too much for most people. One of the few undeveloped beaches left on the Coromandel, with a vista comprising just sand, sea and shore, this gives a taste of what this coast was like before the baches took over. Even on a busy day (maybe 50 people), this is such a long beach that it's just a matter of strolling along the shore until you find a spot you like. However, there is no shade along this beach and it can be quite exposed on a hot summer's day.

Towards the mouth of the river is the Wharekawa Harbour Sandspit Wildlife Refuge, an important breeding ground for several endangered

birds, including the New Zealand dotterel, and the nesting grounds are roped off during spring and summer. (So leave the dog at home.)

The turnoff to Opoutere is 10 km north of Whangamata and the beach access a further 5 km from the turnoff.

Waimama Bay, Whiritoa

From the northern end of Whiritoa Beach, this tiny cove is reached by an easy track over a headland and takes about 20 minutes. Protected by rocky headlands at either end of the beach, this small stretch of white sand has ancient spreading pohutukawa trees, ideal for lounging in the shade on a scorching hot day. The beach drops steeply into the water here and the surf can be surprisingly powerful, so take extra care swimming. At the southern end at low tide are bath-sized rock pools perfect for cooling off while the waves crash against the rocks below.

Whiritoa Beach is 12 km south of Whangamata.

Orokawa Bay, Waihi Beach

A 40-minute walk on a well-formed track winds over a couple of headlands to a long stretch of untouched white sand with a backdrop of old pohutukawa trees just made for picnicking under. If you are in the mood for an extra walk then inland from the beach a track leads to the 25-metre-high William Wright Falls. If you want to get still further away, an even more secluded beach is Homunga Bay, another hour's walking north of Orokawa. The track to both bays traverses bush-clad promontories, with great views along the coast and out to Mayor Island.

The track to Orokawa Bay starts at the north end of Waihi Beach (500 m from the Surf Club) and you will get your feet wet getting to the track at high tide.

◀◀ Coromandel Gold Stamper Battery

Walking into this building is like stepping back in time as the battery has a timeless and hard-working feel that no modern tourist trap could hope to duplicate. One of only three stamper batteries still working, this is the only one still on its original site and the only six-headed stamper battery left in the world. Set up as a teaching facility as part of the School of Mines, the battery also acted as a public facility processing quartz for local miners, and at first was driven by water but converted to a diesel-driven operation in 1899 – a surprising early use of diesel. The water wheel is the largest in New Zealand and you can try your hand at panning for gold in the creek below.

Across the road is the historic Buffalo Cemetery. The burial ground takes its name from the HMS *Buffalo* whose seaman, David Wanks, was killed while loading spars in January 1838 and was the first person to be buried here.

> 410 Buffalo Road, 2 km north of Coromandel town.
> Tours daily but depends on the time of year and it pays to ring ahead, phone 07 866 7933; entrance fee.

◀◀ Hoffman's Pool, Kauaeranga Valley

It was timber, and not gold, that attracted Europeans to this valley behind Thames, and from 1871 through to 1928 the magnificent kauri forests were milled virtually to extinction. While the scars of the forestry era still remain, the bush has reclaimed much of the land, and the old pack trails and tramlines now form part of the extensive track system.

Hoffman's Pool combines a nature walk with milling ruins and is a perfect swimming hole, at a point where the Kauaeranga River divides. The pool is deep and clear, there is a rock to jump off, and even better, part of the pool has a lovely sandy bottom rather than stones. Across the valley is a view of the rock formation called the Chief's Head, an outcrop that really does look like a head. Along the river is an old stone wall, all that remains of the Thames water supply established in 1874, and the concrete slab by the pool is one of the piles of the old Kauaeranga Tramline which crossed the river at this point.

> Hoffman's Pool is 1.8 km from the Kauaeranga Valley Visitor's Centre.

Martha Mine, Waihi

In 1878 gold was discovered at Martha Hill behind what is now Waihi town and work quickly began on establishing a mine. By 1882 a stamper was in operation and later the huge 200-stamper Victoria Battery at Waikino was constructed in 1897. The Cornish pump house (a short walk from the Waihi Information Centre), built in 1904 and used through to the 1930s, is often mistaken for the ruins of an old church. Waihi was the centre of a bitter six-month strike in 1912 that resulted in the death of miner Fred Evans, one of only two deaths during industrial disputes in New Zealand. The Martha Mine was finally closed in 1952 and by that time had produced 174,160 kg of gold and 1,193,180 kg of silver.

During the 1980s, with gold prices on the rise, the Martha Mine was reopened, although this time as an open-cast mine. In 2006 the massive concrete pump house was moved 270 metres as the ground on the original site had become unstable. The Martha mine website has a good series of photos documenting the move (www.marthamine.co.nz). There are two viewing platforms, one on the western side of the pit, the other by the pump house, and the mine offers tours.

> The Martha Mine is located just off the main street of Waihi and the huge hole in the ground is impossible to miss. Tour bookings essential, ph 07 863 9880.

Thames School of Mines and Mineralogical Museum

Thames is the largest settlement on the Coromandel and its main street, Pollen Street, still retains a facade that would be familiar to a visitor from 1900 when the town had a population of 18,000 and over 100 hotels. Thames flourished in the second half of the nineteenth century in response to the gold mined both locally and on the peninsula, and was originally two settlements, Grahamstown in the north and Shortland in the south. Given its close proximity to the mines, Grahamstown dominated early Thames, but after a disastrous flood in 1917, followed by the decline of mining, the retail and service centre of the town moved further south to Shortland, though today it is impossible to tell where either settlement begins and ends.

Mining schools were once common, but of the 30 mining schools established throughout New Zealand, only Thames and Reefton have

survived. This museum comprises two parts: the school and the mineral collection. The School of Mines, opened in 1886 and closed in 1954, was the largest in the country and the current building has largely survived unaltered, with classrooms looking much as they would have a hundred years ago. The Mineralogical Museum was opened in 1900 and has an incredible collection of minerals from both New Zealand and around the world still in their original Edwardian glass cases.

> 101 Cochrane Street, Thames. Open daily, summer 11 a.m. to 4 p.m., winter 11 a.m. to 3 p.m., ph 07 868 6227; entrance fee.

Te Pare Historic Reserve, Hahei

While most visitors to Hahei rush off to the popular Cathedral Cove, at the other end of the beach is one of the most appealing spots on the Coromandel coast. Stronghold of Ngati Hei, who arrived in the area on the waka *Arawa* around AD 1350, this must be one of the most beautifully situated pa sites in the country. The broad terraces that occupy this rocky headland, with the sea on three sides, have the most magnificent outlook over Mercury Bay and Hahei Beach. This is the perfect place to sit for a while and let your thoughts drift off. Another pa is clearly visible on the hill behind Te Pare, while the rocks below are a popular fishing spot and, of course, Hahei Beach itself is very safe for swimming.

> The track to the pa site begins at the end of Pa Road, or leads up from the southern end of Hahei Beach.

The 309 Road

Linking Whitianga and Coromandel town, travelling along this road is a flashback to the early days of travel on the peninsula. Narrow, winding, unsealed, but not too long (42 km), the road wends its way along river valleys and twists up through the rugged Coromandel Range (summit 306 m). It is not really suitable for large vehicles or nervous drivers.

Just past the summit on the Coromandel side is a small grove of massive old kauri that survived the bushman's axe and offers a glimpse of the magnificent forests of the past. This rare patch of mature forest is now

COROMANDEL

accessible by an excellent short track and includes an unusual double-trunk tree, which began life as two seedlings that eventually grew together and fused at the base.

Half a kilometre down the road from the kauri grove are the Waiau Falls, a small waterfall in the bush with a swimming hole. Further still down the Waiau Valley are the fascinating Waiau Waterworks, a 1-hectare garden of water-powered sculptures, a water-driven clock and a pedal-powered pump, and, unlike most gardens, this one has plenty of things to play on.

WAIKATO &
THE KING COUNTRY

WAIKATO & THE KING COUNTRY

The Big Lemon & Paeroa Bottle

In the beginning was the Big Bottle, long before the Big Carrot, the Big Crayfish, the Big Trout or the big anything else. Now, just to be confusing, Paeroa has *two* big bottles, but the 'real' bottle is at the southern end of the town by the Ohinemuru River Bridge so don't go stopping and taking pictures of the wrong one!

Erected in 1969, the bottle stands 7 metres high and celebrates the soft drink Lemon & Paeroa. This drink, more commonly known as just L&P, was created in 1904 using water from a local spring and was originally christened with the reverse name, Paeroa & Lemon. The spring water was well known prior to its use in the soft drink and was reputed to have therapeutic values. The promotional phrase 'World famous in New Zealand since ages ago' has now become part of everyday New Zealand vernacular and has certainly put Paeroa on the map.

Blue Springs, Waihou River

The Waihou as it flows out to sea by Thames is a sluggish dirty-brown muddy-looking river and is a complete contrast to the headwaters near Putaruru. Here, the Waihou River begins its journey to the sea as the most stunningly pure water that has filtered down from the Kaimai Ranges. Remaining underground for up to 50 years, the water that emerges from the Blue Springs is crystal clear and a brilliant blue-green colour, which explains its prosaic name. The stream itself supports an incredible array of aquatic plants that drift languidly in the transparent water while trout, very easy to spot, swim effortlessly in the swift current. However, think twice before leaping into the water even on a hot day as it emerges from the Blue Spring at a very cool 11°C all year round.

> The access to the springs is 4 km down Leslie Road that runs off Whyte's Road/SH28. Whyte's Road/SH28 runs between Putaruru and SH5 (the main road to Rotorua).

The Chainsaw Collection, Putaruru Timber Museum

In a land originally abundant in timber, the early logging industry made a massive contribution to the development of colonial New Zealand. This is the only museum wholly dedicated to the timber industry and is on the site of the original Tuck and Watkins sawmill, while right next door was the pine nursery established in 1926 for New Zealand Perpetual Forests (later New Zealand Forest Products). The original timber mill is now the main museum building, and extensive displays cover every aspect of timber and related industries.

Especially impressive is the chainsaw collection with over 100 old chainsaws on display. Development of the modern chainsaw began in the late 1920s with the first mass-produced saws coming off the production line of Andreas Stihl in Germany in 1926 (Stihl is still a leading market brand). The early models were designed to be used by two people and the Timber Museum has several examples of these enormously heavy and cumbersome machines. It was after World War Two that the chainsaw really took off and quickly became the tool of choice for the substantial New Zealand timber industry. Although there are several examples from the 1940s, this impressive collection is mainly made up of saws from the 1950s and 1960s, in every variety imaginable.

> SH1, 2 km south of Putaruru.
> Open daily 9 a.m. to 4 p.m., ph 07 883 7621,
> www.putarurutimbermuseum.co.nz; entry fee.

HMS Pioneer, Mercer

During the British attack on the Waikato during the New Zealand Wars of the 1860s, gunboats – against which Maori had no real defence – were used to bombard river pa. Several fortifications were abandoned as Maori quickly recognised that they could not fight the iron-clad boats as they churned slowly upriver.

Tucked away in what is left of Mercer's somewhat shabby main street is the gun turret of the HMS *Pioneer*, used by British forces against Maori in the Waikato. The paddle-driven vessel was built in 1862 for the New Zealand Colonial Government and took active part in the attack on Rangiriri pa under

WAIKATO & THE KING COUNTRY

the command of Sir William Wiseman in November 1863. Three years later in 1866 the *Pioneer* was wrecked on the Manukau Bar. The turret, complete with gun loopholes, is all that is left of the gunboat and is now a war memorial.

The remains of another old gunboat, the PS *Rangiriri*, lie on the riverbank at Hamilton's Memorial Park. This boat was launched in 1864 at Port Waikato and in August of that year Captain William Steele stepped off the gunboat to found the European settlement of Hamilton.

◀◀ It's Astounding! Riff Raff Statue

Hamilton is often considered a good solid farming city, so it's a bit hard to believe that it was the inspiration for the 'schlock horror' musical and movie *The Rocky Horror Picture Show* – but it's true!

Richard O'Brien, the show's creator, worked as a barber on the ground floor of the Embassy Theatre in Hamilton's Victoria Street from 1959 to 1964. One of Hamilton's oldest theatres, by that time the Embassy was becoming rather run-down and tired, and specialised in running B-grade double-feature horror flicks. The barber shop was right at the entrance to the theatre and no doubt the low-grade movies were a welcome relief from trimming and snipping the hair of Hamilton's menfolk. The show premiered in 1973 and O'Brien played the character Riff Raff.

The theatre has since been pulled down but in 2004 a life-size statue of Riff Raff was erected in a small square on its former site.

Victoria Street, Hamilton, 100 m north of the museum.

◀◀ Kawhia

This large tidal harbour has a long and important Maori history beginning with the arrival of two important waka, *Tainui* and *Aotea*. The harbour was named by Turi, the captain of the *Aotea*, who then went on to settle in Patea. Kawhia is the final resting place of the *Tainui* waka, which is behind the historic Anaukitirangi marae, marked by two stones, one at either end of the waka and over 20 metres apart. Hoturoa, the captain of the *Tainui*, is featured on the tekoteko (the figure at the top of the front gable) of the meeting house. Just along the beach from the marae, a tree, Tangi te Korowhiti, marks the spot where the *Tainui* waka tied up. The tree is tapu and should be treated with respect.

Now a quiet backwater that is as yet unspoilt by modern development, Kawhia has a relaxed, unhurried atmosphere that is in direct contrast to busy Raglan to the north and a world away from the east coast beaches such as Whangamata and Ohope. Not so well known as Hot Water Beach on the Coromandel Peninsula is the Te Puia Springs. Accessible for two hours either side of low tide, these hot-water springs are situated directly out from the main track to the beach from the car park. This beach is exposed to the westerly wind so bring a substantial digging tool to make a protective wall around your very own hot pool in the sand.

In the small museum in the same building as the information office is a racing whaleboat built of kauri in the 1880s, the only craft of its kind in New Zealand. Longer and narrower than actual whaleboats, these were popular racing craft in the nineteenth century. On New Year's Day crews from communities around the harbour race whaleboat replicas, competing for the appropriately named Whaleboat Racing Cup, in the only race of this type in the country.

Kawhia is also home of the very popular Kai Fest. This annual festival of Maori food and culture is held in Omimiti Park on the weekend closest to Waitangi Day and attracts over 10,000 people. As well as traditional food such as hangi, puha, paua, kanga wai and mussels, there is also Maori craft, art, kapa haka and music.

◀◀ Madonna Falls

New Zealand has very few roadside shrines, but these sacred falls are an exception. In 1980 their water was pronounced to have special healing powers and the falls were declared sacred and named by local Maori as Te Whaea o te Rere/Our Lady of the Waterfall. Although right by the busy main road, the trees and bushes around the falls are festooned with colourful flowers and other bright adornments. A special contraption has been set up making it easier to collect the healing waters.

25 km south of Te Kuiti on SH4.

WAIKATO & THE KING COUNTRY

⟪⟪ Mapara Scenic Reserve

Good news stories about the survival of our unique native birds are relatively rare and usually involve isolated offshore islands. Mapara is one of the last strongholds of the rare kokako and this reserve is the most accessible for those who want to hear or see this elusive and handsome bird. Like so many of our native species, kokako are very vulnerable to imported predators, but with persistent trapping of nasty killers the kokako numbers in the reserve rocketed from just four breeding pairs in 1991 to over 50 pairs in 2008.

The track, which takes only one hour to walk, leads through the territories of several kokako, so the chances of hearing the distinctive song of these birds are very good, though to actually see a bird will require a good deal more patience. The best time is the period two hours after dawn, so you may just have to get up very early, especially in summer.

> To get to Mapara Reserve, travel 26 km south of Te Kuiti on SH4, turn left into Kopaki Road and then after 2 km turn right into Mapara South Road. The reserve is 5.5 km down this gravel road.

⟪⟪ The Marokopa Road

Huge numbers of tourists flock to the Waitomo Caves every year, but few venture much further. On the Te Anga road leading west from Waitomo are a number of natural landscapes that are worth the 45 km drive from Waitomo to Marokopa Beach. Highlights include the following:

Ruakuri Walkway

Only 2 km from the Waitomo Caves and next to the Aranui Cave, this short 30-minute walk along the Waitomo River is crammed with fantastic limestone outcrops, caves, and a huge natural tunnel. The unspoilt bush features luxurious growth – in particular, ferns, mosses and lichens. The area has glow-worms at night but don't forget your torch. The track is well formed and clear even if the signage is a bit confusing.

Mangapohue Natural Bridges

Just a short distance from the road (10 minutes), the Mangapohue natural bridges are two natural arches up to 17 metres high, one on top of the other, cut through limestone by the Mangapohue Stream. The wonderful walk to the bridges passes through the steep cliffs of a limestone gorge, overhung with native trees and featuring glow-worms when it's dark. A torch is necessary if a night walk is planned. Just beyond the caves are the fossils of giant 20-million-year-old oysters clearly visible in the exposed rocks.

Marokopa Waterfall

Especially impressive after rain, the Marokopa River cascades powerfully 30 metres over a limestone bluff creating a spectacular waterfall. The spray from the falls has created bush lush with ferns and mosses that thrive on the permanent damp. The falls are only a short 15-minute walk from the road and are 31 km from Waitomo.

Marokopa Beach

At the end of the road is a small settlement of tiny seaside baches. This is not a beach for brushing up on your tan, but a place to go fishing, for a walk on the shore facing the Tasman Sea, or to just laze around and read a book. There is a camping ground at Marokopa, a pub at Te Anga, and not much else along this road.

The Mokau Mine

In the middle of the road in the centre of Mokau opposite the museum is a German mine found at the mouth of the Mokau River in December 1942. But why would the Germans want to mine the Mokau River mouth? Did they know something nobody else did or was something possibly lost in translation?

Locals tell of a German gentleman who turned up in Mokau well after the war apparently clutching a map of New Zealand with just three places marked: Auckland, Wellington, and Mokau. Another story is that the mine was actually New Zealand-manufactured and just made to look like a German mine to keep the public alert. And yet another rumour claims that a Japanese mine was also found, but that the discovery was hushed up by the government of the day.

WAIKATO & THE KING COUNTRY

The official line is that this mine along with two others just drifted across the Tasman from where the Germans had been laying mines along the Australian coast. But who will ever know the truth of the Mokau mine, that today local schoolchildren nickname 'Da Bomb'.

Mormon Temple, Hamilton

'Knock, knock.' 'Who's there?' 'Mormons!' New Zealand has long been a missionary outpost for the Church of Jesus Christ of the Latter Day Saints, better known as the Mormons. Today most large towns have a temple and, while still considered a bit odd, Mormonism is generally regarded as a mainstream church. What might come as a surprise to most, however, is that this temple situated west of Hamilton is not only the largest Mormon church in the southern hemisphere, but was also the first below the equator.

Opened in April 1958, the church, the village and the school are particularly American in design and layout and even today sit rather uncomfortably in the New Zealand landscape. However, tours of the temple are offered at their visitor's centre, so if you have ever been curious to see the inside of a Mormon temple this is not a bad place to start. Sitting on top of a hill, the floodlit church is particularly prominent at night when it is easily seen from Hamilton. It is also very famous locally for its Christmas lights.

509 Tuhikaramea Road, Temple View, Hamilton, ph 07 8462750.

Pureora Forest

This magnificent forest was saved from the axe by protesters who in 1978 perched themselves on platforms in the trees. Logging was finally halted in the early 1980s and the area is currently a mixture of forest park and commercial forest, providing some interesting contrasts between pristine native bush and clear-felled pine forest. It is also worth noting that the roads in the forest are a combination of forestry and narrow metalled roads, some little better than tracks and rough in parts. Along with the usual bush walks there are three curiosities worth a detour.

The Barryville Road turnoff to the visitor's centre is 56 km from Te Kuiti and 20 km from Mangakino on SH30, and a further 3 km down Barryville Road.

Buried Forest

The idea of a buried forest is much more exciting than the reality, and in fact this must be one of the dullest sights in New Zealand. First you must travel along a rutted narrow gravel forestry road to take a short walk through blackberry-infested pine forest to view a couple of half-buried old logs with absolutely no redeeming features. Rather than the 'buried forest' it should really be labelled 'a half-buried old log or two'.

What is fascinating, however, is the event which caused the forest to be flattened. Over 1800 years ago a cataclysmic eruption blew out the western side of Lake Taupo over 70 km away. Even at this distance the force of the blast was so strong that it decimated the entire forest in the area, knocking over huge mature trees and then burying them under a deep layer of ash and pumice. Part of this forest was accidentally uncovered in the 1970s, and a couple of those ancient preserved logs can be seen along this short track.

Centre of the North Island

Quite frankly, there's not much to see here either, apart from a gigantic rimu right next to a plaque marking the geographical centre of the North Island. Although standing on the plaque and thinking 'this is the middle of the North Island' is a sort of neat, if pointless, thing to do. But let's face it, we don't always have to have a good reason for everything we do!

> 2 km on from the track to Mt Pureora, turn right into Waimanoa Road. The entrance to the track is a further 3 km along this road.

Poukani – the biggest totara tree in the whole wide world!

While everyone flocks to Tane Mahuta, the largest kauri (which by the way is nowhere near the tallest tree in New Zealand), Poukani, the tallest totara tree, only attracts a handful of visitors and it isn't fair. (What's more, the second- and third-largest totara trees are in nearby Pureora Forest.)

Over 42 metres tall and more than 1800 years old, this massive tree is really very impressive – though rather a bit lost and hard to see in the thick bush, let alone properly photograph. The walk takes about one hour return.

Poukani is about 10 km from the Barryville Road turnoff towards Mangakino on SH30.

Railway Houses, Huntly

Manufactured in kitset form at a factory in Frankton, Hamilton, railway houses were transported all over the country (by rail, of course) to provide accommodation for railway workers, who often lived in isolated areas. New Zealand Railways had provided housing since the 1880s, but the cottages regarded today as typical railway houses were built in the 1920s and modelled on the Californian bungalow fashionable at the time. In all, the factory produced nearly 1600 houses until its closure in 1929.

Most of these simple wooden houses are long gone or altered beyond recognition, but numerous good examples still remain – there is even a small cluster in Kingsland, in central Auckland. At Huntly, a group of over 15 railway houses is strung out along Harris Street on the west side of the river. While some have been altered, what makes this collection unique is that the exteriors of most of them are original, including the distinct lattice woodwork around the front door. Once considered inferior, today an original railway house is a treasured gem of domestic New Zealand architecture.

Talking Poles, Tokoroa

While the giant wooden statue of a timber worker with a chainsaw is familiar to those driving along SH1 through Tokoroa, he is in fact just one of over 25 such structures. Labelled the 'Talking Poles', they are incredibly varied in their style, from the Ent-like *Green Man* and the *Timber Worker* through to Maori nui poles and poles with an international flavour from Samoa and Canada.

Although these poles are located all over Tokoroa, the two main clusters are on SH1 by the information centre, and Roseberry Street, which is the main shopping street, is just a five-minute walk away so it is well worth the stop. Every two to three years a pole symposium is held with invited artists who have three weeks to create their own pole that is then added to the collection. The artists work in public so this is a good opportunity to observe creativity in action.

⦉⦉ Taupiri Mountain

Taupiri is the sacred mountain of the Tainui people and on the lower slopes of the mountain are the main burial grounds of the iwi. It is on this mountain that Maori royalty are buried, and in 2006 Te Arikinui Dame Te Atairangikaahu, the Maori Queen, was buried here with great ceremony after journeying down the river from the Turangawaewae marae at Ngaruawahia.

There is a track to the top of the 288-metre peak and the views are fantastic, especially on a clear winter's day when snow-covered Mt Ruapehu is clearly visible. The beginning of the track is to the left of the small marae, which is accessed by the metal road on the north side of the bridge. Use the car park by the river, as the one by the marae is for marae use only.

⦉⦉ Te Aroha Domain

Once a flourishing spa town, Te Aroha has in recent years successfully renovated its Edwardian domain. Modern hot pools (open 10 a.m. to 10 p.m.) with family appeal complement the historical buildings including the 1898 Cadman Bath House, which now houses the local museum, and the renovated No. 2 Bath House. As well as the pools, a restored tearooms and several boarding houses are set out around the attractive domain and each year in March the 'Day in the Domain' festival celebrates Te Aroha heritage as a spa town.

At the back of the domain is Mokena, the only hot soda water geyser in the world. Erupting every 40 minutes to a height of around 4 metres, the soda water is reputed to have medicinal values and a drinking fountain nearby provides an opportunity to taste the unusual liquid.

If you are feeling fit – and you need to be – a track to the top of Te Aroha mountain begins at the rear of the domain by the Mokena geyser and is approximately two-and-a-half hours one way, although steep and rugged in parts. The views from the top of the 952-metre mountain are spectacular over both sides of the Kaimai Range.

www.tearoha-info.co.nz

◀◀ Te Awamutu Museum

This small but professionally curated museum has two outstanding exhibits. The first is the highly unusual and incredibly stylish carving of Uenuku, a god who appears as a rainbow and whose spirit was brought to this country on the waka *Tainui* in the form of a stone. Believed to have been carved around AD 1400, Uenuku is distinctly eastern Polynesian in style and is a very rare carving from this period. A great taonga of the Tainui people, the Uenuku carving has an exceptionally powerful life force and should be treated with the utmost respect.

The second 'must see' is the *True Colours, History Never Repeats* exhibit. Te Awamutu is the home of Tim and Neil Finn, and the museum is developing a unique collection related to the two brothers and their contribution to New Zealand music. Comprising concert memorabilia, records, and a range of Finn items including the distinct suit worn by Tim Finn in early Split Enz concerts, the exhibit is a little thin on material, but that can only improve and it's still worth a visit.

> 135 Roche Street, Te Awamutu. Open Monday to Friday 10 a.m.
> to 4 p.m., weekends and public holidays 10 a.m. to 1 p.m.,
> ph 07 872 0085, www.tamuseum.org.nz; koha/donation.

◀◀ Wairere Falls

Set in attractive native bush, these falls drop 153 metres in two stages over the Okauia Fault, making them the tallest falls in the North Island. The walk to the lower lookout takes around 45 minutes and to the top of the falls a further 45 minutes, and is through very handsome bush following the stream. The stream itself has been subject to dramatic floods and the valley is full of huge boulders scoured by the power of the water.

The falls are at the head of a long narrow valley and in very strong westerly winds the water is blown forcibly upwards back into the bush with the power of a high-pressure hose – an experience not to be missed!

> The track to the falls starts at the end of Goodwin Road. Goodwin Road is
> 20 km south of Te Aroha off the road that runs east of the Waihou River
> from Te Aroha to SH24 near Matamata.

BAY OF PLENTY

BAY OF PLENTY

Haiku Park, Katikati

Haiku is a 17-syllable verse form and consists of five, seven then five syllables arranged in three lines. The world's shortest form of poetry, originating in Japan, it is used to express profound truths in the simplest of natural images.

Here in a small park in Katikati, the locals have been particularly innovative, and rather than just establish yet another walk by a river, there is the Haiku Walk. On rocks and stones along the riverbank are haiku poems from both local and international sources, and this poetry is particularly suited to such a natural environment. So if you're travelling on the busy SH2, stop for a while and contemplate the larger issues of life in this small park behind the shops.

> SH2, Katikati. The entrance is next to the Mitre 10 in the main
> shopping centre.

Karangaumu Pa, Papamoa Hills Regional Park, Te Puke

One of eight pa sites in the Papamoa Hills Regional Park, Karangaumu is very impressive. Located on a high vantage point (224 m), the pa – also known in earlier times as Te Ihu o Ruarangi – covers the entire top of the hill with a narrow ridge being the only access. The ancient ramparts, defensive ditches and terraces are all clearly visible. Established around AD 1500, the strategic advantage of this site is immediately obvious, even to the untrained eye. Watchful sentries would have missed nothing from the vantage of this ancient fortress – the entire bay is clearly visible: north to the Coromandel, south to Mt Ngongotaha, out to sea to White Island and far inland.

It's a steady climb up to the pa along a very good track and partly through a mature pine forest with an unusual understorey made up almost entirely of kawakawa. Take some time to chew a small piece of a new leaf and enjoy the peppery taste followed by a mild numbness as you experience its anaesthetising effect. Early herbalists used this plant to alleviate toothache by packing the infected tooth with kawakawa leaf and thereby numbing the pain.

> 5 km east of Te Puke on SH2 turn left into Poplar Lane and drive 800
> metres to the car park.

Mayor Island/Tuhua

Lying a short distance off the Bay of Plenty coast, this rhyolite volcanic cone has a special appeal all of its own. Dormant rather than extinct, the volcano has on average erupted every 3000 years over a period of 130,000 years and is very similar in shape to the more active White Island further east. The island is mostly comprised of a large caldera containing two small lakes appropriately, but unimaginatively, named 'Black' and 'Green'. In pre-European times it supported a significant Maori population which traded in obsidian or tuhua (and hence the island's Maori name), a rare volcanic glass with a sharp edge that was a highly valued commodity in a stone-age culture. Several major pa sites are still visible.

Captain Cook sighted the island on 3 November 1769, naming it 'Mayor' as that date was also Lord Mayor's Day in London (he also named a group of islands further north 'The Aldermen'). With the advent of iron tools the island population fell substantially, and as the terrain was unsuitable for farming it has been virtually untouched for over 200 years. At one stage the New Zealand Navy considered digging a short canal to one of the lakes to build a secret offshore harbour (which would have been just *so* James Bond), but no doubt some sensible bureaucrat squashed that fabulous idea.

Instead, a superb pohutukawa forest in the crater remains untouched, and recent clearance of pests has led to a recovery of native bird life including bellbirds. A walk around the island will take about six hours and there is a good swimming spot in Sou'East Bay where the boat lands. The waters surrounding the island are renowned for their excellent fishing.

Blue Ocean Charters runs regular trips to the island and the 35-km voyage takes about two hours; www.blueocean.co.nz, ph 0800 224 278.

Omanawa Waterfall

It is rather strange that these beautiful falls are not more easily accessible – and just where does that mysterious door set into the bank at the end of the path really lead to?

The Omanawa Falls plunge dramatically over a bluff in a single drop into a broad pool of dark blue/green water that looks just perfect for swimming. Unfortunately, look is all you can do, and even looking isn't that easy. Poorly

signposted from the road, the track goes down through a bushy glade to a barely adequate lookout point (and the track can be slippery if it is wet). Then there is that solid iron green door at the end of the path. Apparently it provides access to an old power station established in 1915 and long since decommissioned, but of course that's the official story . . .

> From the lower Kaimai road into Tauranga (SH2) turn into Omanawa Road and drive 11 km to the car park.

Opotiki

◀◀ Burial Tree/Hukutaia Domain

Known as the Hukutaia Domain, this small reserve of low rainforest just out of Opotiki was established in 1918 primarily to protect Taketakerau, an ancient burial tree. The large sprawling puriri was used for centuries by the local Upokorehe hapu to conceal the bones of the notable dead from desecration by enemies, a common practice among early Maori. After the tree was damaged in a storm the remains were buried elsewhere. Thought to be over 2000 years old, this mighty old tree is still impressive and highly tapu.

In addition to Taketakerau, the domain contains one of the most extensive collections of native trees and shrubs in the country. From 1933 to 1970 local amateur botanist Norman Potts travelled throughout New Zealand to gather plants that were then established in the domain, and after his death the work was continued by March Heginbotham from 1970 to 1990. While only some of the trees are identified and the tracks are not very well marked, the reserve is actually pretty small and you can't get lost.

> From Opotiki, take the road to Whakatane, and just over the Waioeka River Bridge turn left into Woodlands Road. The reserve is on the left 7 km down this road.

◀◀ Hiona St Stephen's Church, Opotiki

Throughout the 1860s, Maori resistance to the pressures of European settlement grew, and many backed the new religious and political Hauhau

movement, led by the charismatic Te Kooti. The Reverend Volkner, a missionary based at Hiona, regularly reported to the authorities the movement of Hauhau in the area and was, not surprisingly, regarded by local Maori as a government spy. After visiting Auckland, Volkner insisted on returning to the area despite warnings that he was in danger, and in March 1865 was killed by Hauhau in the church in a very grisly manner. However, as is often the case, Maori and settler versions of the incident vary considerably.

To the settlers, the death of Volkner confirmed the savagery of the Hauhau and the need for protection. Maori, on the other hand, contend that Volkner was hanged as a government spy and that the manner of his death was much exaggerated by settlers keen to have government troops stationed in the district – which is precisely what happened. In response to Volkner's killing, the government despatched forces to the Opotiki area, where fighting continued off and on until the final surrender of Te Kooti at Waiotahi in 1889.

Volkner is buried at the back of the church, which, owing to vandalism, is only open when someone is in attendance (check with the Opotiki i-SITE).

Royal Hotel, Opotiki

Built in 1879 entirely of native timber, the Royal Hotel was once the home of opera singer Fannie Rose Howie. Of Ngati Porou descent, Fannie Porter/ Poata was born into a prominent East Coast family in January 1868, the eldest of 11 children. She received her initial music education at home and at Mrs Sheppard's Ladies' School in Napier, but after a public concert in Gisborne moved to Australia in 1891 to study music not long after marrying John Howie.

After returning briefly to New Zealand, Fannie went on to study further in England and in 1901 gave her first performance to much acclaim performing under the name Te Rangi Pai. Between 1901 and 1905 Fannie successfully toured Britain, though she did have a reputation for being somewhat temperamental and unpredictable. After the death of her mother and youngest brother she returned home in 1905 and toured New Zealand several times until ill health forced her to retire in 1907. It was then that she composed the song that was to make her famous – the Maori lullaby 'Hine-e-hine'. Her health continued to deteriorate and Fannie was living at the Royal

when she died on 20 May 1916 in a room directly above the bar. She was buried at Maungaroa under a pohutukawa tree.

Today a gentle presence believed to be the spirit of Fannie is still felt in this fine old hotel, and during a recent renovation the current owners created a special memorial in the restaurant to their most famous guest.

> Corner King and Church Streets, Opotiki, ph 07 315 5760,
> www.huntersbackpackers.co.nz.

Surf Museum, Mount Maunganui

While an astounding 350 old surfboards are on display in the Surf Museum, this is just part of a larger collection of over 750 boards. The oldest are great big heavy wooden planks from the 1950s, followed by their equally big, but slighter lighter, counterparts from the 1960s that were affectionately know as 'dungers'. Many boards are locally made and the collection is a veritable who's who of Australasian board-makers including the likes of Mark Richards, Roger Lane, Bob Davies and Dennis Quane, to name just a few.

Alongside the huge number of surfboards is an equally impressive collection of surfing-related items, ranging from trophies, posters, paddleboards, kneeboards and surf art to a collection of historic surfboard wax. The museum is part of the Mount Surf Shop and is spread over the ground floor and a downstairs basement. At ground level it gets a bit hard to tell where the shop ends and the museum begins, as both new and second-hand boards are for sale.

> Mount Surf Shop, 139 Totara Street, Mount Maunganui,
> ph 07 927 7234, www.mountsurfshop.co.nz.

Te Puna Quarry Park

What do you do with an old quarry in your neighbourhood? Well, lots if you're the locals at Te Puna, just north of Tauranga. With an abandoned quarry on their doorstep, local residents banded together to form the Te Puna Quarry Park and created a whimsical and delightful garden. Leaving some of the infrastructure and machinery in situ, the society has overlaid the quarry with gardens and artwork that not even the meanest and hardest heart will fail to enjoy.

From the old storybook-like digger that children can play on in the car park through to heritage roses, there is plenty here for every age group. Over 30 pieces of artwork are spread around the gardens, including stylised sculptures of Hinuera stone, pottery, and a fabulous mosaic family grouping complete with a small dog. Children in the know head straight for the outdoor percussion area, where young and old can bang and crash to their heart's content on a variety of 'instruments' without fear of disturbing the neighbours.

The more formal plantings are on the lower area near the car park and include a contemplative oriental garden, heritage roses, vireya rhododendrons, bromeliads, succulents, South African natives and even a small kauri grove, while from the higher terraces there are excellent views over the Bay of Plenty. Still a work in progress, these gardens are well worth a detour.

Well signposted off SH2 at Te Puna, just north of Tauranga.

ROTORUA, TAUPO & ENVIRONS

Rotorua

Hinehopu's Track

Linking Lakes Rotoiti and Rotoehu, this track is known both as Hinehopu's Track and Hongi's Track, both names reflecting the importance of this trail in the history of the Arawa people of Rotorua. Halfway along the track (and also accessible from the busy road) is the famous matai tree under which, as a baby, Hinehopu was hidden from enemies by her mother in the seventeenth century. It was also beneath this tree that she met her future husband Pikiao, and many of the Ngati Pikiao iwi trace their lineage directly back to this couple. It was along this track that Nga Puhi warriors, led by Hongi Hika launched their surprise attack on Rotorua in 1823 by dragging their waka along the trail from Rotoehu to Rotoiti.

The track is easy walking through handsome bush of rewarewa, matai, rimu and tawa and takes about one hour one way. The most convenient place to start is at Korokitewao Bay at the eastern end of Lake Rotoiti.

> At the eastern end of Lake Rotoiti turn off SH33 into Tamatea Street and continue for 500 metres to the car park where the track begins. There is very limited parking at the Lake Rotoehu end.

Mamaku Blue

If you didn't think blueberries were the secret elixir to whatever ailed you beforehand, you may well be convinced after a visit to Mamaku Blue. Apparently, blueberries can sort out nearly every health problem from ageing and bad eyesight to preventing just about every sort of cancer.

All the purported health benefits aside, what will surprise anyone who visits here is all the forms and varieties blueberry food takes. Believed to be the first and only blueberry experience of its kind in the world, Mamaku Blue has a dazzling array of blueberry product. There is wine, chutney, jelly, jam, ice creams, juice, chocolate, liqueurs, sauces, sweets, toiletries, and vinegar – not to mention just plain blueberry fruit in season.

Flourishing in the cool climate of the Mamaku Plateau, over 7 hectares are planted out in blueberries and tours are available by appointment, but a good view out over the rows of blueberries from the café could be enough

ROTORUA, TAUPO & ENVIRONS

to satisfy your curiosity. Only blueberry-based food is served, ranging from pancakes to tasty pies and desserts, although many of the dishes on offer are mostly standard fare accompanied by blueberry chutneys and sauces. And if blueberries aren't enough, they also have a small range of produce based on that very old-fashioned fruit, the English gooseberry.

Mamaku Blue, Maraeroa Road (off SH5) at Mamaku, ph 07 332 5840, www.mamakublue.co.nz.

New Zealand Caterpillar Experience

Some people collect stamps and others model cars, but Lindsay Willis has gone straight for the big stuff – he collects old Caterpillar equipment. And what a great collection it is, and thank goodness he had the foresight to save such an extensive range of historic equipment that would otherwise have just ended up as scrap metal. With a background in forestry work, Lindsay was more aware than most as to just what these machines and the men who worked them did to shape the face of this country, from productive farmland to modern roads.

Here, at the world's foremost collection of Caterpillar machinery, he has gathered together a fantastic range of bulldozers and trucks, some of which are the only examples of their type left, including the 1937 Speeder and the Motor Patrol (which is a grader built in 1928). But this isn't just some pile of old machinery chucked in a shed. All undercover, the machines have been lovingly restored and are in perfect working order, with many displayed in bush settings. The displays are accompanied by great film footage and photos, both of the machines in action and also telling the human story of the tough men and brave women who helped shape this nation.

The New Zealand Caterpillar Experience, 171 Fairy Springs Road, Rotorua. Open daily 8.30 a.m. to 5.30 p.m., closed Christmas Day, ph 07 347 3206, www.caterpillarexperience.co.nz.

⫷ Mt Ngongotaha

While today Ngongotaha is better known for the luge and gondola, it is a mountain of great mana and reputedly once a major stronghold of the patupaiarehe or fairy people. Many different legends surround these mysterious folk. Some versions have them normal size with light hair and skin, indicating to some that an ancient Caucasoid race once inhabited these islands. Around Whanganui the tradition is that they were very tall — well over six foot. However, most versions describe the patupaiarehe as small and slim, frequently with red or lighter hair and light-coloured skin. Maori with red hair are often said to be the offspring of a liaison with the patupaiarehe.

Moving only by night, as light would kill them, they dwelt in the deep forest on rugged mountains. Their principal strongholds were Moehau, the Waitakere Ranges, Pirongia, Te Urewera and Ngongotaha in the North Island, and the headwaters of the Arahura River and peaks of the Banks Peninsula and Takitimu Mountains in the South. Usually invisible, they were rarely seen but were often heard talking and playing instruments on dark misty nights. Adept at music, weaving and carving, they lived on only raw foods, were never tattooed, and while they usually resented any intrusion into their domains could also show kindness.

The name Ngongotaha means 'to drink from a calabash' and relates to the story of the explorer Ihenga who became thirsty while climbing the mountain and was given water by a patupaiarehe woman. Another story tells that the patupaiarehe were eventually driven from the mountain by Maori setting fire to bracken on the lower slopes and that they never returned. Or did they? Listen carefully on a dark and misty night and you might just hear soft voices or fairy music wafting down from the heights . . .

⫷ Pukaki

One of the most important carvings in the land is not preserved in a museum but in the Rotorua District Council Buildings. Pukaki is one of Te Arawa's most illustrious ancestors and his massive carving benignly looks down over the central city from the glass gallery on the first floor of the council buildings.

Born in Tutanekai's pa on Mokoia Island around AD 1700, Pukaki led his Ngati Whakaue iwi through a period of major tribal conflict with Tohurangi to the south, eventually forcing their opponents back to Tarawera

and allowing Ngati Whakaue to occupy Ohinemutu.

This marvellous carving was created in 1836 from a single piece of totara by the master carver Te Taupua and commemorates the conquest of Pukeroa-Oruawhata. It was originally a gateway to the pa at Ohinemutu, but the lower part of the gateway was removed in the 1850s, and Pukaki then stood for some time next to the meeting house Tama te Kapua. Eventually the carving was housed in the Auckland War Memorial Museum before being returned home in 1997. The carving shows Pukaki holding his sons, Wharengaro and Rangitakuku, and below is his wife, Ngapuia. It is Pukaki who is featured on New Zealand's 20 cent coin.

Second floor, Rotorua District Council Buildings; entrance at the end of Haupapa Street. Open Monday to Friday, 8.30 a.m. to 4.30 p.m.

Rainbow Mountain/Maungakakaramea

Maungakakaramea, or Rainbow Mountain, lies south of Rotorua and is scarred and torn by a series of volcanic eruptions going back thousands of years. The lakes are old craters and the last eruption is believed to have occurred around 1000 years ago. Today the mountain still steams and boils, and the geothermally active lake near the beginning of the track up the slopes presents the rare sight of ducks swimming unperturbed at one end of the lake, while at the other the water furiously boils. Towering above are raw cliffs of red, orange and brown multi-hued volcanic rock that have been discoloured by continual exposure to steam, giving this mountain its European name. Many of the plants found on the Maungakakaramea are peculiar in that they have specifically adapted to the harsh geothermal conditions.

It takes about 20 minutes return to the lookout over the lake, but around two and a half hours to the top and back. Not a particularly arduous climb, the reward is views over Lakes Tarawera and Rotomahana and in the distance Taupo, and the Tarawera, Tauhara, Ruapehu and Tongariro mountains. The peak is known as Tiho o Rua or 'the owl's perch'. After a hike to the top, reward yourself with a soak in the hot waters of Kerosene Creek, a naturally heated stream a few hundred metres down the road.

Take SH5 26 km south towards Taupo, and Rainbow Mountain is clearly marked on the left, 500 metres past the Murupara/Waikaremoana turnoff.

⟪⟪ Twin Craters/Ngahopua Track

While the twin crater lakes of Rotongata and Rotoatua are the focus of this track, the walk's appeal lies more in the surrounding forest than the lakes. The track begins through a grove of spectacular large totara that have flourished on the rich volcanic soil. The heavy foliage of the totara gradually gives way to tall handsome tawa with a light open canopy that creates a wonderful soft filtered luminance. From a high ridge there are views first to Lake Rotongata, and a little further on, Rotoatua, both of which were formed around 3000 years ago.

> Turn off SH30 at Lake Rotoiti into Okataina Road and the track begins 4 km on the left opposite the turnoff to the Okataina Education Centre. Parking is limited so it's best to park on the road leading to the education centre.

Taupo and Turangi

⟪⟪ Lake Rotopounamu

Mt Pihanga is the beautiful mountain that in Maori legend was fought over by Tongariro and Taranaki, and it is appropriate that this equally beautiful lake is located on the mountain's lower slopes. The name means 'greenstone lake', in reference to the colour of the water, as no greenstone is found here, and even though the water is more often blue than green.

Despite its circular shape and all the nearby volcanic activity, the lake is not in fact a crater but was formed thousands of years ago by a giant landslide. With no visible outlet, it is believed that water seeps out via cracks in the lake bed. The track around Rotopounamu is largely flat, following the lake edge through mature forest of red beech, kahikatea, rimu and matai. On the eastern side is Long Beach, an ideal picnic spot and a good place for a swim on a hot summer's day.

> Travelling on SH47 from Turangi towards Tongariro National Park, the track is located on the left on the downhill side of the Te Ponanga Saddle.

Wairakei Steamfields

The drive to the lookout at the Wairakei Geothermal Power Development leads through and under a fascinating maze of pipes amidst billowing clouds of drifting stream. Underground wells tap into the vents of superheated water over an area of 25 sq km and is then fed via a system of pipes into the geothermal power station down by the river. Built in 1958 and extended in 1996 and 2005, it was the first geothermal plant in the world to use hot water as a steam source to drive turbines. There are over 50 wells that go down an average of 600 metres to tap into the hot water. The lookout provides an overview of the entire field and there is an excellent information board explaining just how the whole thing works.

> 2 km on the right from the junction of SH1 and SH5; poorly signposted and not to be confused with the Wairakei Thermal Valley which is right next door and is a thermal area.
>
> Open 6.30 a.m. to 5.30 p.m. March to September, 6.30 a.m. to 6.30 p.m. October to February.

Tongariro National Trout Centre, Turangi

Wild trout spawning in the rivers and lakes sustain the Taupo fishery, and while trout usually spend some time during their life at sea, in this area Lake Taupo acts as a substitute ocean. The hatchery is a safeguard should a natural disaster such as a volcanic eruption seriously affect trout numbers, though any eruption in the vicinity would surely affect the centre as well.

The complex raises trout from eggs, and at all times of the year there are usually trout in some growth stage on show. The visitor's centre has excellent displays on all aspects of the trout fishery including a fascinating collection of rods and flies. A series of paths links the various pools and leads down to the Tongariro River, and an underground glass viewing chamber allows visitors to see the trout below water. Situated alongside the Tongariro River, which is regarded as one of the best stretches of trout water in the world, the centre has hosted the rich and famous (including royalty – this was one of the late Queen Mother's favourite fishing spots).

While rainbow trout predominate, brown trout are also caught in this very attractive stretch of fast-flowing water. There is a lengthy track along the

eastern bank giving access to a large number of excellent fishing spots, and the Turangi i-SITE in Ngawaka Place has a free and comprehensive map of the river. Several local fishing shops hire fishing gear and local guided trips are also available. A specific licence is required to fish in the Taupo Fishing District and these are available from fishing shops and information centres.

SH1, 4 km north of Turangi.

The centre is open daily 10 a.m. to 4 p.m. from 1 December to 30 April, 10 a.m. to 3 p.m. from 1 May to 30 November; a donation is appreciated.

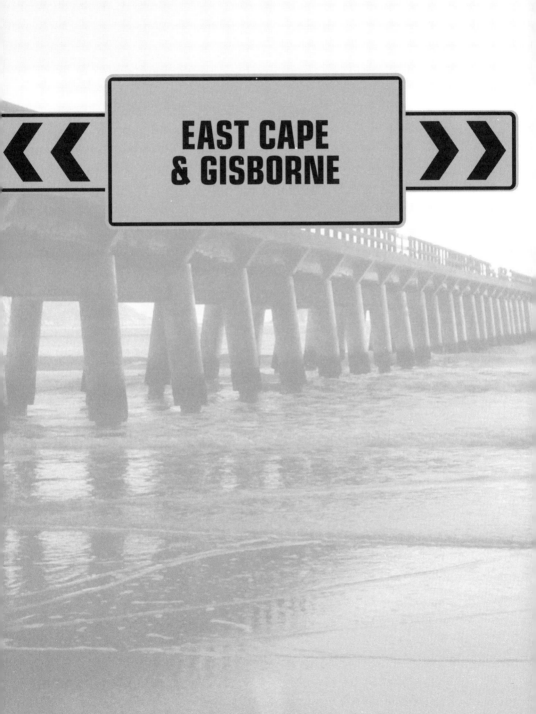

EAST CAPE & GISBORNE

East Cape

Usually treated as one entity, the East Cape in reality is two distinct regions. From Opotiki to Cape Runaway the road hugs the rugged coast, weaving in and out of sandy bays and small rocky coves. The climate is wetter, the landscape more forested, and the iwi is Whanau-a-Apanui. In contrast, the eastern side of the cape is drier and more barren and the road is mainly inland, only touching the coast occasionally. The beaches are wider, more sheltered and sandy, and this is home to the Ngati Porou iwi.

A notable feature of the East Cape is the numerous marae, often with historic carved meeting houses/wharenui. Meetings houses are not tourist attractions or public halls but a living representation of the ancestors of local people. Thus, you should no more walk onto a marae than bowl uninvited into somebody else's house. Please seek permission before entering. Accommodation and facilities in general are limited so it pays to plan ahead, even in the off season.

◀◀ Highway 35, East Cape

Once definitely well off the beaten track, this road from Opotiki to Gisborne is attracting more and more visitors, but it still doesn't carry the coachloads of package holiday tourists and manages to retain a rugged identity all of its own.

The following is the pick of the more unusual and less visited spots along the coast road travelling from Opotiki to Gisborne.

Christ Church at Raukokore

Decorated in Maori carvings and beautiful woven tukituki panels, this small and extremely photogenic Anglican church sits on a flat promontory jutting out to sea, and even manages to accommodate nesting penguins under the floor. In the cemetery behind are the graves of Eruera and Amira Stirling, two eminent twentieth-century Maori leaders.

East Cape Manuka

Manuka was once regarded as little more than a weed or at best a source of good firewood. Today the tree is recognised as playing a vital role in rehabilitating vast areas of marginal land cleared of forest, and here at Te Araroa on the East Cape, one company is turning scrub into gold. Manuka oil is now recognised for its outstanding natural anti-bacterial and anti-fungal properties (for those who take the trans-Tasman rivalry to heart, manuka oil is twice as effective as Australian tea tree oil). The oil has a wide range of uses including soap, cosmetics, massage oil, aromatherapy, food flavouring, sunburn relief, insect bites, dandruff, cold sores and skin irritations. The oil, however, has a low rate of extraction and it requires vast amounts of manuka leaf to produce the quantities required. Fortunately the trees are only pruned and not cut down but, even so, it is now hard for local sources to keep up with demand. Now 100,000 seedlings of higher yielding strains of manuka are being planted to ensure future harvests. Once the green manuka has been reduced by boiling and the oil extracted, the by-product is used for mulch. In addition to manuka oil, kanuka is also used to produce an oil both lighter in colour and density, and kawakawa is being developed for its blood purifying properties.

Almost 90 per cent of the oil is exported but here at Te Araroa there is a retail outlet for the wide range of manuka products, a small café and tours of the factory are available, though it is necessary for visitors to book tours ahead.

3 km north of Te Araroa on SH 35, ph 06 864 4826, www.manukaproducts.co.nz

Te Waha o Rerehou

Located on the beachfront at Te Araroa, Te Waha o Rerehou is the largest pohutukawa tree in the world. Over 20 metres high and 40 metres at its widest point, this massive tree is believed to be over 600 years old. It is also tapu, so please do not climb on it.

East Cape Lighthouse

Located on the easternmost point of mainland New Zealand, the East Cape lighthouse was originally built in 1900 on nearby East Island. Ignoring local Maori advice that the island was tapu, the lighthouse was plagued with problems. Access was difficult, four men were drowned during its construction and, finally, after continuing landslides and

earthquakes, the lighthouse was dismantled and moved to its present position in 1922.

20 km from Te Araroa on a pretty rough gravel road, access to the lighthouse is up a long flight of steps.

Waipiro Bay

In 1900 the largest settlement on the East Coast, shipping out sheep, cattle and timber, it was here that Robert Kerridge opened his first picture theatre in 1923. Now almost a ghost town, the centre of the settlement is the Iritekura marae with its fine meeting house carved in the traditional Ngati Porou style by master carver Pine Taiapa.

Tokomaru Bay Freezing Works

While Tokomaru Bay is a magnificent sweep of sandy beach with plenty of room for everyone, it is the ruins of the old freezing works at the northern end that have special appeal. Although now crumbling, the surprisingly large and extensive freezing works is testament to the size and importance of sheep and cattle farming to this part of the country and the vital role that coastal shipping played before road transport became the norm. Along with the actual freezing works, there are substantial shipping offices and stores and more than a few houses, most of which are now largely in ruins.

Anaura Bay

Generally considered to be one of the finest beaches on the East Coast, this is a beautiful spot for swimming, fishing, taking a walk, diving, or just not doing much at all. This bay was Cook's second landing place in New Zealand, although bad weather prevented him from provisioning his ship and, after two days, on the advice of local Maori, he sailed south to Tolaga Bay. This wonderful stretch of white sand is sheltered a little by Motuoroi Island just offshore.

Tolaga Bay Wharf

Built in 1929 at considerable expense and over 600 metres long, the Tolaga Bay wharf is an indication of the pivotal role played by sea shipping in New Zealand's development. For much of the country's early history, it was the sea and not roads that provided the links

EAST CAPE & GISBORNE

between settlements. Wharves such as the one at Tolaga Bay were key to the success of the fledgling agriculture industry, for without sea access it was virtually impossible to get goods to market. With the advent of better roading, sea transport went rapidly into decline and all along the East Cape flourishing seaside communities such as Tokomaru Bay, Waipiro Bay, Hicks Bay and Te Araroa saw both their importance and populations slowly dwindle.

Cook's Cove Walkway

Captain James Cook's first landing, at the Turanganui River at modern-day Gisborne, was, through a series of misunderstandings, an uncharacteristic disaster. So, in desperate need of water and firewood, he sailed north to this cove in October 1769.

Located on the southern side of Tolaga Bay, this walk mainly through farmland takes two-and-a-half hours return, and from the track there are fantastic views north over the bay.

Wild Stingray Feeding, Dive Tatapouri

Okay, okay, so a stingray killed Steve Irwin, but don't let *one* death put you off meeting these most gentle of sea creatures up close. Just 100 metres off Tatapouri Beach is a reef that becomes almost exposed at low tide, and it is here that Dive Tatapouri have developed a unique attraction and the only one of its kind in New Zealand.

The reef is home to stingrays that live in its deep channels to avoid predators and, attracted by regular feeding, will come right up to people and feed from their hands. Mainly eagle and short-tailed rays, the largest of the regular ray visitors is Brutus, who is estimated to weigh around 200 kg, but the regular food also attracts other sea creatures such as the shy conger eel, kahawai, kingfish and, very occasionally, orcas. The orcas, though, particularly enjoy feeding on stingrays, so it is doubtful how welcome they are.

The trip to the reef is tide and weather dependent, but it is one of those incredibly moving experiences that are well worth more than just a detour. Dive Tatapouri, SH35, Tatapouri Beach, 10 km north of Gisborne, ph 06 868 5153.

Gisborne

Captain Cook Statues, Gisborne

In 1769 Captain James Cook first made landfall at the mouth of the Turanganui River at present-day Gisborne, and it is appropriate that the city has commemorated this occasion with two statues of the famous explorer. One is on Kaiti Hill and the other at the mouth of the Turanganui River near Waikanae Beach.

The bronze figure on Kaiti Hill was erected in 1969 to mark the bicentennial of Cook's landing and was cast from a marble statue purchased in Italy in the late nineteenth century in the belief that it was Captain Cook. It was discovered much later, and to great local amusement, that the reality was quite different. In fact, the facial features of this gentleman bear no resemblance to Cook whatsoever, and the uniform he is wearing is Italian and not British! To their credit, the good folk of Gisborne left the imposter where he was and today this unknown Italian naval hero has entrenched his place in Gisborne folklore.

Gisborne Airport

Usually trains and planes don't really mix, but Gisborne Airport is the only airport in New Zealand (and surely one of the few in the world) where a railway line cuts right across the runway. The railway was there first and that may account for the protocol that the planes give way to the trains. However, for the good of all concerned, this particular railway line is not that busy.

◀◀ The Star of Canada, Te Moana Maritime Museum, Gisborne

This museum within a museum is the wheelhouse and captain's cabin of the steamer *Star of Canada*. Built in Belfast in 1909, the ship ran aground on rocks on the Gisborne foreshore in June 1912 and could not be refloated. The next best thing was to salvage what was possible, and local jeweller William Good purchased the wheelhouse. Towing the structure through town, he placed it on an empty section next to his house in Childers Road where it became a local attraction to many generations of Gisbornites.

In 1983 the *Star* was left to the city of Gisborne and moved to its present location right on the river (the best view of the wheelhouse is on the riverbank opposite the museum). This section of the Tairawhiti Museum naturally houses the maritime history exhibits and includes an amazing collection of old surfboards.

◀◀ Eastwoodhill Arboretum

Billed as 'the largest collection of northern hemisphere trees in the southern hemisphere', Eastwoodhill contains over 4000 exotic trees and shrubs covering over 150 hectares. The arboretum is the life work of William Douglas Cook, who at best could be described as eccentric.

Born in New Plymouth in 1884 to an affluent family, Cook developed an interest in plants from an early age. At just 18 he established an orchard at Hastings with money borrowed from his family, but his venture failed and, after taking various labouring jobs, he sold the orchard and in 1910 bought 250 hectares of rough land at Ngatapa, west of Gisborne. No sooner had Cook established himself on the farm than he was called to service at the outbreak of the First World War.

Wounded at Gallipoli in 1915, Cook then served in France and at one stage lost the sight in his right eye. While recuperating with relatives in Scotland, he became inspired by the great gardens of Britain, and once he returned to New Zealand began a lifetime of collecting and planting trees and plants from the northern hemisphere. On regular trips to Europe he bought thousands of specimens including tulips, peonies and hyacinths from the Netherlands. In addition, he amassed an impressive library of horticultural works.

In 1927 he employed Bill Crooks, who remained at Eastwoodhill for 47 years tending the farm, leaving Cook to tend his trees. He married in 1930,

but the union was not a success and ended just a few years later. During this time he enlarged his farm, but sold parts of it again in the 1950s to fund his tree-buying expeditions. At that time the threat of nuclear war made him even more determined to preserve this oasis of northern flora in the South Pacific. In 1951 Cook established the Pukeiti Rhododendron Trust in Taranaki, as rhododendrons did not flourish at Eastwoodhill.

If Cook's tree collecting was unusual, then his habit of working in the nude wearing just a sunhat and a boot on his right foot was decidedly odd. Over the half-century until his death in 1967, it is estimated that Cook's obsession cost him in excess of £55,000. After his death from a heart attack the arboretum was left to a trust, but the vast preserve gradually became neglected. In 1984 a group of local women formed a garden group to help restore Eastwoodhill to its former glory.

Today the 1-hectare Homestead Garden is recognised as a Garden of National Significance and at every time of the year there is something special to see, though autumn is a particularly popular time to visit. Numerous tracks throughout Eastwoodhill allow the visitor to spend any amount of time from a 30-minute walk to half a day.

2392 Wharekopae Road, Ngatapa, 35 km west from Gisborne.
Open daily 9 a.m. to 5 p.m., closed Good Friday and Christmas Day,
www.eastwoodhill.org.nz, ph 06 863 9003; entry fee.

Manutuke

During the middle and later nineteenth century, Maori carving flourished on the East Coast, and at Manutuke, just south of Gisborne, are two of the most important and finest nineteenth-century meeting houses in the country. The heartland of the Rongowhakaata iwi, Te Mana-ki-Turanga and Te Poho Rukupo were both carved in the distinctive local Turanga style under the influence of local chief Raharuhi Rukupo.

Built in 1883, Te Mana-ki-Turanga is the older house, and features carvings of the separation of Rangi and Papa, and Maui hauling his fish from the sea. Te Poho Rukupo was built not long after in 1887 at nearby Pakirikiri to honour Rukupo and originally stood near his grave, but was moved to the present site in 1913. Manutuke was also home to a third equally impressive and much older meeting house, Te Hau-ki-Turanga. Built in 1842,

this meeting house was dismantled and moved to Wellington in 1867 and is now housed in Te Papa Tongarewa Museum of New Zealand.

14 km south of Gisborne on SH2.
While visitors are welcome at Manutuke, please show respect and do not enter when there is a hui in progress.

‹‹ Matawai Hotel, Matawai

Like many old hotels, Matawai began life elsewhere. Originally built in 1889 at Motuhoura, 18 km from Matawai on the Motu River, the old wooden pub was packed up and moved in 1932 to take advantage of the traffic at the junction of the Motu road and the main route between Gisborne and Opotiki. Today it is one of the country's most original pubs, with its verandahs, high ceilings and period woodwork all intact.

But what makes the Matawai different from other old pubs is the sprawling cluster of outbuildings that surround it. Early hotels were once the hub of the community, providing not only accommodation but also acting as the local store, post office, stables and blacksmith's shop. And for drovers and musterers, obviously a bit too rough to stay in the main hotel, more basic lodgings were on offer. At Matawai most of the ancillary buildings have survived, including the stables and even the old drover accommodation, whereas in other hotels these lesser buildings have long since been demolished.

Lying equidistant between Gisborne and Opotiki, the Matawai Hotel is an ideal spot for a break. Carefully maintained and restored, and providing modern facilities but without losing any of its old-time charm, the large main bar and dining room are packed with old photos, memorabilia, hunting trophies and a glass case enclosing a bizarre stuffed two-headed lamb.

SH2, 70 km from Gisborne, ph 06 862 4874.

‹‹ Millton Vineyard, Manutuke

The Millton Vineyard near Gisborne is possibly the best-known organic winery in New Zealand. Covering 30 hectares in four separate vineyards in the Manutuke region, Millton was established as a biodynamic organic

vineyard in 1984, though grapes had been grown on the property since the 1960s. This means that no insecticide, herbicide, systemic fungicide or soluble fertilisers are used.

As with most Poverty Bay vineyards, Millton is strong on white wine, but also produces Merlot, Pinot Noir, Malbec and Syrah. All the wines are from single vineyards as identified on the label (e.g. Te Arai Chenin Blanc, Opou Vineyard Chardonnay). Millton's premium wines are produced under the Clos de Ste Anne label and come from Naboth's Vineyard, a northeastern-facing hill slope in the Poverty Bay foothills. They also produce two dessert wines from Viognier and Chardonnay grapes.

In addition to its reputation as a leading organic wine producer, the tasting room at Millton is set in a beautiful garden with clipped hedges, under the shade of old olive trees, ideal for a leisurely picnic.

119 Papatu Road, Manutuke, Gisborne. Open Labour Weekend to end of December, Monday to Saturday 10 a.m. to 5 p.m.; January and February, daily 10 a.m. to 5 p.m.; March to Labour Weekend, Monday to Friday 10 a.m. to 5 p.m., ph 06 862 8680, www.millton.co.nz.

Morere Hot Springs and Nature Reserve

New Zealand has more than its fair share of hot springs, but these particular springs are unique for several reasons. They are located in a 364-hectare nature reserve and surrounded by fine native bush that is particularly renowned for the luxurious growth of its nikau palms. The reserve has a number of tracks that take from 30 minutes to three hours, so this is your chance to feel very virtuous and go on a brisk bush walk, rewarded afterwards by a soak in the hot pools. And if you're there at night, take a walk in the bush to see the glow-worms.

The springs produce an astounding 250,000 litres of water per day bubbling up through a crack in the fault line that cuts across the Mangakawa Valley. Even more incredible is that the water is actually ancient seawater that has been trapped for millennia underground, even though Morere is situated inland and at quite a distance from the ocean.

There are a number of pools, indoor and out, for both families and those wanting a more relaxed soak. The mineral pools are reputed to have

therapeutic value, though the water temperature is more warm than hot. The small spa-like pools known as the Nikau Pools are located in a wonderful bush setting thick with nikau and well away from the larger family pool.

On SH2, just north of Nuhaka, ph 06 837 8856.

‹‹ Te Urewera

Te Urewera has always been isolated country. A land of steep hills, deep valleys and a tough climate, Te Urewera is also the home of the Tuhoe people, known as 'the Children of the Mist', fiercely independent and the last Maori iwi to be influenced by Europeans and even today well known for their individuality. The Urewera National Park encompasses much of this inland country and at its heart is Lake Waikaremoana. This large lake, second only to Taupo and formed just 2000 years ago by a massive landslide across the Waikaretaheke River, is over 240 metres deep and has deep bays that reach far into rugged bush-covered terrain. Over 600 native plants have been recorded in the area, and the bush is mostly untouched.

The Lake Waikaremoana Great Walk follows the shore for most of its 46 km. It is by no means flat, but is within the reach of a moderately fit tramper who is prepared for a three- to four-day trip. The weather in the area is very changeable and can be cold and wet even in summer, and it is not unusual to have snow in winter. This tramp is becoming increasingly popular, so it is necessary to book huts and campsites well ahead in the busy season. However, as an alternative, a water taxi is available for those who wish to shorten their journey or even do sections of the walk as a day trip (www.lakewaikaremoana.co.nz).

If you're not up for something so demanding there are a number of much shorter walks ranging from 10 minutes to half a day, most within a short distance of the DoC-administered Aniwaniwa Visitor Centre (ph 06 837 3803), a destination in its own right. Housed within the centre is a small museum, home to the famous Colin McCahon Urewera Mural (valued at well over one million dollars), a huge triptych painting that was stolen from here in 1997 and returned 15 months later.

At the eastern end of the lake, below the distinctive Panakiri Bluff, is the site of the Armed Constabulary Redoubt. Today the bush has reclaimed the

land, and all that remains is the old parade ground, a historic cemetery and a limestone rock poignantly carved with the names and dates of soldiers stationed here in the 1860s and 1870s.

The easiest way to the park by car is the sealed road from Wairoa 72 km away. The road via Murupara from the north is something else: narrow, relentlessly winding and gravel for 100 km, it requires real patience and careful driving, but passes through some of the most wild and untouched bush country in New Zealand.

TARANAKI

Cape Egmont Lighthouse

Solidly built to withstand the furious westerly winds, this cast-iron lighthouse was made in sections in London in 1864 and shipped out to New Zealand. Originally erected on Mana Island north of Wellington, in 1887 it was dismantled and rebuilt at Cape Egmont where it stands today. It was converted to electricity in the late 1950s and automated in 1986. Despite what it looks like on the map, the cape is not the most westerly point in the North Island – that distinction belongs to Cape Maria van Diemen in Northland.

> From New Plymouth, drive 45 km south on SH45. Just south of Pungarehu turn right into Cape Road. The lighthouse is 5 km down the end of this road.

Forgotten World Highway

For a back-country driving experience it's hard to beat a trip along SH43 that runs between Stratford and Taumarunui, a road that has been rechristened the 'Forgotten World Highway'. Rich in both natural and human history, this is not a fast road, continuously twisting and turning through broken hill country and over numerous saddles. From the higher points there are marvellous views of Taranaki and the mountains of the central North Island. Even though it is now sealed all the way, it will still take three to four hours to travel the 155-km extent.

Highlights along the road include:

The Moki Tunnel

Known as the 'Hobbit Hole' long before the *Lord of the Rings* films were made, this narrow 180-metre one-way road tunnel was built in 1936 and has wooden beams supporting the portals and peaked roof.

Mt Damper Falls

A 16-km detour off the highway near Whangamomona, at 74 metres these falls are the highest single drop in the North Island. A local story tells of their discovery by a sheep farmer who lost his prize sheep dog after it was dragged over the cliff by a wild boar. From the road it is a 45-minute return walk mainly across farmland to the falls. Though not hard, the track is pretty rough and muddy.

TARANAKI

Whangamomona

Established in 1895, this historic village is now famous for its January Republic Day Festival that attracts thousands to a township that normally has a population of just 16. The festival was first held in 1989 and declared the Whangamomona area a republic (complete with its own passport) as a protest against regional government boundary changes that took the district out of Taranaki and into the Manawatu. The focal point of the rebellion was the Whangamomona Hotel, one of New Zealand's most iconic pubs.

Hawera

Elvis Presley Memorial Record Room

Born and bred in Hawera and a rocker from way back when, Kevin Wasley is a long-time Elvis fan and in his garage has created a monumental collection dedicated to 'The King'. The garage, more correctly known as the 'Elvis Presley Memorial Record Room', is absolutely packed from floor to ceiling with Elvis and general rock 'n' roll memorabilia and souvenirs including over 5000 recordings and a jukebox that only contains Elvis records.

Kevin has visited Elvis's former home 'Graceland' no less than 17 times and the highlights of his collection are a 1968 autographed Christmas album, original concert tickets and a scarf from a 1974 Memphis concert. While this is a private collection and viewing is strictly by appointment only, Kevin is a friendly and accommodating guy, but the room is part of his family home so don't just turn up unannounced.

51 Argyle Street, Hawera. By appointment only, ph 06 278 7624, 027 498 2942; donation.

Tawhiti Museum

In 1975 Nigel and Teresa Ogle bought the old Tawhiti cheese factory and eventually transformed it into one of New Zealand's best private museums. What makes this museum so special is the wonderful models, both miniature and life-sized, that are dazzling in their attention to detail. The diorama of a

91

Maori raiding party, comprising hundreds of tiny figures threading their way through a variety of landscapes, is just superb. The life-size models will make you jump with surprise.

While the focus is on South Taranaki history, this museum's appeal extends way beyond the region. Don't miss the working reconstruction of a water wheel, the vintage tractor collection, and the special display on Chinese settler and entrepreneur Chew Chong (Chau Tseung), who developed a fungi export business that provided local farmers a much-needed source of cash during difficult times.

> 401 Ohangai Road, well signposted from both Normanby (north) and
> Hawera (south). Open September to May, Friday, Saturday, Sunday,
> Monday 10 a.m. to 4 p.m., January daily 10 a.m. to 4 p.m.,
> ph 0800 921 921, www.tawhitimuseum.co.nz; entry fee.

◀◀ Koru Pa, Oakura

Situated on a loop of the Oakura River, Koru pa is located on some of the oldest inhabited land in New Zealand, dating from around AD 1000. Occupied until 1826, the pa was finally abandoned when invading Waikato forced Taranaki tribes to flee further south to safety.

Use of stone by early Maori is uncommon and the pa is highly unusual in that this material is used extensively on the outer facings of the defensive ditches. This is especially obvious on the upper terraces. (Some theorists claim that the use of stone indicates a much older culture stretching back thousands rather than hundreds of years.) The outlines are very clear, in particular the deep kumara pits, ditches and terraces. The pa also has an unusual feel in that it is totally bush covered, though there is an excellent view of the Oakura River from the top terrace. While the pa site is well maintained, the access is an unformed track across farmland.

> From Oakura, turn left into Wairau Road. The pa is 4 km down this road and
> is well signposted.

New Plymouth

⫷ Govett-Brewster Art Gallery

In 1963 Monica Brewster bequeathed £50,000 to the New Plymouth City Council to create a trust to establish the Govett-Brewster Art Gallery (combining both her maiden name, Govett, and her married name). Now one of the finest contemporary art institutions in the country, the gallery is dedicated to exhibitions that are intellectually challenging, visually exciting and at the cutting edge of contemporary art. This is no mere collection of modern paintings, but a mixture of contemporary art expression in the broadest possible terms. A special feature is a collection by the artist and kinetic sculptor Len Lye, who left a significant portion of his work to the gallery.

But what of the benefactress who endowed such a gallery to the city? A private person, Monica Brewster was also a very shrewd connoisseur and collector herself. Hailing from a long-established local family, she travelled widely and developed a love of modern art – a style she much preferred to the more traditional art common in the grand European art galleries she had visited. Accordingly, along with the £50,000 gift came a deed that included some very carefully drafted provisions to ensure the gallery would focus on contemporary work. One of the key stipulations was that its director should be an art professional with a national reputation.

The opening of the initial exhibition in February 1970 shocked locals, but 30 years later New Plymouth folk take new installations at the gallery in their stride. Monica Brewster died in 1973 and was buried without a headstone, preferring her memorial to be the art gallery she founded. Love or hate the Govett-Brewster, the one thing you won't be is indifferent.

40 Queen Street, New Plymouth. Open daily 10.30 a.m. to 5 p.m., ph 06 759 6060, www.govettbrewster.org.nz; koha/donation.

The Swanndri Collection, Puke Ariki Museum, Library and Information Centre

In 1913 local Taranaki tailor William Broome developed a strong woollen overshirt for farmers and bushmen that he waterproofed with a secret formula and registered under the name 'Swanndri'. The origins of the special formula are uncertain, but a recipe for waterproofing clothing was available in a book that William owned called *Fortunes in Formulas and Facts* and may have been adapted and further developed to produce the Swanndri garment.

Made in limited quantities in Taranaki until 1952 when new techniques permitted much greater production, the Swanndri became hugely popular during the 1950s and 1960s, and virtually anyone who worked or played outdoors owned a 'swannie'. Mostly they were long, almost reaching the knee, and always an olive-green colour, though coloured checked Swanndris become more common later. Subsequently, production moved to the South Island, and more recently overseas. No one now knows the reason for the double 'n' in Swanndri and whether the idiosyncratic spelling was deliberate or, as some might claim, simply a spelling mistake.

Proactive in collecting vintage Swanndris, Puke Ariki has a small collection of about 20, of which around five are on display. Swannies are not the sort of clothing to be left hanging in the cupboard, but were worn until they fell apart and then biffed out, making older versions very rare.

1 Ariki Street, New Plymouth. Open Monday, Tuesday, Thursday, Friday 9 a.m. to 6 p.m., Wednesday to 9 p.m., weekends 9 a.m. to 5 p.m., closed Christmas Day, www.pukeariki.com.

Okurukuru Wines

Located high above the sea on the Taranaki coast just south of New Plymouth, Okurukuru has one of the most spectacular sites of any New Zealand vineyard – but what a tough place to grow grapes! In contrast to the warm, dry climate usually associated with grape-growing, Okurukuru is exposed to cool prevailing westerly winds, receives high rainfall, and is a test to any grape-grower. Planted in Pinotage, Pinot Gris and Pinot Noir, the vineyard produced its first vintage in 2006 with a Taranaki Rosé.

Okurukuru has taken full advantage of a stunning site by building a

modern and very stylish restaurant accentuating views both of the coastline and the mountain. Blending into the hillside and imitating an ocean wave, extensive use of huge glass windows ensures a view in every direction. Whether it is for weekend brunch, lunch, dinner, coffee and cake, or just a relaxing glass of wine, Okurukuru is not to be missed in any visit to the Taranaki.

> 738 Surf Highway 45. Open Tuesday to Sunday from 9 a.m.,
> ph 06 751 0787, www.thevineyard.co.nz.

Parihaka Village

Parihaka, south of New Plymouth, has today become the symbol to many of the power of peaceful protest. The village grew up after the land confiscations of the 1860s and was at the time the largest Maori settlement in New Zealand.

In 1880, in a series of remarkable actions, the people of Parihaka began protesting against continued land sales. Time and again, under the leadership of Te Whiti o Rongomai and Tohu Kakahi, they met armed force with peaceful action and courteous resistance, using tactics such as pulling up survey pegs and ploughing confiscated land, but never resorting to violence. However, by September of that year, hundreds of men were either exiled or imprisoned in the South Island, and finally, on 5 November 1881, in front of a silent crowd of 2000 Maori, the army moved in, arresting the leaders Te Whiti and Tohu. The militia then spent two months destroying the houses and crops and occupied Parihaka for the next five years. Many of the menfolk never returned from the south, and of those who did, the last arrived back in Parihaka in July 1898.

Parihaka as a village never recovered and today is a small cluster of houses around a central monument. Nevertheless, while the protest ultimately failed, the actions at Parihaka and its leaders Tohu and Te Whiti have come to symbolise the fight for indigenous rights through non-violent resistance and have inspired books, music and art. The tiny village is the location of the Parihaka International Peace Festival held in January each year (www.parihaka.com), and today the spirit of Parihaka fulfils Te Whiti's prophetic words: 'Those who are bent by the wind shall rise again when the wind softens.'

Parihaka Road, off SH45, Pungarehu, south of New Plymouth. Visitors are welcome at Parihaka – but remember, these are people's homes and not a tourist attraction, so please show respect.

Patea

Aotea Waka Monument

New Zealand doesn't really have a tradition of folk art, but the memorial to the *Aotea* waka is one of the country's best-known such works. Constructed (and possibly designed) by Jones Brothers, monumental masons based in Hawera, the waka was built of concrete with paua-shell inlays. Nearly 17 metres long, the monument was originally the gateway to the town hall (since demolished).

Unveiled on 2 April 1993, the *Aotea* was the brainchild of Messrs Panenui, Tupito and Wakarua and commemorates the settlement of the district in the fourteenth century by Turi and his wife Rongorongo. The figures, which all resolutely face forward – no doubt excited at the prospect of settling in Patea – were originally carved from punga wood. Turi was specifically told about the land around the Patea River by the explorer Kupe, and although the waka actually landed at Kawhia, Turi and his hapu travelled through dense bush and rugged hill country to settle here – a walk that even these days would be a challenge.

An annual Waitangi Day celebration called 'Paepae in the Park' is held in the park behind the monument and attracts top musical acts and large crowds.

Electrical Displays, Patea Museum

When it comes to electricity, Patea was at the forefront of adopting this new technology, and in 1901 was the first municipality to build its own power station. The borough continued to run the power station until it was sold to the South Taranaki Power Board in 1958. It was a simple operation and initially the power was just for electric lighting, but later the generating hours were extended to Monday afternoons to allow women to do their ironing!

Very little remains of the original power station, but the museum,

housed in Patea's oldest building (dating from 1869), has a great display of electricity-related materials. Here you will find collections of light switches, electricity meters and a dazzling array of historical light bulbs, along with other electricity paraphernalia. Patea is one of those wonderful small-town museums that looks like a cluttered antique shop and will appeal to those who enjoy an enthusiastic and eclectic style of collection rather than the sparser modern kind.

127 Egmont Street, Patea. Open Tuesday to Saturday 10 a.m. to 3 p.m., closed public holidays, ph 06 273 8354; koha/donation.

Pukerangiora Pa

This major pa has a magnificent location high on a rocky bluff overlooking the Waitara River with wide views back to the coast, and its strategic advantage is obvious. Pukerangiora saw bitter fighting during the Musket War period in the 1820s and 1830s and at one stage fell to invaders, forcing many of the defenders to attempt escape by leaping from the cliffs above the river.

During the bitter land wars in Taranaki in the 1860s the pa was a major centre of Maori resistance and the focus of a campaign led by the elderly Major-General Pratt. Advocating slow-siege tactics, Pratt constructed a complicated series of redoubts and a long sap, or trench, the latter still clearly visible today just below the pa. Pratt's technique, described as 'a mile a month', drew criticism from the colonists and prompted the ironic remark in one report: 'The war in Taranaki maintains its peaceful course.' However, Pratt's persistence eventually paid off and the pa fell to his war of attrition.

The site is not well maintained and the signage minimal and confusing, but don't let that put you off. The main car park is about 200 metres past the first sign and is easy to miss. The military sap to the pa is behind the trees to the left of this sign.

From New Plymouth, turn right into Waitara Road about 2 km before the turnoff to Waitara. The pa is 8 km on the left down this road.

◀◀ Sentry Hill Winery

Green ginger wine enjoyed popularity in the eighteenth and nineteenth centuries as prevention for cholera, though the health properties of ginger have long been recognised in folk medicine. Today, ginger in all its incarnations has a reputation as a good aid for digestion and other stomach ailments – but why not take your medicine in an enjoyable form?

Green ginger wine is made from fresh root ginger, not the dried variety, and the Sentry Hill fruit winery near New Plymouth produces an excellent traditional version known as Trooper's Green Ginger Wine. This small, award-wining winery, which takes its name from the 57th Regiment of the British Army who established a garrison in the area in 1864, also produces a boutique range of fruit wines.

> 152 Cross Road, Lepperton. Open October to March, Monday to Friday
> 11 a.m. to 3 p.m., Saturday, Sunday and public holidays 10 a.m. to
> 4 p.m.; April to September, Thursday and Friday 11 a.m. to 3 p.m.,
> Saturday, Sunday and public holidays 10 a.m. to 4 p.m.,
> ph 06 752 0778, www.sentryhillwinery.co.nz.

WHANGANUI

Right, before we start – a spelling lesson and an introduction to a lively local debate. Maori words beginning with 'wh' are usually pronounced with a soft 'wh' sound, though some iwi leave the 'h' silent. However, debate rages over whether or not the correct spelling of Wanganui is with or without the 'h'. The current position is that the city is spelt *Wanganui* without the 'h' and the river and the national park (and sometimes the region) are spelt *Whanganui* with the 'h'.

◀◀ Whanganui River Road

The legendary Whanganui River Road begins at Upokongaro, just north of Wanganui on SH4, and ends 91 km later at Raetihi, traversing some of New Zealand's most fascinating back country. Settlements along the river were originally only accessible by riverboat, but once the road was built in 1935 river traffic slumped.

Following the river closely for much of the way, this is not a road that can be hurried, as it is narrow and winding and a long stretch is still unsealed and with few facilities. What's more, the locals drive fast and are disinclined to give way. Many of the names of the settlements along the bank are of biblical origin – Hiruharama/Jerusalem, Atene/Athens, Koriniti/Corinth – a legacy of their origins as missionary settlements. Though quite how Ranana/London crept in is anyone's guess! In recent years, the population has drifted away and today these once thriving villages are little more than tiny collections of old houses.

Now based in Wanganui City, the restored riverboat *Waimarie* was built in 1899 as a kitset in London, and was one of a fleet of 12 such boats owned by Alexander Hatrick. Working the river between the coast and Taumarunui, the *Waimarie* was finally taken out of service in 1949. Salvaged from the mud in 1993, she was back on the river in 2001 and is now New Zealand's only authentic coal-fired paddle steamer, running regular cruises up the river to Upokongaro.

Highlights along the river include:

Jerusalem/Hiruharama

Once a thriving settlement, Jerusalem is set in a bend of the river above which sits the pretty church of Hatu Hohepa (St Joseph), one of New Zealand's most photographed houses of worship. The convent next to the church was the home of Mother Aubert (1835–1926), who came from France and established the order of the Sisters of Compassion in 1892. Mother Aubert was well known in the district for her charitable work and use of native plants for medicinal purposes.

The acclaimed poet James K. Baxter established a short-lived commune settlement at Hiruharama in 1969, and his *Jerusalem Sonnets* and *Jerusalem Daybook* were written here. Just downriver is Moutoa Island, site of the historic battle of 1864 when upriver supporters of the anti-British Hauhau were defeated by their lower-river opponents.

Kawana Flour Mill, Matahiwi

In 1854 Governor ('Kawana') Grey presented the Poutama people with the machinery to build a flour mill. Operating until 1913, the mill then fell into disrepair until being faithfully restored in recent years. The mill contains the original millstones and upstairs the walls are lined with historic photographs and an excellent diagram as to how it operated. The cottage next to the mill was moved to the site from its original position across the road.

Koriniti

This beautiful historic marae features three carved meeting houses: Poutama (1888), Te Waherehere (1845), and Hikurangi Wharerata (1975). The marae is open to visitors except when a function is being held. A koha is appreciated.

Pipiriki

The stretch of the river above Pipiriki, which is not accessible by road, is considered to be the most attractive part of the Whanganui as it meanders through the Whanganui National Park. Once a busy river port, Pipiriki is now a base for tramping, jet boating, kayaking and other adventure trips along the river and access to the historic 'Bridge to Nowhere'. The bridge was constructed in 1936 to improve access to the Mangapurua Valley, an area specifically allocated to resettling soldiers after WWI. While 35 farms were developed the area was so remote and totally unsuitable to farming that by 1942 only three farms remained occupied and these too were eventually abandoned.

Cooks Gardens

While the origins of the name are a bit clouded (it is believed the area was once a vegetable garden), today Cooks Gardens is best known as the athletic stadium made famous when Peter Snell ran New Zealand's first sub-four-minute mile in January 1962 in front of a packed crowd of over 13,000 people. In fact, the gardens began their life as a sports arena in 1896, when the local athletics, cycling, rugby and cricket clubs got together to jointly develop the area for their club activities.

Generally, the gardens are open to the public and anyone can test their pace over the very track that Snell ran (though don't get in the way of the real athletes training!). If the stadium is closed there is an excellent view over the grounds by the old wooden fire-tower with bells dated 1874.

St Hill Street, central Wanganui.

Durie Hill Elevator and Tower

Across the river from the city and giving access to the suburb of Durie Hill is the only public underground elevator in New Zealand. Durie Hill became part of Wanganui Borough in 1910, but there was no easy access to the area high above the river. Dismissing a cable car as too costly, the council opted for a unique solution – an underground tunnel and elevator. While work began in 1916, the elevator was only finally opened in August 1919. The 205-metre-long tunnel and the 66-metre elevator are now a Category 1 historic place. Not fast, the elevator rattles and shakes, but it is much more convenient than the path with 191 steps from the river to the top.

Not part of the elevator development, the 33-metre tower is in fact a World War I war memorial opened in 1925. From the top, views include not only the city and environs, but also on a fine day Mts Taranaki and Ruapehu.

The suburb of Durie Hill is also unique in its own right. Considered to be New Zealand's first modern suburb, it was planned by architect Samuel Hurst Seager and is properly known as the Durie Hill Garden Suburb.

The tunnel to the elevator is opposite the City Bridge at the end of Victoria Street, Wanganui. Open Monday to Friday 7.30 a.m. to 6 p.m., Saturday 9 a.m. to 5 p.m., Sundays and public holidays 10 a.m. to 5 p.m.; small charge.

Lindauer Gallery/Te Pataka Whakaahua, Whanganui Regional Museum

While this excellent regional museum focuses on the Whanganui district, it also contains some of the country's most important artefacts and is not too big to be overwhelming. Not to be missed is the Lindauer Gallery/Te Pataka Whakaahua, one of the largest collections of this colonial artist's paintings in the country with around 20 works on display at any one time (only Auckland has a larger collection and most Lindauers are in private collections).

Born in Bohemia (modern-day Czech Republic), Gottfried Lindauer began painting at a young age and in 1860 produced a series of large murals for a church in Moravia where they remain today. In 1874, to escape the army, he jumped aboard the first ship leaving Hamburg thinking he was going to America, but instead landed in Wellington in August of that year. Initially, Lindauer wandered around the country, picking up commissions from leading colonists, and eventually settled in Woodville, built a studio and continued to paint until his death in 1926.

In 1885 Sir Walter Butler commissioned Lindauer to paint a series of portraits of rangatira (a chief or noble person) for a London exhibition, and afterwards the paintings returned to New Zealand and have been on display at the museum since 1928. While today Lindauer is best known as a painter of Maori subjects, the majority of his thousand-odd paintings comprise family portraits of important and wealthy Europeans. Indeed, he repeated many of his most popular pieces several times, so what might appear to be copies are in fact originals.

In addition to the Te Pataka Whakaahua, the museum boasts one of the most important collections of moa bones, with a number of complete skeletons of several species. And located in the central hall is the magnificent waka taua (war canoe) *Te Mata*. Over 22 metres in length, this waka was built before 1810 from a single totara log and took part in several battles – and has the musket holes to show for it!

Watt Street, Wanganui, adjacent to Queen's Park. Open daily 10 a.m. to 4.30 p.m., www.wanganui-museum.org.nz; donation/koha.

◀◀ Ratana Temple, Ratana

Every year in February, Ratana pa springs into the news headlines as politicians vie for attention and support of the influential Ratana church. For the rest of the year, this is a quiet place dominated by the distinctive Ratana temple that is well worth a short detour off SH3 just south of Wanganui.

During the 1918 influenza epidemic, the very worldly Tahupotiki Wiremu Ratana was told during a vision that he was to unite Maori and return them to God, for now Maori were to replace the Jews as God's chosen people. After studying the bible, Ratana, now known as the Mangai (Mouthpiece of God), began preaching and quickly began attracting increasingly large congregations. In order to improve the conditions of Maori, Ratana gradually turned to politics and through the 1920s and 1930s become more influential resulting in his taking two seats at the 1935 election. In 1936 Ratana and the Labour Prime Minister Michael Savage brokered a deal that saw the political arm of the Ratana movement come under the Labour banner. T W Ratana died on 18 September 1939 and, while the influence of the Ratana movement has waned during the second half of the twentieth century, it still claims to have around 65,000 adherents.

Te Tempara Tapu O Ihoa (Holy Temple of Jehovah) was dedicated in 1928 and, while it has features common to Christian churches, it is at the same time distinctly different. The interior of the church is very simple but strong in symbolism; in particular the five-pointed star and the crescent moon representing divine enlightenment are repeated throughout the church. The carefully chosen colours all have meaning: blue symbolises The Father, white The Son, red The Holy Spirit, purple angels, and pink Ratana himself. The symbol of the sun unusually represents both the second coming of Christ and a unique spiritual relationship established in 1924 between Ratana and Bishop Juji Nakada of Japan. On the two domed towers are written Arepa (Alpha) and Omeka (Omega). Set in beautifully kept gardens, the grave of the Mangai is in front of the church. Visitors are welcome but are requested not to take photos inside the gates.

23 km south of Wanganui and 2 km off SH3

MANAWATU, RANGITIKEI & KĀPITI

◀◀ The German Metal Press, Tokomaru Steam Engine Museum

Dedicated to the industrial and agricultural use of steam in all its amazing manifestations, this museum is the private collection of Colin and Esma Stevenson. With machinery collected from all over the country, the Tokomaru collection includes New Zealand's oldest steam engine, dating from 1869 and used for hauling ships to the Wellington dry dock.

In the extensive workshop area (which is not always open to the public) is a metal press rescued from a factory in nearby Palmerston North. The press originated in Germany, where during the Second World War it manufactured parts for the Luftwaffe. As part of Germany's vital war industry the factory came under fire on numerous occasions and the metal press was hit several times by rockets fired from Typhoon fighters. But this huge heavy machine is made of solid steel and built to last, and although it received several direct hits, the worst they could do was leave the occasional shallow dent.

On SH57, 18 km from Palmerston North.
Open Monday to Saturday 9 a.m. to 3.30 p.m., Sunday 10.30 a.m. to 3.30 p.m., closed Christmas Day and Good Friday, ph 09 329 8867, www.tokomarusteam.com; entry fee.

◀◀ Feilding Sale Yards

While so many smaller sale yards have disappeared over the years, they are a vital ingredient of the rural economy, not only for trading sheep and cattle, but also as a venue where rural folk can meet. Feilding in the Manawatu still has one of New Zealand's largest yards where each week on a Friday morning around 15,000 sheep and 1400 cattle are sold.

For those not directly involved in agriculture, the operation of a sale yard can be just noisy and plain confusing. Fortunately for the uninitiated, a tour is available at Feilding, with local farmers acting as guides. These personable and friendly tours unlock the mystery of how a sale yard works and why these sales are a key indicator to the health of the rural economy. Don't forget to wear sensible shoes and bring a rainproof jacket.

Manchester Street, Feilding. Guided tour Fridays 11 a.m., bookings essential, ph 06 323 3318, www.feilding.co.nz; small charge.

Foxton

◀◀ De Molen Windmill

Some men build sensible things like decks or a garden shed, but for Dutch immigrant Jan Langen nothing but a full-sized seventeenth-century Dutch windmill would do. So, today, after years of fundraising and planning, the main street of Foxton is home to the unusual sight and sound of windmill arms whirring in the wind.

This working windmill was built from actual Dutch plans from the seventeenth century, with only minor adaptations to comply with the New Zealand Building Code, and the machinery was imported from the Netherlands. The windmill operates during opening hours (except in very high winds) and processes New Zealand wheat into flour that can be purchased at the shop on the ground floor. There is a tour of the working areas of the mill. This is a very strange sight and well worth the short detour off SH1.

> De Molen Windmill, Foxton. Open daily 10 a.m. to 4 p.m.,
> www.windmill.org.nz; a small charge applies for the tour.

◀◀ Foxton Flax Stripping Museum

Flax was an important industry not just in the Manawatu, but throughout colonial New Zealand. In the heyday of the industry the stretch of the Manawatu River between Foxton and Palmerston North supported 70 flax mills. Foxton alone had eight mills as late as 1912, sourcing huge amounts of flax from the vast swamps along the river. Different regions produced different types of flax fibre, used for everything from rope to very attractive matting.

Today flax has long been superseded by imported and synthetic yarns, and this museum now houses the only working stripping and scutching (fibre separating) machines in the country. Every bit as interesting as the machinery is the man in charge, Gordon Burr. Known locally as 'Mr Chatterbox', Gordon has worked all his life in the flax industry and what he doesn't know about flax isn't worth knowing. Also for sale is unusual flax soap! Whether you are interested in flax or not, Gordon's enthusiasm and charm make this one of New Zealand's best working museum experiences.

The museum is behind De Molen Windmill.
Open daily 1 p.m. to 3 p.m., closed Christmas Day, Good Friday and
Anzac Day, ph 06 363 7095; entry fee.

◀◀ Trolley Bus and Doll Collection

There must be something about Foxton that attracts unusual collectors. Yet in a town that is home to a windmill, a sound museum and a flax museum, the doll and trolley bus collection of this enthusiastic husband-and-wife team, Christina and Ian Little, is not so unusual.

Ian claims to have the largest private collection of trolley buses in the world, with over 14 from Auckland, Wellington, Christchurch and Dunedin (only the capital still uses trolley buses). His interest in these vehicles began in 1949 when as a boy he stood on the wharf with his father watching the new Dunedin trolley buses being unloaded from a ship – one of which he later purchased in 1966 for just one pound. Opened to the public in 1986, the buses are all in working order and rides are available along the 4 km of overhead wire set up in Foxton streets.

While Ian collected buses, Christina set about making and collecting dolls. Her collection includes a 160-year-old French wax doll and a kewpie doll collection the oldest of which dates from 1910, but it is the Princess Diana dolls that really catch the eye. Christina has an amazing collection of around 12 Diana-lookalike dolls all dressed in miniature versions of the People's Princess's most famous frocks.

55 Main Street, Foxton. Open Tuesday to Sunday 10 a.m. to 5 p.m., ph 06 363 6656; entry fee and charge for the trolley bus rides.

◀◀ Kapiti Island

One of New Zealand's most important bird sanctuaries, Kapiti Island lies 5 km off the coast, is 1965 hectares in area, and its highest point, Tuteremoana, is at 520 metres. Occupied by Maori around AD 1150, Kapiti originally was part of the territory of Rangitane, ancestor of the iwi of the Manawatu. In 1822 the island was occupied by Te Rauparaha, driven south from Kawhia, and it was from this offshore base that the great fighting chief launched his devastating

attacks on the South Island. A small area of 13 hectares at Waiorua Bay is still held by Maori.

In 1987 the management of the island was handed over to the Department of Conservation, which set about removing sheep and possums. In an operation thought impossible, rats were also eradicated in 1998, and now Kapiti is an important nature sanctuary and home to a wide range of native bird life including many rare birds such as the little spotted kiwi (extinct on the mainland), weka, kaka, kakariki, tieke (saddleback) and hihi (stitchbird).

The island is reasonably accessible, with two companies operating a ferry service (weather dependent). However, visitor numbers are regulated and you must obtain a permit from DoC first (kapiti.island@doc.govt.nz, for more information). It is also possible to stay overnight at the Nature Lodge in the north of the island.

Lake Papaitonga

For those used to the open and often windswept landscape of the Horowhenua, this small lake surrounded by the finest lowland bush remnant between Wanganui and Wellington will come as a surprise. Now just covering 122 hectares, including the lake, the reserve forest is dominated by titoki, kahikatea, nikau, karaka and kiekie. It is just so hard to believe that this whole coast was once blanketed in such dense and luxurious bush and that so little has survived. Early settlers were nothing if not thorough when it came to clearing the land for farming . . .

Within the lake are two small islands, Motukiwi and Motungarara, both of which were the site of pa of the local Muaupoko iwi. The smaller of the pair was artificially constructed in the shallow lake water to afford greater protection for the pa. Even so, the lake was the scene of a bloody massacre when the invading Te Rauparaha captured both pa and took revenge on the inhabitants who had earlier killed his son and daughter.

In 1897 the land was acquired rather deviously by the noted naturalist Sir Walter Buller, though it was Buller who recognised its value and preserved this small piece of lowland forest for future generations. Today the lake is an important bush and wetland preserve.

Signposted 4 km south of Levin off SH1.

Our Lady of Lourdes, Paraparaumu

High on a hill overlooking the Kapiti Coast is an enormous 14-metre high statue of Our Lady of Lourdes. The idea for the statue came from local Waikanae parish priest Father Dunn, who wanted a monument to celebrate 100 years since the first appearance of the Virgin Mary at Lourdes in 1848. Early in 1958 he commissioned Martin Roestenburg to build the statue after a previous one built by enthusiastic, but inexperienced, Marist brothers blew down. Born in Eindhoven in the Netherlands in 1909, Roestenburg always had an interest in religious art and intriguingly spent some time studying at the Munich Academy of Fine Arts in 1941 and 1942. In 1951 he immigrated to New Zealand and, while this statue is his most prominent work, he is best known for his stained glass windows. Constructed over a period of six months, the statue is concrete plaster over a wooden frame and was dedicated in August 1958 to a crowd of over 6000 people. Roestenburg returned to the Netherlands and died there in 1966 aged just 56. The statue is simplistic in form, with strong angular lines and rather roughly finished. Located on a small hill, the rather steep and bumpy track to the statue is lined by the 14 Stations of the Cross in various states of repair. At night the statue is floodlit, though the halo is separately lit.

Tongariro Street, Paraparaumu.

Palmerston North

Hoffman Kiln

Despite being listed by the Historic Places Trust as one of the country's 10 most important industrial sites, the Hoffman Kiln is rather neglected and is only visible through a wire fence. This type of kiln was developed in Germany in the 1850s, though the Palmerston North one is an updated version of the original design.

The kiln was unique in that it was fired continuously, with each chamber being loaded, heated and unloaded one after the other. While most firings lasted around six weeks, the longest continuous firing of this kiln was three months, and when running at full capacity it produced an incredible 9000

bricks per day. To keep the kilns running, coal was fed into the chambers through small holes in the top by men working under the corrugated-iron roof structure. Talk about hot work!

The kiln is located at 615 Featherston Street, Palmerston North.

‹‹ The Bald Kiwi, New Zealand Rugby Museum

Regardless of your level of interest in rugby, this small museum is crammed full of every conceivable type of rugby memorabilia and is well worth a visit – rugby fans should plan to spend at least a few hours here. But what is a stuffed kiwi with a bald patch doing in a rugby museum?

On the 1925/26 tour of Great Britain, the New Zealand team took along a stuffed kiwi in a glass case to give to the first team that beat them. But the All Blacks won game after game and the stuffed kiwi kept touring on and on. Unfortunately, the bird was just a bit too tall and every time it moved, its head rubbed against the top of the case. Undefeated, the All Blacks returned home, still clutching their flightless talisman. By this time the kiwi had lost all the feathers on the top of its head and today is bald, but still proud to have been part of that extraordinary team.

87 Cuba Street, Palmerston North. Open Monday to Saturday
10 a.m. to noon, 1.30 p.m. to 4 p.m., Sunday 1.30 p.m. to 4 p.m.,
www.rugbymuseum.co.nz; entry fee.

‹‹ Savage Crescent

Few communities in New Zealand are without a larger or smaller neighbourhood of state houses. Actively promoted by the first Labour Government under Michael Joseph Savage, state houses popped up everywhere and today, in the 'leaky home' era, are considered to be very well built if a little lacking in style.

What makes Savage Crescent unique is that the whole development is still original. Constructed from 1939 to 1946, the crescent is a mixture of housing designs from this period, with some of the homes being quite different in style from those typically associated with state housing. A walk round the entire crescent will take less than an hour.

Savage Crescent can be accessed off either Park Street or College Street, both of which run off Fitzherbert Avenue, Palmerston North.

Sanson Rugby Grandstand

It isn't large or fancy or even that well maintained, but this iconic grandstand is symbolic of the enthusiasm of grass-roots rugby that has made such a small nation a major international player in this sport. Simply built of corrugated iron with a sign proudly proclaiming 'Manawatu Rugby', the stand overlooks a single and rather lumpy football field and it is doubtful whether it would hold 100 people – which for most matches is probably plenty.

On SH1, 500 metres south of the Sanson–Palmerston North intersection.

Stormy Point Lookout, Rangitikei

While there are a number of good view points overlooking Rangitikei, by far the most spectacular is from Stormy Point. Of particular interest are the broad river terraces considered to be one of the best-preserved sequences of their type in the world and each formed during a period of climatic cooling, the oldest of which dates back 350,000 years. There used to be a very good sign indicating the points of interest and giving an explanation of the area's geology, but that seems to have vanished – quite possibly blown away by the strong winds that give the lookout its name!

On SH54, 15 km from the turnoff on SH1, 6 km north of Hunterville.

The views over the Wairoa River are exceptional from Tokatoka Peak.

Ratana churches are both distinct in their architecture and unique to
New Zealand.

The legendary Puhoi Pub — 'Up the boohai' is a corruption of 'Up the Puhoi'.

Ninepin Rock at Whatipu overlooks the treacherous Manukau Bar.

Mazuran's is the lone survivor of the old time wineries along Lincoln Road.

The waterwheel at the only surviving six-stamper battery at Coromandel.

Tiny Waimama Bay is the perfect Coromandel beach.

The Riff Raff statue in Hamilton is a tribute to Richard O'Brien, the creator of The Rocky Horror Show.

This German mine was washed up at the mouth of the Mokau River in 1942.

The giant chainsaw man at Tokoroa is a tribute to forestry workers.

The Green Man is just one of Tokoroa's Talking Poles.

Located just off Waihi's main street is the giant Martha goldmine.

Picturesque St Stephen's in Opotiki was the site of a gruesome murder.

The mosaic family group is just one of the entertaining exhibits at the Te Puna Quarry.

The steam pipes at Wairakei look like a demented hydroslide.

Stroll out on the country's longest wharf at Tolaga Bay.

Extensive ruins of the old freezing works at Tokomaru Bay.

Manutuke is home to two of the country's finest carved meeting houses.

Over 20,000 items pack the Elvis Memorial Room in Hawera.

Electricity meters in the Patea Museum reflect the town's early adoption of electricity.

The Whangamomona pub is the ideal spot for a break on the Forgotton World Highway.

HAWKE'S BAY

Dannevirke

Danish Hair Embroidery, Dannevirke Gallery of History

Dannevirke, meaning 'Danes work', is named after a fortification in Schleswig (now part of Germany) and, like nearby Norsewood, was settled by Scandinavians. On 15 September 1872 two ships carrying Scandinavian immigrants landed at Napier. They were the *Hovding* from Christiania (now Oslo) and the *Ballarat* from London, and their passengers were Norwegian and Danish families sponsored by the New Zealand government and destined to develop the rugged southern Hawke's Bay. Initially, 19 families settled in Norsewood and Dannevirke, and over the years many more Norwegians, Danes and Swedes joined them.

In the local museum, known as the Gallery of History, is the 'Danish Hair Embroidery' exhibit. While ornaments made of human hair were not uncommon in Victorian times, the pieces were usually confined to rings, lockets and small personal items. What makes this particular item so special is that not only is it large but it is also totally embroidered using human hair. The embroidery celebrates the marriage of Brendt and Lisbet Johannsen and their offspring and was completed in 1886. What is not known, however, is just whose hair was used or whether each name was embroidered using the hair of the individual concerned.

> 14 Gordon Street, Dannevirke. Open Monday to Friday 9.30 a.m. to
> 4 p.m., Saturday and Sunday afternoons, ph 06 374 6300.

Dave's Den and Pauline's Patch

It all started on a holiday to Norfolk Island in 1981 when Dave Pawson purchased his first model car. Over 25 years and 8000 die-cast model cars later, Dave's Den on the north side of Dannevirke is a collector's Valhalla. Models under the Matchbox, Lledo, Dinky and Trax brands form the heart of the collection, but he does occasionally get sidetracked. Meticulously organised, the collection is arranged in series order and many still have their original boxes alongside. The earliest models date back to the early 1950s,

and a small range is available for sale. While Dave caught the collecting bug in Norfolk Island, you might just catch it in Dannevirke.

Not to be outdone, Dave's wife has her own domain known as Pauline's Patch. Pauline is an artist using both watercolours and oils, and her paintings are on display and for sale. If a painting isn't in your budget, there are also postcards of her work available to send to your friends.

363 High Street (SH2), Dannevirke. Open most days between 10 a.m. to
4 p.m. (if the sign is out Dave's is open), ph 06 374 8432; entry fee.

◀◀ Kahungunu meeting house, Nuhaka

This magnificent meeting house in Nuhaka was built as a war memorial after the Second World War to honour the large contingent of Maori soldiers from this area who fought overseas. Traditional in style and elaborately carved, in pride of place at the apex of the front of the house is Kahungunu himself, the central ancestor after whom the iwi of the Hawke's Bay and Wairarapa take their name. In contrast is the modern and more colourful meeting house Tane nui a Rangi two miles north.

300 metres from the roundabout on SH2, Nuhaka.

◀◀ Morris Minor Collection, British Car Museum, Haumoana

Ian Hope just can't stop collecting Morris Minors. Only a few years ago he had 30, now he has in excess of 70, and after packing the cars in closely to accommodate the growing collection, he has had to resort to stacking them.

In 1998 Ian moved his growing collection of cars into an unused packing house and now has over 400 vehicles of British origin. Cars are jammed in everywhere and in every sort of condition, though Ian claims 80 per cent are in working order. In addition to the Morrie Minors there are over 50 Vauxhalls and the rarest car is a 1958 Vanguard Sportsman. Not content with cars, Ian also collects old petrol pumps, car manuals, number plates, car badges and road signs.

The British Car Museum is unique, but come with the expectation of an experience rather than to view a collection of pristine showroom models.

63 East Road, Haumoana, on the road to Cape Kidnappers. Opening
hours are when Ian Hope is there, which is most days between 10 a.m.
and 4 p.m., but ring ahead on 027 231 3916 just to make sure;
entry fee.

Napier

Joan Wiffen Exhibition, Hawke's Bay Museum

New Zealanders have always had a 'give it a go' attitude, and no one sums
up that approach like Joan Wiffen. Born and raised in Hawke's Bay, Joan was
intrigued by rocks even as a child, and had often wondered how seashells
turned up in rocks high in the hills behind the Hawke's Bay plains. But there
weren't too many career options open to girls in the 1930s and, with minimal
education, Joan – like most other young woman of her generation – married
and had children.

However, her natural interest in science took an unexpected turn when
(mainly because she didn't want to waste the fees) she attended a geology
class that her husband had enrolled in, but had been unable to attend. From
geology her interest slowly turned to fossils, and outings for the family then
began to take the form of fossil-hunting expeditions. In a local toy store she
found two geological survey maps with a reference on one to reptilian bones
in the Te Hoe River. In typical fashion her reaction was, 'Oh, perhaps we could
go there, you never know what we might find'. At that time it was believed
that New Zealand had never had land dinosaurs as all the fossils found to
date had been marine specimens.

When Joan found a fossilised bone at Mangahouanga in 1975, she
was convinced that it was from a land-dwelling dinosaur, but her lack of
confidence in her own scientific training made her hold back from announcing
the discovery. It wasn't until 1980 that a leading American palaeontologist
confirmed that the bone she had found was that of a theropod dinosaur
that lived on land. The find also connected the dinosaurs of supercontinent
Gondwanaland to New Zealand. Joan Wiffen's tenacious work radically
altered the perception of prehistoric New Zealand and, since 1980, she and
other palaeontologists have gone on to discover the fossils of yet more land-
dwelling dinosaurs, though some are only represented by a single bone and
are yet to be identified.

Along with the Joan Wiffen exhibition, the museum has the superb Nga Tukemata Maori section with an exceptionally fine group of carvings of four brothers, and of course there is an extensive display relating to the 1931 Hawke's Bay earthquake.

Marine Parade, Napier. Open Monday to Friday 10 a.m. to 4.30 p.m., weekends and public holidays 11 a.m. to 4 p.m., ph 06 835 7781, www.hawkesbaymuseum.co.nz; entry fee.

Napier Botanical Gardens

One of New Zealand's oldest botanic gardens is tucked away in a gully on Bluff Hill, and often bypassed by visitors who flock to the famed art deco wonders of Napier. Established as early as 1855, the gardens contain a number of very large specimen trees that must count among the oldest exotics in the country. The gardens had a tough start, as the site was steep and difficult to work. As always, public money was short, so the development had to rely on prison labour. Today the gardens are an attractive mix of wonderful old trees, specialised plantings such as the subtropical garden with palms and cycads, formal gardens, a duck pond and an aviary that unfortunately is a bit tired.

Right next door is the oldest cemetery in the area, established just a year before the gardens in 1854 and which includes the graves of early missionaries William Colenso and Bishop William Williams. In keeping with the custom of the time, most gravestones are large and elaborate, but there are also a number of very rare wooden memorials dating from the 1860s. As was typical of the period, the cemetery is carefully laid out by religious denomination.

The gardens are also a good place to start a walk on Bluff Hill.

Spencer Street, Napier.

Napier Prison

In 1858, £125 was allocated for the construction of a prison in Napier, and in 1862 the penitentiary opened with a muster of 25 male and 24 female inmates, but which included lunatics, alcoholics, children and dispossessed Maori. The prison was harsh and the regime included hard labour in the

117

quarry opposite under the watchful eye of Officer Jack 'the Bastard' Adams. The quarry is now the Centennial Gardens.

The current building, constructed of sandstone blocks, is still largely in original condition and includes the solitary confinement cells, the hanging yard with a public gallery, a small graveyard, and cells complete with original bunks. It was in this prison that those found guilty of killing the Reverend Volkner in Opotiki were hanged. Finally closed in 1993, the prison is now a popular backpackers complete with regular ghost sightings! Tours are conducted daily and the prison was also the setting for the reality television show 'Redemption Hill'.

> 55 Coote Road, Napier. Daily tours 9.30 a.m. and 3 p.m., ph 06 835 9933, www.napierprison.com; entry fee.

◀◀ Onga Onga Public Toilets

Once a thriving farming community, progress bypassed Onga Onga – and what a good thing too. This small township has 11 registered historic buildings and some of them, such as the old butcher's shop and school, are tiny. Several have been shifted to an historic park next to the Department of Conservation office, including a back-country hut.

But the best thing to do is save your toilet stop for Onga Onga. Not a community to let a good historic building go to waste (so to speak!), the public toilets are housed in the old police cells. Built to last, the sturdy wooden cells still have barred windows over their heavy doors, but thank goodness the peephole covers have been firmly closed!

> Just off SH50, 18 km west of Waipawa, central Hawke's Bay.

◀◀ Rush Munro Ice Cream Garden, Hastings

Having worked with his father in the confectionery business, Frederick Rush Munro arrived in the Hawke's Bay from Britain in 1926. With just £10 to his name, he started selling hand-made ice cream, taking advantage of the abundance of local fresh fruit. From this small beginning he established his Ice Cream Garden in Heretaunga Street, only to have the building completely destroyed in the 1931 earthquake.

In its heyday, the Ice Cream Garden was a very popular attraction and a special treat for local children, and while today the gardens themselves are a little on the shabby side, the ice cream is most certainly not – Rush Munro ice cream is superb. Still made to the original recipes with no artificial flavouring or additives, Rush Munro uses only natural ingredients and the fruit ice cream contains a minimum of 25 per cent real fruit. The range today also includes organic ice creams.

704 Heretaunga Street West, Hastings, ph 06 878 9634.

Shine Falls

Picture a hot Hawke's Bay summer's day, with a deep blue sky and a temperature nudging 30 degrees. Then imagine the picture-perfect waterfall, with water tumbling down a rocky face into a large cool swimming hole, surrounded by native bush alive with birds. Now you have Shine Falls.

At 58 metres, this is the highest waterfall in the Hawke's Bay, and certainly one of the most attractive in the North Island, with two streams breaking into a myriad of rivulets spreading down over a broad rock face into a wide and deep pool. The falls are located in an 800-hectare 'mainland island', an area where predators are intensely managed, resulting in an obvious recovery of both bird and plant life in the reserve, and where recently both kokako and kiwi have been reintroduced.

It is a bit of a walk to get there – about 45 minutes from the road – but it isn't too hard and the track meanders through a handsome limestone gorge with rocky bluffs towering above the stream amid cool, deep-green native bush. You don't get to see the falls until you are there, which in itself increases the trek's appeal.

While it is a bit of a journey to get to Shine Falls, and much of the road from Tutira is winding and gravel, it is well worth the effort and you can stop off for a short walk around the very pretty Lake Opouahi just down the road.

At the Tutira Store on SH2, 45 km north of Napier, turn left into Matahorua Road. At the junction with Pohokura Road veer to the right (this is still Matahorua Road), and after 5 km veer to the left into Heays Access Road and the beginning of the track is on the left 7 km down this road.

◀◀ Waikare Beach

Wild and empty, Waikare Beach was once the main highway down the coast both in pre-European times for Maori, and for Pakeha prior to the road further inland being built. Today the long sweep of beach with mounds of driftwood and backed by high cliffs mainly attracts just a few fisher folk, but it has an untamed beauty all of its own and is an ideal place to slow down and do not much at all.

The flat farmland on the other side of the river from the camping ground was the location of an early whaling station, though nothing now remains. Clearly visible to the south is the massive Moeangiangi Slip, created when a 3-km section of the huge crumbling cliffs collapsed during the 1931 earthquake.

To get to Waikare Beach, at Putorino 60 km north of Napier on SH2 turn into Waikare Road and follow this narrow and unsealed road for 13 km to a camping ground by the river at the very end.

◀◀ Wimbledon Tavern

Typical of late-nineteenth-century rural hotels, the Wimbledon is quite possibly the most original pub in New Zealand. The exterior is no different from when built in 1889, apart from a couple of chimneys that toppled after earthquakes and were never replaced. This is not the first hotel on the site; an earlier hotel built around 1880 went up in flames. The narrow front bar is typical of the older hotels, with standing room only for drinkers and a small separate dining room for meals. The walls are still lined in scrim and the foundations are still piled by the original wooden blocks, so if you find you're a bit unsteady on your feet after a beer or two it may not be the drink alone!

Like most small pubs, not only did the Wimbledon provide drink, food and lodgings, but also a wide range of services for both the local community and travellers, while the publican often doubled as postmaster, storekeeper, and even local magistrate. The narrow bar occupies the entire front of the building, with a pleasant outdoor area off the eastern end. With wooden fixtures, historic photos and local farming memorabilia, including a small collection of old shearing combs, the Wimbledon Tavern is worth the long 65-km drive from Dannevirke (the road is sealed but winding).

The township of Wimbledon takes its name from Wimbledon, England,

which was originally better known for rifle shooting championships rather than tennis. Legend has it that the name stuck after a farmer shot a cattle beast at such a distance that a local remarked the shot 'was good enough for Wimbledon'.

SH52, Wimbledon, ph 06 374 3504.

WAIRARAPA

⟨⟨ Anzac Bridge, Kaiparoro

It is easy to overlook this war memorial as you speed along SH2 in the northern Wairarapa. The simple concrete Anzac Bridge was built in1922 over the Makakahi River. When a new bridge proved a necessity, the Anzac Bridge was turned into a war memorial in a joint community and government project. The idea behind the bridge as a war memorial was to remind travellers crossing the bridge of those who had died in war. The impetus for the bridge came from local mill owner Alfred Falkner, who had lost his youngest son Victor and his nephew Donald Pallant during World War I. Falkner, a draughtsman, drew up the plans while the local community provided half of the 800 pounds to build the bridge. The bridge was open in December 1922, and the plaques unveiled on Anzac Day the following year. After World War II further names were added to the bridge and Anzac Day commemorations are still held each year at the bridge. The Anzac Bridge was replaced with a new bridge in 1956.

Kaiparoro, on SH2 just north of Pukaha Mt Bruce Wildlife Centre, Northern Wairarapa.

⟨⟨ Castlepoint Lighthouse and Lagoon

With a reputation for safe swimming, surf and fishing, the setting of Castlepoint is dramatic. Facing the small settlement is a wide surf beach partially protected from the worst of the southerly weather by the raw cliff face of Castle Point. High on the point is one of New Zealand's most stylish lighthouses, with a slender taper from 5 metres at its base to 3 metres at the top. Built in 1912, the lighthouse can be seen 30 km out to sea and was automated in 1988.

Below the lighthouse huge waves, directly off the southern ocean, hammer the cliffs and thunder and crash over the rocky reef that protects the lagoon. In rough weather this place has a wild seascape that is nothing short of spectacular. The rocky reef overlooking the lagoon is a very popular fishing spot, but as a plaque commemorating the dead and injured reminds, this is a very dangerous spot – a powerful wave or single careless step and you could be lucky to come back in one piece.

Castlepoint is also famous for its beach races that have been held in March annually since 1872. The races apply the sweepstake form of betting where punters place their bets and are then allocated horse numbers after the tote has closed.

65 km from Masterton on a sealed road.

Fell Locomotive Museum, Featherston

The Rimutaka Ranges between Wellington and the Wairarapa once presented a major obstacle to the easy movement of people and goods between the two provinces. The solution was the unique Fell railway system where the train used a third track to brake the engine on the steeper sections. This smart little museum tells the marvellous story of the famous Rimutaka Incline and John Fell's ingenious system designed to tackle the most difficult terrain.

Now housing the only remaining Fell engine in the world, known as Mont Cenis H199 and built in Bristol in 1875, the museum also contains the only piece of the original track, the Fell brake van built in Petone in 1898, an audiovisual presentation of original archive film, and a great display of photographs. A small pit allows the visitor to look under the Fell engine, and a model of the Incline gives a graphic impression of the rugged terrain the track formerly traversed.

For those feeling fit, the Rimutaka Rail Trail is a 17-km walk along the old railway line from Kaitoke to Cross Creek, 10 km south of Featherston.

SH2, Featherston (middle of the main street). Open daily 10 a.m. to 4 p.m., closed Anzac morning and Christmas Day, ph 06 308 9379, www.fellmuseum.org.nz; entry fee.

The Cricket Oval, Queen Elizabeth Park, Masterton

For fans of the traditional game, with men dressed in white and a polite audience lounging under leafy trees, the cricket oval in Queen Elizabeth Park is the place to go. What must be the most attractive ground in the country, the oval lies in the middle of this huge park established in 1877 alongside the Waipoua River in the heart of Masterton.

Traditionally English in style, the beautifully kept green is surrounded

by mature European trees (not a native specimen in sight), and contains a tiny Victorian grandstand built in 1895 and, alongside, an Edwardian band rotunda erected to celebrate the coronation of Edward VII in 1902. Whether or not a game is in progress, the oval is well worth a visit, along with the rest of the gardens renamed in 1954 to commemorate the visit of the young Queen Elizabeth. As well as the attractive formal gardens, the park also features aviaries, a miniature railway, a children's playground, a swing bridge over the river, and across the road a modern swimming pool complex.

Dixon Street, Masterton.

Shear Discovery

Shear Discovery is a fitting tribute to the sheep farming industry on which the prosperity of the Wairarapa region was founded. The first sheep arrived in the district in 1844 after being driven around the coast by five Wellingtonians (who had obtained leases from local Maori), and today the Wairarapa is home to three million of the woolly critters.

Shear Discovery is housed in a building that is actually two historic shearing sheds: Glendonald (built 1903) and Wilton (built 1900). Masterton folk were originally horrified at the sight of two dilapidated old woolsheds being dumped in the centre of town right across from their splendid Queen Elizabeth Park, but the museum now does the town real credit. It is the only museum in the country dedicated entirely to the history of the wool industry, and the well-presented exhibitions of every aspect of this very Kiwi industry include the Trethewey statue 'Shearing a Ram' (commissioned in 1925 for the Great Empire Exhibition in London), a range of historic shearing gear, and the Golden Shears Hall of Champions.

Masterton is home to this most famous shearing event, which attracts both national and international competitors to New Zealand's shores (and includes a trans-Tasman test). The Golden Shears competition was first held in 1960 and quickly became a major event on the national calendar, especially when televised during the 1960s and 1970s. As well as shearing, other events include wool classing and wool handling, and there is also a 'wool triathlon' – a combination of all three disciplines. The main events are always held on the first Saturday in March.

◀◀ Papawai Marae

Established only in the 1850s, this marae, under the leadership first of Te Manihera Te Rangi-taka-i-waho and then Tamahau Mahupuka, became one of the most influential and important in the country. It played a major role in the Kotahitanga (Maori Parliament) movement in the late nineteenth and early twentieth century, and was the focus of many key meetings to address important Maori issues, including an end to the sale of Maori land. The leadership also actively supported and encouraged close involvement with Europeans. The meeting house Hikurangi was opened in 1888 and the lively Maori newspaper *Te Puke ki Hikurangi* was published here from 1897 to 1913.

Of particular note are the unique tekoteko. These carved figures representing ancestors on palisades surrounding the marae usually face outwards to protect the pa. However, the 18 tekoteko at Papawai erected in 1940 face inwards, representing peace between Maori and Pakeha, and include one which represents a Pakeha, the surveyor, artist and run holder William Mein Smith (1799–1869).

Through the remainder of the twentieth century Papawai declined in importance and fell into disrepair. However, in recent years the marae has revived, with the buildings being restored, and is now the centre of local Maori life.

> From Main Street, Greytown, turn into Papawai Road and the marae is
> 2.5 km on the right.

◀◀ Putangirua Pinnacles

The Putangirua Pinnacles are the most extensive example of 'badlands' or 'hoodoos' erosion formations in the country, and are reached by an easy walk up a rocky stream.

Over many thousands of years the Putangirua Stream eroded the loose gravel soils to form a series of deep gullies, including the tall gravel pinnacles called hoodoos. These pillars are topped by rock which protects the underlying soil from the rain and prevents the soft gravels from eroding and thereby creates high fluted formations. The result is a fascinating landscape comprising tall towers of loose gravel with deep gullies and channels carved

in between. There is a picnic area and camping ground at the entrance to the walk.

12 km south of the junction of the Cape Palliser road and Lake Ferry Road, south of Martinborough.

Stonehenge Aotearoa

Anyone interested in astronomy will find immediate appeal in this full-scale model of Stonehenge that looks completely lost in the foothills of the Wairarapa. Opened in 2005, this southern Stonehenge is built on a hill overlooking the plains, and has been adapted to function for the sky in this hemisphere. More than just a replica, Stonehenge Aotearoa also details ancient and modern methods of astronomy, chronometry (time measurement) and navigation, including early Polynesian celestial seafaring techniques, Maori astrology, and Celtic, Egyptian and Babylonian astronomy.

Take Park Road out of Carterton and follow the signs.
Guided tours for the public on weekends only, bookings essential,
ph 06 377 1600, www.astronomynz.org.nz.

Ngawi, South Wairarapa Coast

Facing the wild southern ocean, with nothing much between Ngawi and the Antarctic, this rocky coastline is hammered by some of the fiercest weather in the country – which does not deter a small fishing community from using it to launch their boats into wild waters in quest of a catch. With no sheltered harbours, the boats are hauled in and out of the water by a collection of bulldozers that are as varied as the craft they pull, and indispensable for grading a usable track in the ever-changing shingle beach.

Five km along the coast from Ngawi is the striking Cape Palliser lighthouse, smartly painted in red-and-white horizontal stripes in the most traditional manner. Located 78 metres above the sea, the 18-metre tall lighthouse was built in 1897 to guide shipping around the perilous Cape Palliser, a coastline that combines rocky headlands and shoals with ferocious weather. From the lighthouse keeper's cottage the steps lead straight up the rocky bluff to a

fantastic view along the coast. Succulents and coprosma struggle to survive in the crevices of the raw, dry hillside.

About halfway between Ngawi and the lighthouse keep an eye out for the seal colony on the rocks below, but take care if you plan on taking a closer look, as many seals rest right beside the road and are not easy to spot until you are almost on top of them (and they may not appreciate being disturbed).

> The road to Ngawi is excellent. Sealed and mainly straight, it follows the coast with just one or two rough patches through the unstable terrain, though the last section from Ngawi to the lighthouse is unsealed.

The *Aotea* Waka Monument in Patea is a rare example of folk art.

The tower on Durie Hill in Wanganui was built as a World War I memorial.

A long tunnel leads to the unique Durie Hill Elevator opened in 1919.

Huge arms of the full-size replica of a seventeenth century windmill whirr over Foxton.

Built by a Dutch immigrant in 1958, Our Lady of Lourdes looms over Paraparaumu.

Unique tours of the Feilding stockyards are held every Friday morning.

Ian Hope with just some of his Morris Minor collection at the British Car Museum in Hawke's Bay.

A make-shift hut provides basic shelter on windswept Waikare Beach.

The Anzac Bridge in the northern Wairarapa was designed by Alfred Falkner as a tribute to his dead son.

The Cape Palliser lighthouse overlooks the coast near Ngawi.

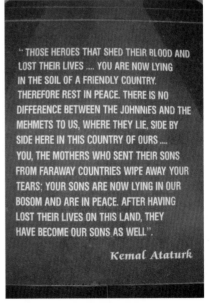

" THOSE HEROES THAT SHED THEIR BLOOD AND LOST THEIR LIVES .... YOU ARE NOW LYING IN THE SOIL OF A FRIENDLY COUNTRY. THEREFORE REST IN PEACE. THERE IS NO DIFFERENCE BETWEEN THE JOHNNIES AND THE MEHMETS TO US, WHERE THEY LIE, SIDE BY SIDE HERE IN THIS COUNTRY OF OURS .... YOU, THE MOTHERS WHO SENT THEIR SONS FROM FARAWAY COUNTRIES WIPE AWAY YOUR TEARS; YOUR SONS ARE NOW LYING IN OUR BOSOM AND ARE IN PEACE. AFTER HAVING LOST THEIR LIVES ON THIS LAND, THEY HAVE BECOME OUR SONS AS WELL".

Kemal Atatürk

Written in 1934, this moving statement graces the Atatürk Monument in Wellington.

The remains of the gun emplacement on Matiu/Somes Island, now a wildlife sanctuary.

Wild and untamed, the Makara coast near Wellington has a special appeal.

Glistening piles of salt are the product of New Zealand's only saltworks at Grassmere.

The tiny totara slab cottage in the Rai Valley once housed a family of six.

A rusting stamper battery is all that remains of the once bustling town of Lyell.

Moria Gate limestone arch is just one of the attractions of the Oparara Basin.

Over 2000 dolls are packed into Bev Donaldson's garage at Reefton.

Time for a cup of tea at the Bearded Mining Company in Reefton's main street.

WELLINGTON

‹‹ The Addington Bat, New Zealand Cricket Museum

This compact and fascinating museum holds a surprising array of cricket memorabilia and will appeal to all sports fans, not just enthusiasts of the 'gentleman's game'. Housed under the old members' grandstand built in 1920, historic items and photos are professionally combined with good text to create entertaining and informative displays on this ancient and often confusing game.

For those familiar with the modern form of cricket, the oddest exhibit must be the 'Addington' bat. Dating from 1743, this is the third-oldest cricket bat in the world, but what makes it unusual is that it looks more like a hockey stick than a modern cricket bat. The shape is a clue as to how cricket was played in the eighteenth century when the ball was not bowled overarm, but underarm along the ground. To their horror, New Zealanders found this style of delivery was still permissible in the modern game when, in a one-day match against Australia on 1 February 1981, Trevor Chappell bowled the final ball along the ground, denying the Kiwis a chance to win.

Other items of interest include the retired Plunket Shield, Dennis Lillee's famous aluminium bat, a ball cleverly made of cork and parcel string in Stalag 180 prison camp during World War II and special displays featuring cricketing greats such as Richard Hadlee, Bert Sutcliffe, Martin Crowe, Clarrie Grimmet and even Donald Bradman.

The entrance, off the busy roundabout that is the Basin Reserve, is not that easy to find, but make the effort, as this museum is worth it (there is a small car park just inside the gate).

> Rugby Street (southern side of Basin Reserve), Wellington.
> Open daily 10.30 a.m. to 3.30 p.m. November to April (and all day on match days) and 10.30 a.m. to 3.30 p.m. weekends only May to October, www.nzcricket.co.nz; entrance fee.

‹‹ Atatürk Memorial

War memorials are usually erected to commemorate victory, but in New Zealand (and Australia, for that matter) it was a great defeat that seared itself into the national memory and today the country has an intriguing connection to its old WWI enemy Turkey. Anzac Day was initially established to honour those who fought and died in the disastrous Gallipoli campaign in 1915, and today it is generally recognised that this military assault was the birth of a strong and independent national identity for both New Zealanders and Australians. Rather than harbour bitter feelings towards the Turks (who were, after all, justly defending their homeland), a rare reciprocal bond has formed between two old opponents. The Atatürk Memorial on Wellington's south coast is a tribute to Kemal Atatürk who led the defence at Gallipoli.

The memorial is located on a rather bleak hill overlooking Cook Strait and the entrance to Wellington Harbour – a site deliberately chosen as a reminder of the harsh terrain encountered by New Zealand soldiers landing on Anzac Cove on the rugged Gallipoli Peninsula. Unveiled on Anzac Day 1990, the monument was part of an agreement in which Turkey officially renamed Ari Burnu, Anzac Cove, and Australia and New Zealand created memorials to the conflict in both countries. Wreath-laying ceremonies are held each year on both Anzac Day and in August to commemorate the battle for Chunuk Bair. While it is a simple memorial, it is the inscription of a statement penned in 1934 by Atatürk that is both moving and gracious and very hard to read with a dry eye:

Those heroes who shed their blood and lost their lives, you are now lying in the soil of a friendly country. Therefore rest in peace. There is no difference between the Johnnies and the Mehmets to us where they lie side by side in this country of ours. You, the mothers who sent their sons from far away countries wipe away your tears, your sons are now lying in our bosoms and are in peace. After having lost their lives on this land they become our sons as well.

◀◀ The Board Room, Museum of Wellington City and Sea

Located in the historic Bond Store (dated 1892), this excellent museum is often overlooked in a city well endowed with galleries and museums. With a focus on Wellington maritime heritage, the entry to and from the museum is through a re-creation of the original 1890s Bond Store.

The highlight is the incredible Wellington Harbour Board Room. This was the meeting room of the Wellington Harbour Board from the 1920s through to 1987, and walking in here the immediate thought is 'Just who did these people think they were?'. Forget about the usual image of a boardroom with a large wooden table. This room is massive and set out like a very grand

courtroom. Beautiful wood panelling lines the walls, and at the front of the room, arranged like thrones, are three heavy carved leather chairs flanked by large Greek columns. Before them is a long table along which, no doubt, sat the lesser members of the board. Huge double-height windows flood the room with natural light and the overall effect is an opulent display of privilege and power.

Among its many other displays, the museum has a Wahine Disaster section that includes a 12-minute film as well as memorabilia from the ill-fated vessel.

Queens Wharf, Jervois Quay. Open daily 10 a.m. to 5 p.m., closed
Christmas Day, ph 04 472 8904, www.museumofwellington.co.nz.

◀◀ Cuba Street Bucket Fountain

Originally called the Water Mobile, this fountain was part of the redevelopment of Cuba Street in the late 1960s when the tramlines were removed. Designed by architects Burren and Keen and erected in 1969, the fountain works a simple bucket system that in theory should merely fill and empty on a regular basis. In reality, however, the whole thing works erratically, with the water either missing the buckets altogether, tipping when partially full, or swinging completely upside down, often splashing passers-by. It is this unpredictability that gives the fountain its enormous appeal, as it is immensely enjoyable just to sit, watch and wait . . .

◀◀ Hutt River Trail

Feel like getting out and about for a bit of exercise? Extending nearly 30 km from the Hikoikoi Reserve in Petone to Birchville in Upper Hutt, this flat trail is a dream for cycling, walking and running, as well as giving great access to the Hutt River for kayaking, swimming and fishing (there are good trout to be had in these waters). Of course, you don't have to go the whole way and can do short stretches, as numerous bridges cross the river.

For those less keen on physical activities, the trail offers easy access to quiet picnic spots on both banks. The scene in the *Lord of the Rings* movie trilogy where the Fellowship travel down the River Anduin was filmed on the

Hutt River between Moonshine Bridge and Poet's Park in Upper Hutt, with the Elven boats being launched from Poet's Park.

Johnsonville Line, Wellington Rail

Of all the cities in New Zealand, Wellington has the most extensive and best patronised rail network, linking the northern districts with the central station. And for the visitor, and especially anyone interested in railways, the most interesting and scenic line is out to Johnsonville.

Work began on the Johnsonville line in 1879, a project undertaken by the Wellington and Manawatu Railway Company as the main railway line from Wellington to Palmerston North. Now a branch line, this track weaves precariously along steep-sided valleys, trundles over small bridges and, although covering only 10.5 km, passes through no fewer than seven tunnels. Linking eight stations, the trip takes 21 minutes and trains depart from the main Wellington Railway Station.

Built in the classical tradition with massive Doric columns and opened in 1937, it is believed that this station's huge entrance foyer in the beaux-arts style was modelled on Pennsylvania Station in New York. Now looking decidedly shabby, Wellington Railway Station was at the time the largest public building in New Zealand, and employed the latest earthquake protection technology available in its construction.

www.tranzmetro.co.nz.

Katherine Mansfield's Birthplace

The surprising thing about this house is that Katherine Mansfield never had good memories of the place, describing it as 'that dark little cubby hole'. And yet the house regularly features in her writings, especially her short stories.

Katherine was born in this house in 1888 and lived there until 1893 when the family moved to Karori. Eventually, at the age of 19, she left Wellington for Europe and died at Fontainebleau, France, of tuberculosis in 1923. Now recognised as one of New Zealand's greatest short story writers, the house she once lived in has been immaculately restored to reflect a typical lower-middle-class family home of the late Victorian period. With its dark stained wood, heavy drapes and furniture, and overdecorative wallpapers, the

house has a somewhat overbearing and melancholic feel, but then so can Mansfield's writing. A useful handout relates each room of the house to her stories, while the main bedroom has a detailed display of her life. For those not familiar with the author or her life an excellent range of books is available for purchase.

> 25 Tinakori Road, Thorndon. Open Tuesday to Sunday 10 a.m. to
> 4 p.m., closed Christmas Day and Good Friday, ph 04 473 7268,
> www.katherinemansfield.com; entrance fee.

Krupp Gun

Located next to the old Dominion Observatory, this is the only surviving example of 190 such guns manufactured by F. Krupp in Essen, Germany, in 1907. The 8.2-metre-long gun weighs 6.7 tonnes and was captured by the Wellington Regiment near La Vacquerie in northeastern France in 1918 and brought back to Wellington as a war trophy.

The site of the gun is the old Botanic Garden Battery, established in 1894, and one of six such batteries established to defend the city during the 'Russian Scare' at a time when Russia was actively expanding into the Pacific.

Makara

For many Wellingtonians, Makara is a special place. Definitely not a spot for a dip in the sea, the bay, exposed to both northerly and southerly winds, opens directly onto the wild waters of Cook Strait and in summer or winter is a place of solitude, wild winds, crashing waves and dramatic seascapes. However, it wasn't always as barren and devoid of vegetation as it is today. Several Maori pa sites in the area are testament to the former richness of both sea and shore life, and Captain Cook remarked on the din of the dawn chorus from the forest even though he was anchored almost a kilometre offshore.

The Makara Walkway begins at the southern end of the beach, and crossing farmland the track climbs solidly uphill, with magnificent views along the way, steadily unfolding as you climb. A track along a narrow ridge leads to an ancient Ngati Ira pa, and higher still is Fort Opau, a WWII gun emplacement built to protect Cook Strait.

The strategic value of this site to both Maori and Pakeha is immediately apparent. The whole of Cook Strait is in clear view, with Mana and Kapiti islands to the north, the Marlborough Sounds to the west, and the Kaikoura mountains to the south. The fort was extensive in its heyday, but now only the lookout posts and the gun emplacements partially dug into the hillside remain.

«« Matiu/Somes Island

Located in the heart of Wellington Harbour, this 25-hectare island has a long history of human occupation and is now an important nature sanctuary free from predators. Named Matiu by the legendary explorer Kupe, who discovered the harbour around AD 1000, Maori have long occupied the island, although mainly as a refuge as it lacked permanent fresh water. Purchased by the New Zealand Company and renamed Somes after the deputy governor of the company Joseph Somes, the island was used as a quarantine station from 1872 for both people and animals.

During both wars the island was a detention centre for alien residents. Oddly enough, among the WWI detainees were a Dutchman, a Swiss and a Mexican, all from countries that weren't even involved in the conflict. WWII detainees included members of Wellington's Italian, German and Austrian communities, even though many were in fact refugees from Nazi Germany. Most of the surviving buildings are from the animal quarantine period, though the barracks (1890) and a hospital (1915) still stand. There are also remains of WWII anti-aircraft gun emplacements, but these guns were never fired and have long since been removed.

In its new role as an important native wildlife sanctuary the island is slowly being replanted in native bush, and several bird species as well as tuatara have been reintroduced. In particular, the rare kakariki is common on the island. The circuit track is easy walking and for the most part is high up on the island with excellent views all the way around and will take about two hours.

East By West stops at the island on their cross-harbour ferry route, ph 04 499 1282, www.eastbywest.co.nz.

The Treaty of Waitangi, Archives New Zealand

It is an odd experience seeing the actual Treaty of Waitangi. For such an important document, there isn't too much to it, and the first page that contains the main text and the Waitangi signatures is pretty battered and torn. Most of the document is made up of the signatures of the chiefs. At the time, there were several copies circulating, though this is the main version and the only one remaining. After the northern chiefs signed the Treaty at Waitangi on 6 February 1840, the document then travelled the length of Aotearoa to be signed by chiefs at various locations (though many refused to sign).

Archives New Zealand holds a number of the country's key founding documents and is often overlooked in favour of the more spectacular Te Papa. However, if you are idly strolling around Wellington this place is well worth dropping in on, and as it is not that big it will appeal to those with a short attention span. The key documents are held in the Constitution Room that is not only light and temperature controlled but also protected by a massive vault-like door. Along with the Treaty, also on display is New Zealand's earliest document, the 1835 Declaration of Independence of the Northern Chiefs, all in Maori, the elaborate Charter of 1840 which constituted New Zealand as a separate colony, and part of the massive petition to government in 1893 that led to New Zealand being the first country in the world to grant voting rights to women. The Archives also holds temporary exhibitions in the foyer.

10 Mulgrave Street, Thorndon. Open Monday to Friday 9 a.m. to 5 p.m., Saturday 9 a.m. to 1 p.m., ph 04 499 5595, www.archives.govt.nz.

Tinakori Road Houses, Thorndon

Wellington's steep and hilly terrain has given rise to some intriguing local architecture as builders devise innovative ways to construct houses on some extremely difficult building sites. The main problem is the scarcity of flat land, and the obvious solution to this is to build close and build high. This approach is best expressed in the houses at 296 to 306 Tinakori Road in Thorndon. Here, the six narrow wooden houses built in 1903 are just one room wide but rise three to four storeys above the road with steep steps climbing to the main entrance at the side of the house.

While the fronts of these houses are ornate, several have corrugated-iron-

cladded sides – a very common feature on many old Wellington buildings. The use of corrugated iron was primarily one of economy as it was light, inexpensive and easy to use, though it also acted as fire protection for Wellington's closely packed buildings. The grand frontage coupled with more modest sides and back gave rise to the comment 'Queen Anne at the front, meat safe at the back'. Number 306 has a shop at street level that was once the local butcher's.

Diagonally across from these tall houses is the Shepherds Arms Hotel. Built in 1870, this tavern has undergone numerous style changes since. Adjacent is narrow Ascot Street where small cottages are packed in tightly, one of which, the tiny dwelling at number 30, unbelievably housed a school run by one Granny Cooper between 1867 and 1888.

The oldest house in the neighbourhood, built in the 1860s, is at 251 Tinakori Road, while the Prime Minister's official residence, Premier House, is at number 260.

《《 Wallaceville Blockhouse

In any other town or city, this blockhouse would be an historic attraction, but here in Upper Hutt the local authorities have completely ignored this interesting structure, which is somewhat surprising given that the area has little other historic architecture. The two-storey building, complete with musket loopholes, was built in 1860 for hostilities that never eventuated and is one of the very few wooden blockhouses of the time to survive. Once the threat of war had passed, the blockhouse became the local police station from 1867 to 1880. Completely original and now a sports clubrooms, the building has no signage or any other indication of its historical significance.

McHardy Street, by Heretaunga College, Upper Hutt

《《 Wellington Airport

Everyone has a horror story of landing at Wellington airport, and this single runway (1936 metres) is the busiest in New Zealand and just about the best spot in the country to watch aeroplanes taking off and landing. For close up, comfortable viewing, the main terminal has massive windows overlooking the runway and is replete with comfy chairs, food and drink.

But if you want action then head to Wexford Road, just off Calabar Road on the northeastern corner of the airport. Here the view is right down the runway and at eye level with the planes taking off and landing. The wilder the weather, the more interesting the experience, and in a turbulent northerly wind you'll be especially glad you're on the ground watching and not clutching your armrests in the plane as it bumps and lurches in to land!

Nelson

Blenheim

⑥

①

Greymouth

⑦

Kaikoura

⑥

①

Christchurch

①

Ashburton

⑥

Timaru

⑧

①

Queenstown

Oamaru

⑥

⑧

Dunedin

①

Invercargill

SOUTH ISLAND

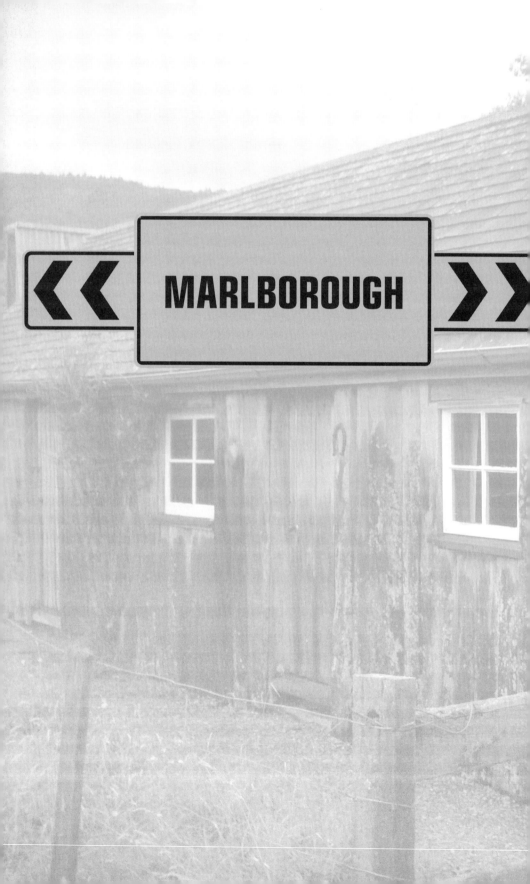

⟪ Dominion Salt Works, Lake Grassmere

New Zealand's only solar salt works, the system at Lake Grassmere is pretty simple. Salt water is pumped from the sea into huge shallow ponds on the northern side of the naturally shallow lake and is gradually evaporated by the action of wind and sun until the salt is sufficiently concentrated to be cleansed of impurity and as dry as natural salt. Covering almost 700 hectares, Lake Grassmere is ideal for the operation and is in fact more a sea lagoon than a lake. Located in Marlborough, a region with a naturally dry, sunny and often windy climate, the lake has no natural inflow other than rainwater, is shallow and exposed to wind and sun. However, Grassmere was not used for salt production until the 1940s when manufacturer George Skellerup needed a solution to salt shortages during the Second World War – though in the end construction delays meant that salt was not produced until long after the war had ended.

Today, Grassmere produces 60,000–70,000 tonnes, though it is significantly supplemented by imported salt. Towering structures supporting the large conveyor belts (and looking very much like a roller coaster) pile the salt up to 20 metres high before it is bagged and freighted by train around the country. Beyond the works, hectare after hectare of shallow ponds with salt water at various stages of evaporation stretch across the lake. These ponds on occasions turn vivid pink, coloured by both algae and tiny pink-coloured shrimps that thrive in the briny water. Unfortunately, daily tours have been discontinued and the company only takes group tours by arrangement, but it is worth the short detour as the ponds and salt piles are right by the road and all the operations are clearly visible.

> The salt works are just off SH1 between Ward and Seddon, south of Blenheim.

⟪ Marlborough Sounds

When waterborne transport was common, the bays and inlets of the Marlborough Sounds formed a natural highway and were reasonably accessible. The sheltered waters were ideal for Maori waka, while Captain James Cook and French explorer Dumont d'Urville used the Sounds as a base during their voyages of discovery. Early whalers were also attracted to the area for easy and safe access to Cook Strait. Much of the land was cleared for

143

farming, though not very successfully on this steep and rugged terrain. Once road transport became the norm, the area became a backwater, and for most people the experience of the Sounds is limited to the ferry trip from Picton to Wellington or motoring along Queen Charlotte Drive.

The Sounds are an intricate and complex system of drowned valleys with fingers of bush-clad land and islands reaching well out into Cook Strait. With over 1500 kilometres of coastline, many of the myriad bays, beaches and coves are only accessible by water. It is the perfect place for boating, kayaking, tramping, fishing (blue cod is the prized fish in this area), and just getting away from it all.

For the casual visitor, the Sounds are not the easiest place to explore. Picton in Queen Charlotte Sound and Havelock at the head of the Pelorus and Kenepuru Sounds both have boat operators offering everything from boat hire to day trips for pleasure, fishing, or access to accommodation. The Queen Charlotte Track winds 71 km through marvellous landscapes, and while the full track will take four days, the proximity to the water means that short options are readily available. Even driving in the Sounds is not so straightforward. Hilly and steep with endless bays and channels, roads in the area are almost without exception narrow, winding and slow, and often gravel. But take your time and discover the hidden beauty of this wonderful corner of New Zealand, from the tree-lined coves of Tennyson Inlet through to the wild waters of French Pass and the old whaling station at Port Underwood.

◀◀ Molesworth Station

New Zealand's largest station, covering over 180,000 hectares of inland high country, has had a very mixed history. Established as a merino sheep station in the middle of the nineteenth century, farming initially flourished and in 1900 the run supported 50,000 sheep. By 1925 the station's flock had dropped to just 1400 sheep. The cause was simply a plague of rabbits in such proportions that Molesworth and other runs like it were virtually turned into deserts. When the lease ran out on the station in 1938, Molesworth and neighbouring Tarndale returned to the Crown, and from 1949 these two stations (together with yet two more failed stations) have been managed by a government agency and today are under the care of the Department of Conservation. Through careful management of stock and land, Molesworth has slowly returned to production and now supports the largest herd of cattle in New Zealand, numbering over 10,000.

This is tough country at best. The climate is hot and dry in summer and very cold in winter with frequent snow, and frosts occurring over 200 days a year. Varying in altitude from 500 to over 2000 metres, the station is the source of the Acheron, Clarence and Waiau rivers, and much of the terrain is mountainous and rugged. While not as spectacularly alpine as the Southern Alps, this high country has a natural beauty and appeal all of its own, with a vast landscape empty of people, subtle vistas of muted colours, and a quiet solitude like few other places. At Acheron the history guesthouse is open to the public. Built of cob in 1863, it was part of a number of such accommodation houses built between Canterbury and Nelson to provide shelter for men moving stock through the mountains (Tophouse south of Nelson still operates as a hotel).

Open only through summer, the public road from SH1 just south of Blenheim runs 182 km through the heart of the station to Hanmer, and the 1437-metre-high Island Saddle is the highest point in New Zealand on any public road. While mostly gravel, and often winding and narrow, it is not a difficult road and it makes a comfortable day's drive with plenty of time for stops along the way. The station is more accessible from Hanmer, so if the long drive is not an option, then a trip from Hanmer is a pleasant outing. Along the Acheron Road there is camping at both Acheron and Molesworth, and also at Lake Tennyson and Coldwater Creek, but no other accommodation or facilities. Make sure you also bring a fit passenger as there are plenty of gates to open and close!

Rai Valley Cottage

Once a very common type of house construction, few totara slab cottages have survived beyond the nineteenth century. The cottage was built in 1881, with the totara slabs cut on site and fixed with hand-forged nails; the fireplace is constructed of local river stones and the roof of wooden shingles. It is not a big house by any standard, and with a low-pitched roof it feels even smaller, so it is difficult to imagine how such a small and basic cottage housed the Turner family of six until 1909 in addition to providing food for passing travellers. The small main room is both the living area and kitchen all rolled into one and must have been a real squeeze on a cold winter's evening. Maybe everyone just went to bed early.

1.5 km north of Rai Valley village (SH6) on the road to Tennyson Inlet.
Open at all times. Interior is visible through glass panels.

145

Whites Bay

This small, sandy, bush-clad bay on the northern side of Cloudy Bay is in direct contrast to the dry open country south of the Wairau River. Sheltered from the worst of the weather, the bay is popular and safe for swimming, and in certain conditions even has good surf. Important to Maori, Pukatea pa is located on the southwest corner of the bay and the Treaty of Waitangi was signed just north of here on Horahora Kakahu Island. The first Cook Strait telegraph cable was hauled ashore here in 1886, linking the South Island to Lyall Bay in Wellington, and the telegraphers' building, prefabricated in Australia and housing staff from 1867 to 1873, is still on site today.

A number of short and attractive bush walks lead up from the bay. However, it is its name that adds greatly to the appeal of the place. In 1828 an African-American slave with the intriguing and rather colourful name of Black Jack White jumped ship at Port Underwood, just to the north, making the bay which was eventually renamed after him his new home.

Whites Bay is 15 km from Tuamarina off SH1 via Rarangi.

NELSON & GOLDEN BAY

Golden Bay

◀◀ Cape Farewell and Farewell Spit

Just a few kilometres apart, the sheltered waters of Golden Bay are in direct contrast to the wild seascape of the Tasman Sea, and in between these two bodies of water is the unique sandbank that is Farewell Spit. Over 30 km in length, Farewell Spit is one of the longest recurved sand spits in the world and protects a delicate ecosystem, the shallow tidal flats of Golden Bay. Home to a rich variety of bird life, over 90 species have been recorded here, including migratory birds such as godwits and red knots that arrive in their tens of thousands in the spring to feed. However, the very shallow water is also a death trap for whales and the bay is the site of regular strandings, mainly by pilot whales.

At the end of the spit are an old lighthouse and a gannet colony. In order to preserve the environment only a small area at the spit's base near Puponga is accessible to the public, although two tour operators have a licence to take visitors out on to the spit itself (Farewell Spit Eco Tours, www.FarewellSpit. com; and Farewell Spit Nature Experience, www.farewell-spit.co.nz).

As well as the spit itself there are several excellent short walks to the Pillar Point Lighthouse – that has the best views over the spit (and on a clear day as far north as Taranaki), Cape Farewell with its dramatic cliffs and sea arches, and to the windswept sands of Wharariki Beach. This surf-pounded beach of fine golden sand directly faces the wild Tasman Sea, has magnificent wind-sculpted rock formations and is a popular resting place for fur seals.

◀◀ Grove Scenic Reserve, Takaka

Easily overlooked, this tiny bush reserve just outside Takaka is the place to let your imagination run wild. This is the forest of every child's storybook, with paths that weave through a fantastical forest of twisted and gnarled old rata trees whose roots entwine weathered limestone rocks and hide secret caves. This place just makes you want to stop and start building a hut! Best, however, is the narrow path that leads through a cleft in the rock to a wonderful lookout point high above the plain over Golden Bay from where you can survey your entire kingdom. If you are there in mid-December when the rata is a blaze of crimson, then the reserve takes on an even more magical glow. Every child should have their own Grove Reserve to play in!

Grove Reserve is on the road from Takaka township to Pohara Beach, signposted from Clifton.

⟨⟨ Harwood's Hole, Takaka Hill

The entire Takaka Hill area is a great place to explore, but the highlight has to be the amazing Harwood's Hole. Over 170 metres deep, this dramatic tomo is the deepest vertical cave shaft in the country. You could drop Wellington's tallest building at 116 metres high into this hole and not even miss it. Harwood's wasn't properly explored until December 1958, and the following month the Starlight cave, which leads from the bottom of the hole, was also discovered. It is actually hard to see into the hole, but soaring cliffs on all sides give a very good idea of the extent of the drop. A short side track up to the Gorge Creek lookout not only gives you an incredible prospect from the top of the escarpment over Gorge Creek, but also has a view back toward Harwood's Hole giving a much better idea of the tomo's sheer size. While the walk to the hole is easy and takes around one-and-a-half hours return, the last section involves a bit of a scramble over rocks – and as there are no barriers, one slip and it's curtains! Cavers regularly use the hole, so don't go biffing rocks into the shaft.

From SH60 (Takaka Hill road), turn into Canaan Road and follow this unsealed narrow road for 10 km to the car park at the end. From the car park, the walk to the hole is around 90 minutes return.

⟨⟨ Wainui Falls, Takaka

While most visitors join the mad rush to Totaranui, not so many people bother stopping to visit these falls that are actually inside the Abel Tasman National Park. While the 20-metre falls and the deep shady pool below are an attraction in their own right, the easy bush walk has an appeal all of its own, and on the several times I have visited the falls I have not met another visitor. The mature bush is a fine mix of beech, rata and nikau, and the boulder-strewn stream is in itself impressive with huge water worn rocks the size of small trucks littering its course. The walk takes around one hour return and the track is in good condition, though the wire suspension bridge might be a little challenging for those a bit unsteady on their feet.

From Takaka, take the road to Totaranui. At the Wainui Inlet, a clearly marked road sign to the right leads to the falls.

Nelson

Botanic Reserve

While William Webb Ellis is credited as the first person to pick up a soccer ball and run with it, the rules of rugby were not formalised in Britain until 1862. Gradually, the game was imported to this country, and the first officially recognised match in New Zealand was played on this field, known as the Botanic Reserve, on 14 May 1870 between Nelson Football Club (Town) and Nelson College. The Nelson Football Club originally played an odd mix of soccer and Victorian (Australian) Rules football, but in 1870 changed its name to the Nelson Rugby Club, thereby becoming the first rugby club in the country. At that stage rugby was played by large teams of 20, and points could only be scored by kicking goals. However, to be able to kick a goal the ball had to be touched down first, which then gave that team the right to 'try' for a goal. For the record, Town beat College two goals to nil and rugby is still played on this field today.

From the centre of Nelson, the Botanic Reserve is over the footbridge at the end of Hardy Street.

The Boulder Bank

The Boulder Bank is a fascinating natural phenomenon, though at first glance it is hard to believe that such a prominent and clearly defined breakwater is natural. Over 13 km in length, the bank has been formed from large granodiorite boulders moved southwest from MacKay Bluff during northerly storms. That these large stones have been moved by wind, water and tide to form a precise line for such an extent is extraordinary, and it is not surprising that this boulder bank in Nelson is one of the very few examples of its type in the world.

The bank originally extended to Haulashore Island near Tahunanui Beach, but in 1906 a substantial gap was cut near its western end to provide better

access to the harbour. The lighthouse at the end of the bank was originally cast in Bath, England, shipped to New Zealand in sections, and reassembled in 1861 to begin working in August 1862. While it might be tempting to walk the length of the bank, it is made up of loose stones and the traverse is really hard work.

Access to the bank is off Boulder Bank Drive off SH6, 7 km north of Nelson.

Broadgreen House

What's another old historic house, you say? Well, two things in particular make this house very special. Firstly, the original condition of the building is amazing, having been owned by only two families prior to being purchased by the city in 1965. Built in 1855 of cob construction, Broadgreen House is typical of a comfortable home of the mid-Victorian period, and some rooms still retain Victorian wallpaper. The second reason this house is special is the fantastic kitchen. Packed with every conceivable Victorian gadget available at the time for cooking and baking, there is both an open hearth and a coal range, a special oven for bread baking, and a separate dairy for the cool storage of butter, cheese and milk. The floors are the original smart red-and-black tiles and the feel of the whole place is so inviting that you just want to fire up the range, open up Mrs Beeton's *Book of Household Management* and get going. In short, this is a kitchen even a modern chef would die for. The cellar under the house is the hole from which the mud for the cob walls was extracted; and if you feel the urge to dress up, then the upstairs costume room has a collection of original nineteenth-century dress.

276 Nayland Road, Stoke. Open daily 10.30 a.m. to 4.30 p.m., closed Good Friday and Christmas Day, ph 03 547 0403; entrance fee.

WOW World of WearableArt and Classic Car Museum

It is debatable whether WOW should be in a book about 'detours', as displays of both cars and clothes are not that unusual in New Zealand and the World of WearableArt is extremely well known. However, what makes WOW unique in New Zealand is that the display treatment of both clothes and cars is so imaginative and inspiring that even if you are not remotely interested in

either vehicles or fashion you will not fail to be impressed.

The WearableArt show was first held in Nelson in 1987 and quickly became hugely successful, so much so that eventually it outgrew the city and was moved to Wellington. This collection holds the supreme winners from each year, and while the costumes themselves are by their very nature spectacular, the theatrical and dramatic display will make you gasp with delight. Alongside the WearableArt Gallery is the Classic Car Gallery, which, like its fashion counterpart, is no mere collection, but displays the cars in such an imaginative way, combining high standards of excellence with style and humour, that you will not fail to say 'wow!'. Even better is that the entire contents of both displays change every six months, so there is no reason not to keep coming back and back and back for more. The building housing the displays was originally the Honda Assembly Plant, now transformed into an imaginative modern museum complete with café, a very smart shop and local artists' work for sale.

95 Quarantine Road, Nelson. Open daily 10 a.m. to 5 p.m.,
ph 03 548 9299, www.wowcars.co.nz.

◀◀ Tophouse Hotel, Nelson Lakes

Tophouse is the only survivor of a string of similar guesthouses through the mountains that were built to provide basic food and lodgings for travellers between Nelson, Marlborough and Canterbury. A licence for a hotel was granted in 1844 and the original Tophouse was built in 1846 on the road from Nelson to the lakes, taking its name from its position at the top of the Wairau, Motueka and Buller rivers. The building standing today, and now a Category 1 historic building, was built in 1881, and both internal and external walls are entirely of cob construction. Cob is an ancient building material and is a combination of straw, soil, sand and water – or whatever variations of this mixture were to hand. More suitable for drier climates, cob was often used in areas of New Zealand where wood was scarce. An exposed section in the hallway of the Tophouse Hotel demonstrates how cob was used in its construction.

Even today the hotel has a cosy and welcoming feel, but it wasn't always the case. Tophouse was supposedly haunted by a resident ghost called Sidney (and never, ever Sid!) who disturbed the guests by shaking them awake

NELSON & GOLDEN BAY

during the night. Sidney was a tinker who, after being thrown from his horse-drawn cart, died in the hotel. But apparently even ghosts have their price – after a stern talking to and the promise (a promise so far kept) of a slice of Red Leicester cheese for Christmas, Sidney has left the guests to slumber on in peace. Accommodation is still available in the original hotel as well as in adjacent cottages.

Tophouse is 9 km from St Arnaud, Nelson Lakes, ph 03 548 9299,
www.tophouse.co.nz.

BULLER

Buller River at Westport

Beginning as the outlet for Lake Rotoiti, the Buller River passes through some of New Zealand's grandest scenery on its 169-km journey to the sea. Draining a substantial and very wet catchment area on its final stretch to the coast at Westport, the river is narrowly confined between two long breakwaters. With a heavy swell running, the river mouth is a place of great drama, especially if a fishing boat or coal barge is navigating the bar. There is easy access out to the end of the breakwater on the north side and the views along the coast are superb – and besides, there's not a lot to do in Westport so this is a great spot to while away a bit of time, especially in the evening with the sun setting over the Tasman Sea. The rare Hector's dolphins are often seen in the area, and if you're lucky to strike stormy weather there's no better place to be.

> From the west end of Palmerston Street (the main street), turn right into Gladstone Street and then left into Derby Street, and finally left into Coates Street, which leads to the beach and breakwater.

Charming Creek Walkway

One of the best short walks in the country, this walkway is a great combination of superb natural scenery – such as the Mangatini Falls and the Ngakawau Gorge – with appealing man-made features such as old railway tunnels and a swing bridge. The private Charming Creek railway was opened in 1914 to bring coal down from the Charming Creek coal mine, but was also used to extract timber as well. When the railway closed in 1958, the line was abandoned, and today much of the infrastructure is more or less intact. Much of the track is still in place, the old bridge foundations still remain, as well as the concrete foundations of the 'bins' (an area used for sorting coal). The three tunnels are still useable and are short enough that torches are not needed.

Recent slips and rock falls demonstrate what a daunting task it must have been to both build and maintain this railway line in such steep and rugged country with a very high rainfall. The bush along the way is thick and luxurious and glow-worms can be found in the tunnels and some of the railway cuttings. At the base of the Mangatini Falls is the rare daisy *Celmisia morganii*, found only in the Ngakawau Gorge (most Celmisia are alpine plants). Beyond the falls the track goes through a tunnel to Watson's Mill, a pleasant

155

picnic spot at the confluence of the Ngakawau River and Charming Creek, and the old site of a timber mill. As the walkway follows the railway line, it is for the most part flat; and if you intend to do the whole walk it will take three hours one way.

The Charming Creek Walkway begins at Tylers Road, Ngakawau, on the southern side of the bridge over the Ngakawau River.

◀◀ Denniston and the Incline

On a bleak plateau high above the sea, only a handful of houses now remain of the once bustling coal-mining village of Denniston, famous for its spectacular Incline, and in more recent years for historical novel *The Denniston Rose* by Jenny Pattrick, New Zealand's answer to Catherine Cookson.

Opened in 1879 to carry coal from the Rochfort Plateau down to Conn's Creek, the Incline rail system dropped 518 metres in just over 1610 metres. The Incline was a simple arrangement, with the down wagons counterbalancing the up load. Until the road was built in 1900, the Incline was the only way in and out of Denniston, and it carried people, furniture and all manner of goods as well as coal. In 1887 the population of Denniston was 500, and supported three hotels, and eventually peaked at 1500 people in 1911. However, the isolation, improved road transport, and the bleak soil-less landscape slowly led to a decline in the town, and finally the Incline itself closed in August 1967.

At the time it was constructed, locals called it the 'eighth wonder of the world', and today the Institute of Professional Engineers recognises the Incline as one of New Zealand's outstanding engineering feats. Substantial sections of the track, working gear and buildings still remain, and a walking track following the old bridle track weaves its way from Conn's Creek to the top of the Incline. Information panels at the summit feature many historical photos showing the Incline and Denniston in its glory years. The huge brake drum, as well as an original wagon displayed at the actual angle (45 degrees) of the Incline, can be seen in the Coaltown Museum in Westport.

Denniston is 25 km north of Westport.

Inangahua Hall

Now doubling as the Inangahua Museum, this simple wooden building is typical of local halls that for so long formed the very centre of life for small communities. Built in the early 1930s and largely in original condition, the plain timber building has a varnished wooden interior, a small stage accommodated in a corrugated-iron extension, and a kitchen annex for preparing suppers. Like all such halls, every local event would have taken place here, from meetings and concerts through to dances and weddings.

On 24 May 1968 at 5.24 a.m. an earthquake measuring 7.1 on the Richter scale hit Inangahua. While only three people died in the quake, damage to the area was compounded by continual strong aftershocks for the next four weeks, 15 of which registered over 5 on the Richter scale. This small museum has an extensive display of newspaper clippings and photographs of the quake as well as historical information of the surrounding district.

Inangahua Landing (SH69). Open daily except Saturdays 10 a.m. to
3 p.m., September to May; koha/donation.

Lyell

If it wasn't for the information boards with photographs showing a flourishing town it would be very difficult to believe this area was once home to thousands of people and the valley alive with feverish activity. Gold was discovered in Lyell Creek in 1862 and, like so many other gold mining settlements, a township mushroomed virtually overnight. By 1873 the busy town of Lyell boasted a school, post office, church, six hotels and even its own newspaper. While other gold towns succumbed to gorse and blackberry, at Lyell the town has not only disappeared but also the bush has returned and today looks virgin and untouched.

But on closer inspection faint traces of the past do remain. Here and there in the deep bush stands an old fireplace or the remains of concrete steps. Of special interest is the old cemetery where old decaying headstones enclosed by rusting wrought-iron railings are laid out on a hillside looking like a quintessential horror-movie set graveyard. Further up the creek are the substantial remains of the old stamper battery, rusting and abandoned in the beech forest. Just south of Lyell is the historic Iron Bridge (built 1890),

towering over 30 metres above the Buller River on massive stone pylons. If nothing else, Lyell perfectly sums up the old biblical saying, 'Men come and go, but the earth abides'.

Lyell is north of Inangahua on SH6.

Maruia Falls

On 17 June 1929 at 10.15 a.m. an earthquake measuring 7.8 on the Richter scale struck the northwest of the South Island. Centred on the Lyell Range west of the township of Murchison, the quake killed 17 people and caused damage as far away as Nelson and Greymouth, much of the destruction coming from slips or the floods created by them. Very little evidence of the earthquake remains, but the most dramatic of these transformations to the landscape is the Maruia Falls.

The falls were created in mere seconds by the power of the quake causing a sharp 1-metre drop directly across the Maruia River. The rushing water has since eroded the riverbed further so the falls are now much higher than in 1929, and today are a popular drop for the more adventurous kayakers.

On SH65, 11 km from the junction with SH6 west of Murchison.

Mitchell's Gully Gold Mine, Charleston

The real thing is always far more appealing than a replica, and Mitchell's Gully gold mine is no tourist mock-up. An actual working mine from 1866 to 1914 and again from 1977 to 1998, the mine today is maze of old gold workings tucked away among regenerating bush. A trail follows a tramline through short tunnels, past the old workings, and if you bring a torch you can explore some of the mine shafts. There is a water-driven stamper battery, and you can try your hand at panning for gold as well.

Mitchell's Gully was just one of the many gold mines in the Charleston area, extracting gold washed down from the Alps over thousands of years and mixed in with beach sand. When gold was discovered in August 1866, the area boomed, and by October of that year the population had risen to 1200 and by 1869 to almost 20,000. The town supported 80 hotels, three breweries and even a casino, 'Casino De Venice'. Robert Hannah opened his first shoe shop in Charleston (now the Hannah's chain of shoe stores), and when the postmaster was moved from Wellington to Charleston it was considered a promotion! Today just one pub and a handful of houses remain.

Mitchell's Gully Gold Mine, SH6, 22 km south of Westport. Open daily 9 a.m. to 4 p.m.; entrance fee.

The Oparara Basin, Karamea

The Oparara Basin lies just north of Karamea and is accessed by 15 km of pretty rough road, but it is well worth the effort as this area has some of the most stunning limestone landscapes in the country. In addition to these dramatic limestone formations, the magnificent virgin bush is prolific with bird life, including the cheeky weka that are so common you need to keep a good eye on your belongings if you don't want to find them whisked off to a weka nest. Highlights of the basin are the three short walks to the Oparara Arch, Moria Gate, and Crazy Paving and Box Canyon caves.

Oparara Arch

An easy 40-minute walk leads to what is believed to be the largest natural arch in New Zealand. In fact, there are two arches over the Oparara River and huge limestone cliffs enclose both. The main arch is over 200 metres long and has the river flowing through it, while a second gigantic arch towers far above the river and is so huge and yet appears so fragile that it's uncomfortable standing below it.

Moria Gate

Moria Gate is lower and far more delicate compared to the massive Oparara Arch, and is accessible through a small side cave that takes you directly into the arch itself. The rocks within the cave have a dimpled pattern from the action of water over the years, and if the water is low you can wade upstream for a view of the arch from outside. The walk through mature beech forest is easy and takes around one hour return.

Crazy Paving and Box Canyon Caves

These two caves lie right next to each other and are situated 2 km beyond the Oparara Arch and Moria Gate car park. The 'crazy paving' on the floor of this particular cave comes from the patterns formed by mud that over time has dried and shrunk into geometrical patterns. This cave is also home to New Zealand's only cave spider, and while the elusive creature is not visible, the delicate egg sacs hanging from the roof are plain to see. A little further along and accessed by steps is Box Canyon Cave, a large roomy cave deep in the limestone hill. The short walk to these caves is through beautiful beech forest and a torch is necessary for both. The walk is easy and takes around 20 minutes.

From Karamea, drive north for 10 km, then turn right into McCallums Mill Road and follow the unsealed, narrow road for a further 15 km. The road into the basin is narrow, winding and unsealed, with stretches where it is difficult to pass. A DoC sign at the beginning advises that the road is unsuitable for caravans and campervans, and while not an easy road, those campervans with a shorter wheelbase will manage it.

❮❮ Six Mile Hydro Station, Murchison

Commissioned in 1922, Six Mile is New Zealand's oldest hydro power station and operated right up until 1975 supplying power to the Murchison district. While early power stations such as Six Mile are not so unique, what makes this place special is that most of the infrastructure is still in place. Especially well preserved and protected from the elements is the tiny powerhouse, where the equipment appears in such good working order that it looks as if it would start today with the mere push of a button.

An easy walk from the power station follows the intake pipe up a short hill to the holding pond and beyond that the water race. Still in working order, the water race winds through mature beech forest thick with moss to the intake by a small weir on the Matakitaki River. Even if you are not an old hydro station aficionado, this easy walk of around one hour will be a very pleasant outing.

Turn off SH60 into Fairfax Street (where the museum is) and continue down the Matakitaki Valley for 10 km to the powerhouse.

WESTLAND

≪≪ Arahura and Taramakau Road Rail Bridges

With the demise of road/rail bridges over the past decades, a unique and exciting part of the New Zealand motoring experience has disappeared. The combination rail and road bridges were once very common throughout the country when bridge building was expensive and cars relatively scarce, but very few survive today. The bridges were a treat – often very narrow with barely adequate passing lanes in the middle, they also invariably had loose timbers that rattled and shook beneath the car giving the impression that the bridge was about to collapse into the river at any moment. Of course, there was always the exciting possibility that a train might be coming, and the whole experience was – for some drivers – quite nerve-wracking.

To the best of my knowledge, the only two surviving road/rail bridges are both just north of Hokitika over the Arahura and Taramakau rivers. The Arahura Bridge is the older of the two, built in 1887, and is a typical late nineteenth-century wooden truss bridge, though plans are now in place for a new road bridge due to be completed in 2010. The Taramakau Bridge is a more modern steel construction and is likely to be the sole survivor once the Arahura is replaced.

> The Arahura and Taramakau bridges are between Kumara Junction and Hokitika on SH6.

≪≪ Formerly The Blackball Hilton Hotel

Blackball is one of those unique places in New Zealand where fact has blended with fiction, but there is no doubt that the township has had a special role to play in New Zealand's industrial relations history and this hotel has been at the heart of it all. The town itself evolved around coal mining and rocketed to fame in 1908 when miners went on strike for three months to extend 'crib time' (lunch) from 15 minutes to 30 minutes. The miners were taken to court and, as they were breaking the law, fined for their actions – though in a supreme instance of irony the judge hearing the case adjourned for a lunch break of 80 minutes!

It was from the actions of this strike that New Zealand's Labour Party arose, and it is said that the political party was actually formed in the hotel. Without a doubt, the town was a stronghold of militant unionism, and in 1925

the New Zealand Communist Party moved its headquarters from Wellington to Blackball. Today the town is rather run-down, with dilapidated houses huddling amongst the scrub, but the famous Blackball Salami Company and the 'Formerly The Blackball Hilton Hotel' make this detour worthwhile.

Built in 1910 as 'The Dominion', the hotel's current name has a story all of its own. In the late seventies its owners changed the name to 'The Blackball Hilton' – a rather tongue-in-cheek name but with strong local connections as the main street is called Hilton after one of the early mine managers. However, after fierce objection and threat of legal action in 1992 by a well-known hotel chain, the name was altered by adding 'Formerly' to the title. Today the large two-storey wooden hotel is a great place to visit and offers simple accommodation, food and good company. Crammed with memorabilia, old photos and newspaper clippings, the pub exudes old-world charm and successfully treads the very fine line between rustic and run-down.

26 Hart Street, Blackball, ph 03 732 4705, www.blackballhilton.co.nz.

Greymouth

◀◀ Point Elizabeth Walkway

Greymouth isn't exactly New Zealand's most attractive town, but just to the north the Point Elizabeth Walkway is a real treat. The track is actually part of an old gold-mining trail as, originally, wandering gold miners used the beach as a highway to travel north and south along the coast. However, the high cliffs of Point Elizabeth were a major obstacle in the coastal journey and in 1865 this track was constructed to make access much easier. Following the coastline, the track is never far from the roar of the sea just below, and at the point itself a lookout has views both north and south along this wild coast.

For the most part, the native flora has regenerated from early clearances and today dense groves of kiekie and nikau palm give the track the feel of a tropical jungle. Nikau at Point Elizabeth is at its most southerly growing limit, making these palm trees the most southerly naturally grown palms in the world. Apart from a modest uphill section at the beginning, the track

is fairly level all the way and takes around three hours one way at a modest pace or two hours return to the lookout.

> From Greymouth, take the road north to Westport over the Grey River Bridge. Immediately over the bridge, turn left and follow the road along the coast 6 km to the very end.

On Yer Bike

You like mud and plenty of it? The West Coast is famous for its rain, and with rain comes mud. So if you are a messy child at heart, then 'On Yer Bike' is just perfect, rightfully claiming to be 'New Zealand's muddiest off-road adventure'. Here you can hire motorbikes and drive on tracks that are a mixture of mud, water, narrow bush trails and puddles the size of small lakes. The motorbikes can be operated by those 12 years and older, with passenger options for younger children on the go-karts. Even though protective clothing is available, dig out some old gear, as it is guaranteed you will get very dirty and wet!

In addition to the motorbikes, On Yer Bike also includes miniature models of the townships of Waiuta, Reefton and, under construction, an English village. The huge outdoor model of the mining town of Waiuta, the site of one of the West Coast's last gold rushes, is built to scale and is impressive in detail. The Reefton model is inside (in case it is raining too hard) and lights up, reflecting Reefton's early experiments with electricity. The models can be visited separately if you don't want to go on the bikes, and there is an excellent café on site as well.

> SH6, 5 km north of Greymouth. Open daily 8.30 a.m. to 5 p.m., ph 03 762 7438, www.onyerbike.co.nz.

Jones Creek, Ross

Forget about Lotto and Big Wednesday, Jones Creek at Ross is the place to strike it rich! Gold was discovered at Ross in 1864, and the largest gold nugget ever found in New Zealand was discovered in Jones Creek in 1909. Named the 'Honourable Roddy' after the then Minister of Mines The Honourable Roderick McKenzie, the nugget weighed a hefty three

kilograms. Interestingly, this creek is now open to public gold panning, and what you find you can keep! If you don't have your own gold pan then they are available for hire from the friendly visitor's centre.

Panning for gold is best just after heavy rain, so if you strike the Coast on a very wet day don't stay inside grizzling about the rain, head off to Jones Creek and find a nugget to beat the Honourable Roddy! Gold continues to be extracted at Ross, so your chances are still good. And if you have no luck you can always drown your sorrows like every other miner over the last one and a half centuries, just down the road in the 140-year-old Empire Hotel.

Jones Creek is right behind the visitor's centre in Ross.

Munro Beach

If pristine Westland wilderness and wildlife is what you are looking for, then Munro Beach should fit the bill perfectly. The actual beach is a small sandy cove pounded by the wild weather straight off the Tasman Sea and backed by mature rainforest. While the beach is appealing in its own right, it is also favoured by fur seals and is the home of a colony of the very rare Fiordland crested penguin. Only 1500 pairs remain in the world, and like most penguins they are somewhat timid. The best time to see them is early morning or late afternoon, and it is best to sit still rather than wander all over the beach. Once disturbed they will return to the sea, leaving chicks unfed and the adult tired and unrested. It takes about 45 minutes to walk to the beach along an easy flat track through a beautiful coastal forest of magnificent rimu.

Off SH6, 30 km north of Haast at the southern end of
Lake Moeraki.

Okarito

The area around Okarito sums up the magnificence of southern Westland. To the east tower the Southern Alps, with Mt Ellie De Beaumont, Aoraki/ Mt Cook, Mt Tasman and the Franz Josef Glacier all clearly visible on a fine day from vantage points such as the Okarito trig or lookout point on the Pahiki Walk. Near the sea is the Okarito Lagoon, home to the famous kotuku, or white heron (*Egretta alba modesta*). Found throughout the South Pacific,

166

Australia and Asia, but rare in New Zealand, this elegant bird gave rise to the traditional Maori proverb, 'He kotuku rerenga tahi' — 'A kotuku of a single flight' – referring to a once-in-a-lifetime event. The kotuku is the bird featured on the New Zealand two-dollar coin.

Okarito is also home to the rare Okarito brown kiwi, now identified as a separate species – and while often heard, it is only occasionally seen at night. Vast native forests stretch in every direction and the Okarito area has several good examples of virgin pakihi swamp. Peculiar to the high rainfall areas of the West Coast, the wetlands are almost permanently wet and are characterised by low stunted vegetation, the result of nutrients being rapidly leached from the waterlogged soils.

The township itself is just a small collection of seaside cribs and is the base for kayak trips on the lagoon and several excellent short walks that range from an hour or two through to half a day or longer.

Reefton

⟪ Bearded Mining Company

Not so long ago a service group in Reefton built a replica of an 1860s miner's hut in Broadway, the town's main street. Constructed of kaiwaka, or mountain cedar, several local men decided that this was a much more interesting place to spend their day than sitting at home and duly set up camp and added their own touches to the wooden hut. Today, Gavin, Peter and Geoff – now known as the 'Bearded Mining Company' – can be found every day at the hut dressed as old-time miners, playing old songs on the guitar and accordion or brewing a cup of tea and ever ready for a chat with passers-by about life on the old goldfields. With all sorts of old equipment, they have built an eccentric collection of contraptions, ranging from a stove and blacksmith's forge through to innovative 'central heating'. So, if you're passing through Reefton, stop in and sit a while and maybe there will be a cup of tea going or a song to be sung.

> Broadway, Reefton – you won't be able to miss these guys; and while there is no charge, a donation is appreciated.

Bev's Dolls

Packed into the converted garage of the Donaldson home in Reefton is an astounding collection of over 2000 items, mainly dolls, but also including doll's clothing, prams and even an old wooden horse from an American carousel. What makes this place astounding is that everything is crammed into such a small space and yet it's all so clean, tidy and extremely well organised. The walls are stacked high, with every conceivable space covered in dolls that range from tiny little kewpie dolls through to almost life-size schoolgirls. From the ceiling hang doll's clothes, and you have to carefully make your way around to avoid knocking anything over.

The oldest item is a 180-year-old German stone doll, and the more recent additions include an extensive Harry Potter collection. Tucked away in there somewhere are Bev's childhood dolls that originally sparked her interest. Over the years, the garage has been modernised and extended to accommodate the ever-increasing collection, although I did forget to ask just where Mr Donaldson puts his car these days!

35 Main Street, Reefton. Ring first to check that Bev's at home, ph 03 732 8597; entrance fee.

Blacks Point Stamper Battery

Blacks Point, just east of Reefton, was once a flourishing gold-mining town and home to large numbers of immigrant miners from Cornwall. Today the old Wellesley Methodist Church built in 1876 has been turned into a wonderful local museum. No fancy lighting or designer displays here, the Blacks Point Museum is just packed with fascinating historical items relating to gold mining and the hardy people who once lived here. Bearded patriarchs and stoic women gaze out of old photos high on the wall, and a special display is given over to Blacks Point's greatest son, Olympic gold medal winner Jack Lovelock.

The highlight of this gold-mining museum is the working stamper. The water-driven machine crushed the quartz in order to extract the gold and is unique in that so few working stampers have survived. Stampers often worked 24 hours a day, and in some areas where a number of stampers were operating the noise was constant and overwhelming, only being relieved at midnight on Saturday through to midnight on Sunday, as Sunday was the only day on which they didn't operate.

> Franklin Street, Blacks Point (SH7). Open October to April, Wednesday,
> Thursday, Friday and Sunday 9 a.m. to 12 noon and 1 p.m. to 4 p.m.,
> Saturday 1 p.m. to 4 p.m.; the stamper works Wednesday and Sunday
> afternoons; entrance fee.

⟨⟨ Reefton School of Mines

Opened in 1886 and not closed until 1970, the School of Mines has altered little from the nineteenth century. Partially constructed of timber and partly corrugated iron, the school still retains original mining equipment and has a great mineral collection, sourced both locally and from around the world and spaciously laid out in wonderful old glass cases. Next door, the single classroom has an extensive collection of old technical books on every aspect of mining.

Nicknamed 'Quartzopolis', Reefton flourished in the early 1870s, and in keeping with its boom-town image was the first town in New Zealand to have electric street lighting – just a few years behind New York. Driven by gold-obsessed speculators, investment in local mining companies reached such inflated prices that the market finally overheated and crashed in 1883, causing many companies to fail. There is a short walk around the town, with information boards giving details of the town's history, and the excellent visitor's centre has a reconstruction of the Quartzopolis mine and a huge operating winding engine.

> Shiel Street, Reefton. Entry by arrangement with the Reefton Information
> Centre, www.reefton.co.nz; entrance fee.

⟨⟨ Waiuta

Though very little remains, Waiuta has a special place in the hearts of West Coasters. Site of the Coast's last great gold rush, in 1905, it was also the richest and most productive of the area's gold mines, with around half of all the gold mined on the West Coast coming from this one mine. In 1939 the mine had a workforce of 250 and the town a population of over 600, but in 1951 the shaft

suddenly collapsed. Overnight the town was abandoned and within three months only 20 people remained. By 1952 the town virtually disappeared as houses, buildings and anything else worthwhile was scavenged to be used elsewhere. Today only six original buildings remain, though oddly enough the rugby field complete with goalposts still survives intact.

It is a rather peculiar place to visit, with the odd building still surviving here and there and the remains of others poking out from the scrub and blackberry. Excellent information boards with photos and maps bring the old township alive and there is also a good camping area. The road to Waiuta is only partly sealed and is narrow and winding in places, but the compensation is the lovely beech forest along part of the way. At 'On Yer Bike' near Greymouth (see page 165) a full-scale model of the town has been recreated in miniature.

Take SH7 north towards Reefton, and 3 km north of Ikamatua, turn right to Waiuta and follow this road for 17 km (only partly sealed).

West Coast Washing Lines

New Zealand has very little in the way of regional architecture, with the exception of the half brick, half stucco houses common in the southern part of the South Island. However, here on the West Coast there seems to be a peculiarly local version of the washing line. The line itself is fairly simple – two posts are set a small distance apart and attached to the top of each is a short movable arm. Wire is strung from ends of the shorts arms to the other pole and its on this wire that the washing is hung The movable arms allow the line to be lowered on one side to make pegging out the washing easy, and then lifted to clear the ground and catch the breeze. Once you notice these lines, you can't help seeing them everywhere behind older homes on the West Coast, but not elsewhere in New Zealand. It is possible that these washing lines were once common throughout the country and have only survived into the twenty-first century here on the Coast.

WORTH A DETOUR

◀◀ Blackwells Department Store, Kaiapoi

O lucky people of Kaiapoi! So fortunate to have such an amazing shop as Blackwells, once typical of many department stores throughout New Zealand, most of which have long since closed down or been bought out by larger concerns. The minute you walk into this shop, you just know it is going to have something you need. From carpets and camping gear through to socks and stockings and every other necessity in between, Blackwells has it all and more besides. No fancy store displays, just plenty of everything – and at a good price, too. It is not surprising that many local families have been shopping at Blackwells generation after generation since it first opened for business.

Established in 1871 by George Henry Blackwell, who emigrated from England to New Zealand in 1840, this store has now been in the Blackwell family for five generations and these days is ably run by Andrew Blackwell. Not that it has been plain sailing all the way. The store standing on Williams Street today was built in the early 1920s and was at that time a grand affair with two floors of retail as well as elegant tearooms. However, the 1930s Depression hit hard and the top floor closed, never to reopen. Fire nearly destroyed the store in 1927, but sound financial management and good friendly service has allowed Blackwells to survive where other similar stores have long since failed.

In addition to a store packed with stock, a magnificent ornate till, originally purchased in 1885 and last serviced in 1893, is still in use today – so even if the power goes off, Blackwells can still keep trading. It is heartening to see such an establishment survive in the era of mass-market chain stores and 'box retail', and let's trust that the good folk of Kaiapoi know what a real treasure they have in their midst. If you live in the area, don't go to Blackwells when you can't find what you want anywhere else – go there first and save yourself a lot of trouble.

131 Williams Street, Kaiapoi, ph 03 327 8029.

◀◀ Cave Stream

If, like so many, you are not so crazy about narrow creepy caves, then this cave is the perfect adventure – challenging, but not too demanding. Almost

600 metres long, the cave is part of limestone country in the Castle Hill area and was created by an underground stream wearing away the soft limestone. This is great fun for those with no caving experience, taking about an hour to work from one end to the other, following the stream for the most part, but with a little climbing as well.

That said, this cave is not to be taken lightly, and every precaution should be taken before entering the system (people have died in here). While it is easily accessible to anyone moderately fit, you will get wet, and the water can be very cold, especially in winter, so warm clothing is essential, as is a torch along with a back-up. Do not enter the cave after heavy rain or if the water is discoloured.

On SH73, 3 km west of Castle Hill, on the road to Arthur's Pass.

Glentunnel Library and Post Office

If this isn't the smallest library in the country, then it must be pretty close. Built in 1886, the Glentunnel Library is beautifully constructed of bricks and tiles made at the nearby Homebush Pottery. In some respects the library is that pottery's showroom as the construction of the library utilised every type of tile and brick produced by the pottery at that time. With handy sources of coal in the vicinity, the Homebush Pottery was just one of many such potteries that thrived in the Glentunnel and Coalgate area up until the 1980s, producing bricks, ceramic pipes and domestic pottery.

The library's proportions are perfect, with ornate tiles decorating the external walls, while still surviving inside is a wonderful original fashion poster taken from the 'Supplement to the Young Ladies' Journal' in 1894! Today the library still operates and doubles as the local post office. It is also the beginning of the Millennium Walkway, which follows an old mine tramway and ends at the now closed Glentunnel mine. Just up the road from the library are the old stables that once housed the pit ponies, and just beyond that are the remains of a small kiln.

The library is on SH77 at Glentunnel.

Kaikoura

Fyffe House

New Zealanders have always been good at making do. No doubt this stems from a pioneering spirit in both Maori and Pakeha, who both settled a long way from home and from where it was impossible to 'nip back' for anything forgotten! Kaikoura, occupied by Maori for over 700 years, attracted early European whalers, and what they had an abundance of in Kaikoura was whale bone. Not to let a good thing go to waste, when Captain Robert Fyfe, who established his whaling station at Waiopuka near Kaikoura, built his simple cottage by the sea in 1843, he very conveniently used that excess of whale vertebrae for the piles of the house. Later, in 1860, the house was extended by Robert's cousin George Fyffe (*his* surname had two 'f's), but this time he used more conventional timber piles. The house is virtually unaltered from that time and the whalebone vertebrae are clearly seen at the front. Imagine getting that past the Resource Management Act these days!

62 Avoca Street, Kaikoura. Open daily November to May 10 a.m. to 6 p.m., June to October 10 a.m. to 4 p.m.; entrance fee.

Kaikoura Wine Company

This must be one of New Zealand's most spectacularly-sited vineyards – where it is actually possible to watch whales and taste wine at the same time. Granted, it's not *that* common, but on occasion humpback whales do come right into the shallow waters of South Bay just below. Dolphins, however, are more frequently spotted in the bay – but let's be honest here, do you really need whale or dolphin watching as an excuse to drink wine?

The winery sits atop a limestone bluff with views out over the sea, while at your back are the rugged Kaikoura Ranges, shimmering blue in the summer and snow-topped in the winter. On a fine day it is a hard spot to beat. But it's also a tough place for growing grapes, so the vintages are variable and the winery supplements its supply with grapes from Marlborough, producing a good range that includes Sauvignon Blanc, Pinot Noir, Pinot Gris, Gewürztraminer, Late Harvest Riesling, Chardonnay, and Rosé. For something different and very warming on a cold day, try Kaikoura Cream, a wine-based cream liqueur.

174

Kaikoura Winery has an intriguing underground barrel hall and tours are available on the hour from 10 a.m. to 4 p.m. Over 30 metres long, and buried deep into the hillside, the cellar is a consistent 12 degrees all year round, and the tours, which take around 30 minutes, cover local history, wine types, wine equipment and wine processes, and finish with wine tasting underground. The hall is the setting for the local 'Trash Fashion' competition where clothing is made from discarded rubbish, and several dramatic examples of earlier entries feature at the entrance to the barrel room. Not content simply to host 'Trash Fashion', the winery also holds an 'Art in the Dark' exhibition in the barrel hall in March, and a '48 Hours in Kaikoura' photography competition in July (refer to the website for details).

2 km south of Kaikoura township on SH1. Cellar door open 10 a.m. to 5.30 p.m., tours on the hour until 4 p.m., ph 03 319 7966, www.kaikourawinery.co.nz.

◀◀ Maruia Springs

You will think you've wandered onto a leftover set of *The Last Samurai* when you stroll into the Maruia Springs Thermal Resort in the Lewis Pass. In direct contrast to the busy Hanmer hot springs over the pass, Maruia Springs is a unique blend of New Zealand high country and the best of Japan. Set in a forested mountain valley, the springs stand alone in a magnificent alpine setting, with the hot pools overlooking the Maruia River below.

Under Japanese ownership for the past 12 years, the complex features private pools, a segregated Japanese-style bathhouse, outdoor rock pools styled to resemble a small mountain tarn, massage and a fine Japanese restaurant. The distinct Japanese architecture sympathetically blends into the unique New Zealand landscape and the result perfectly combines oriental elegance and style with relaxed high-country living.

In use for over 100 years, the pools draw from a natural hot spring from the other side of the river, piped untreated to the complex. Free from additives, the water is high in mineral content and reputed to have healing properties, particularly for the skin. The pools are drained every day and can vary considerably in content and colour.

Lewis Pass road, SH7. Ph 03 523 8840, www.maruia.co.nz.

◀◀ Weka Pass Railway

The Waiau Branch railway line, which first opened in 1884, was originally intended to be the main line north from Christchurch, but in 1945 the line via the coast was finally opened making this a branch line that serviced a sparsely populated district. Not surprisingly, it closed down, though not until 1978, and in 1982 local people together with railway enthusiasts joined to preserve this piece of rail heritage and acquired the track and much of the rolling stock.

Today, the Weka Pass Railway owns five locomotives with A428, the steam engine, the darling of the fleet. Running 13 km between Waipara and Waikari, the highlight of the trip is negotiating the rugged open limestone country of the Weka Pass, after which the railway takes its name.

Glenmark Station, Glenmark Drive, Waipara. Trains run every first and third Sunday of each month, and every Sunday in January; www. wekapassrailway.co.nz.

The old gold-mining town of Waiuta in miniature at On Yer Bike, Greymouth.

Tiny Glentunnel Library is beautifully built from tiles and bricks from the old Homebush Pottery.

A portrait of Dame Ngaio Marsh dominates the Long Room at her home in Christchurch.

Homebuilt cribs shelter under the cliffs at Taylors Mistake.

Rugged and beautiful, this is the pass used by the legendary sheep rustler James McKenzie.

Loyal beer drinkers know exactly where they stand at the Kurow Hotel.

Limestone formations known as the Elephants are part of the dramatic landscape near Duntroon.

This modest house in Oamaru was the childhood home of New Zealand writer Janet Frame.

Directly exposed to the southern ocean are the heated saltwater pools at St Clair, Dunedin.

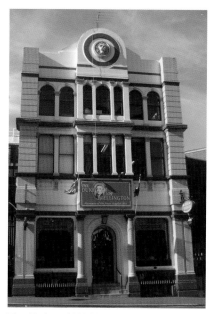

The Duke of Wellington pub was the original clothing factory of Hallensteins.

Traditional long borders, each in a different colour, flourish in the Dunedin Botanic Gardens.

Dating back to the 1840s, the simple but stylish farm buildings at Matanaka are the oldest in New Zealand.

The Chatto Creek Post Office, built in 1892, is New Zealand's smallest.

Just a sample of over 500 ceramic Jim Beam decanters in the collection at Naseby.

The saucy 1970s are on display at the Museum of Fashion, near Naseby.

The restored Traills tractor at Cook's Sawmill in the Catlins.

Even the macrocarpa hedge bows to the relentless wind at Slope Point.

St Mary's Basilica in Invercargill is one of the many F W Petre churches in the South Island.

An old wooden lighthouse graces Waipapa Point, scene of a tragic shipwreck in 1881.

Lonely Lake Hauroko in Fiordland is New Zealand's deepest lake.

CHRISTCHURCH & BANKS PENINSULA

Christchurch City

Barnett Park Walkway

What a perfect hidey-hole this lava cave located high on the Port Hills above the Heathcote and Avon rivers would make for every adventurous 10-year-old. Not too big to be scary, but big enough to be dry and sheltered, the cave is accessed by a well-formed track that winds its way up the side of a valley through regenerating bush and past rock bluffs. Finally, a flight of 70 steps leads to the cave mouth, from which there are great views to the north over the Heathcote and Avon river estuaries, along the coast to the pier at New Brighton, and beyond over Pegasus Bay.

> Barnett Park is well signposted to the right at Moncks Bay on the main road to Sumner, and the track begins at the far end of the playing fields.

Dame Ngaio Marsh's House

Best known for her detective fiction, Ngaio Marsh wrote over 30 novels from 1934 to 1978, as well as numerous articles, short stories, plays and works of non-fiction. Born in 1895, Dame Ngaio Marsh lived in this house for 77 years from the age of 10 until her death in 1982, and during this time she cast a wide and domineering shadow over Canterbury literary and theatrical life.

The house is not large, but beautifully proportioned and full of family treasures, books and paintings, including the famous portrait of the Dame by Olivia Spencer Bower painted in the early 1950s. Ngaio Marsh was also an accomplished painter in her own right, and some of her early works are on display in the house. However, it is her detective fiction for which she is best known and Ngaio Marsh stands among the 'Great Ladies' of the English mystery novel, such as Dorothy Sayers and Agatha Christie. Her first novel, A Man Lay Dead, was published in 1934; her last novel, Light Thickens, was published shortly after her death in 1982; and only four of her novels were set in New Zealand. Curiously, she always wrote with a Waterman pen in green ink.

While her mother was a New Zealander, Ngaio's father was English, and during her later life she spent considerable time in England. It is not surprising,

then, that the house is very English in style, with a beautiful wood-panelled dining room, a very chintzy bedroom, and a wonderful period kitchen. The living room, complete with a grand piano and known as the 'Long Room', is both stylish and comfortable and was once the scene of many an elegant party. The house is only open by appointment, but it is well worth making the time to visit the home of this extraordinary woman.

37 Valley Road, off Sherwood Lane, Cashmere. Guided tours daily (except Monday), by appointment only, ph 03 337 9248, www.ngaio-marsh.org. nz; entrance fee.

Nurse's Chapel

Tucked in front of the Christchurch Hospital, the small but beautiful chapel has on more than one occasion narrowly escaped demolition. Built in 1927, the chapel is the only memorial specifically to commemorate New Zealand women killed in war, and the impetus for its erection came from the deaths of three Christchurch nurses during World War I when their transport ship the *Marquette* was torpedoed in 1915 in the Gulf of Salonika (31 New Zealanders died on this vessel). Since then, many other women have been remembered on the chapel's stained-glass windows and brass plaques on its walls. The beautifully timbered interior with its fine parquet floor is complemented by a stunning modern aisle carpet designed by artist Nicola Jackson.

Riccarton Avenue near the Christchurch Hospital. Open daily 1 p.m. to 4 p.m.; donation.

Riccarton Market

This large bustling market with over 300 stalls operates on a Sunday morning (except Easter Sunday when it operates on Easter Monday), and sells everything from fresh vegetables and food through to clothing and craft and a lot more besides. What makes this market so appealing and different is that, unlike most other markets, Riccarton is not stuck in some ugly car park, but situated in an attractive leafy park alongside Riccarton Racecourse with plenty of space and parking. The friendly atmosphere under the trees on a warm summer's day while munching on a tasty treat and looking for

that special bargain is a great way to idle away a Sunday morning in the 'Garden City'.

Riccarton Racecourse, Racecourse Road. Every Sunday 9 a.m. to 2 p.m.

Rutherford's Den

New Zealand's most famous scientist, Ernest Rutherford, was born at Brightwater, Nelson in 1871 and studied mathematics and physics at Canterbury University in the early 1890s. Rutherford left New Zealand in 1895 to study at Cambridge University and he is best remembered for his pioneering work in nuclear science, for which he is often called the 'father of the atom'. He died in 1937 and is buried in Westminster Abbey near two other great scientists, Sir Isaac Newton and Lord Kelvin. Ernest Rutherford appears on the New Zealand $100 note.

At the Art Centre is a series of superbly preserved rooms that Rutherford once used reflecting university life in New Zealand around 1900. The lecture theatre comes complete with desks absolutely covered in student names and doodles carved in the wood over many decades, while downstairs is a tiny basement room where Rutherford conducted his experiments. It is amazing that these rooms have survived all these years virtually unaltered, and it really is like walking back into the past. Also on display are the replicas of the 36 medals awarded to Rutherford for his contribution to science and gifted to the University of Canterbury.

Access through the Art Centre visitor's centre, Worchester Boulevard.
Open 10 a.m. to 5 p.m.; donation.

The Stone Chamber, Canterbury Provincial Council Buildings

Christchurch's finest historical buildings, the Canterbury Provincial Council Buildings housed the Provincial Government from 1859 until 1876 when the system was abolished. Constructed in three distinct periods, the buildings are a mix of wood and stone, with the wooden, rather plain, section being the oldest. Reflecting the increased prosperity of new settlement, the second group of buildings was more elaborate, and displays the taste for Gothic Revival popular at that time. Continuing in the Gothic theme, the third

section, built in 1861, was yet even more ornate and includes the magnificent Stone Chamber.

Used for government meetings, the Stone Chamber is highly decorated, with beautiful stained-glass windows, kauri and rimu ceiling, and intricate stone carvings, and will instantly appeal to every Harry Potter fan as it looks very much like the perfect movie set. The upper gallery is accessed by a staircase on the other side of the main entrance and gives an excellent vantage point over the chamber. In addition to housing the provincial officials, the building was also, for a short period, home to the Canterbury Museum.

Corner Cambridge Terrace and Armagh Street. Open 10.30 a.m. to 3.30 p.m. seven days.

Taylors Mistake

As hard as it is to believe, this bay takes it name from the incredible coincidence that three sea captains all with the unlucky surname Taylor wrecked their ships on this short stretch of sand just over the hill from Sumner. While the origins of the name are somewhat clouded, the bay was first marked on maps as Taylors Mistake as early as 1853, in an apparent reference to ships wrecked there earlier. However, the name finally stuck after the unfortunate Captain Taylor of the American ship the *Volga* apparently mistook the bay for the entrance to Lyttelton Harbour and came to grief here in 1858.

Today the beach is best known for both its collection of home-built cribs, some of which are nestled right into the rocky cliffs, and also for its very lively surf (check out the live webcam, www.taylorssurf.co.nz). It is also a start point for the very popular Godley Head Walkway, and the Taylors Mistake to Sumner walk via the dramatic coastal cliffs of the Giant's Nose, Whitewash Head and Sumner Head.

Taylors Mistake is 10 km from central Christchurch.

The Whare, Halswell Quarry Gardens

Halswell was once the site of an extensive quarry, providing stone for many of Christchurch's best-known buildings including the Provincial Council Chambers, the 'Sign of the Takahe' rest house and the Canterbury Museum.

Opened in the late 1850s and known as Rock Hill, the quarry finally closed in 1990, and today the 55-hectare site is gradually being transformed into extensive gardens, though the quarry itself remains largely untouched. Newly established, six of the gardens represent Christchurch's various sister cities, while another garden focuses entirely on the Canterbury region's native plants.

However, it is the old stone building known as 'The Whare' that is the draw card in the gardens. Constructed in 1922 of locally quarried stone (naturally) to replace a wooden building that burnt down, this small low building was the single men's quarters and provided accommodation for up to 12 quarrymen at any one time. While The Whare is simple and sturdy, it was not exactly homely, with the men sharing two large bedrooms and a single living area. The highlight is the huge deep bath, a necessity for what must have been a very dirty job, but which constructed entirely of concrete must have taken an age to heat up!

The main entrance is off Kennedy Bush Road, Halswell.

◀◀ Wild West Adventure Mini Golf

A mini-golf course with its own fan club? There are mini-golf courses everywhere and they are the sort of places where anyone of any age can go and have a good time. Most courses try to be amusing, but many just end up looking tired and tattered, relying on a few short summer months for good business. However, Wild West Adventure Mini Golf is head and shoulders above the crowd.

The course takes its name from the themed outdoor course that by any standard is pretty good, but it is the indoor course that really takes the cake. Combining fluoro lighting and 3-D effects, the indoor course is a sensation overload. Wearing those very cool cardboard 3-D glasses, everything takes on a new dimension and the special carpet is designed to give the illusion of being multilayered. Fortunately, the ball is fluoro as well, so you can sort of keep track of things. Young or old, this place guarantees a good time. While you are there, check out the 'haunted house' shooting range that has special surprise pop-ups every time you hit the target. And yes, Wild West really does have its own fan club on Bebo.

Wild West Adventure Mini Golf, 455–471 Blenheim Road, Sockburn, ph 03 343 2055.

Banks Peninsula and the Port Hills

Okains Bay

Settled by Europeans in the early 1850s, Okains Bay flourished on the back of a timber industry supplying the growing town of Christchurch. Farming followed on from timber, but the isolation of the bay led to a declining population and to the small seaside settlement that it is today. Unspoiled, Okains Bay has a very good swimming beach and two nearby caves large enough to picnic in. The now restored historic library was first opened in 1865.

Okains Bay Maori and Colonial Museum

One of the most extraordinary collections anywhere in the country, this originally began as the private collection of Murray Thacker and is now housed in the old cheese factory. The Maori collection alone rivals any of New Zealand's major museums, and in addition to a complete meeting house includes an 1840 kareto, or puppet, a god stick dating back to 1410, a pre-European waka huia from the East Coast, superb greenstone tiki, and even a Chatham Island dendroglyph – human figures carved into the bark of a tree.

Murray has also been busy collecting buildings: the old Akaroa Grandstand, a totara slab cottage built in 1884, and a complete 1871 blacksmith's workshop. The Colonial Room houses artefacts relating to the history of the bay, and among a vast array of items includes an impressive collection of tobacco-related objects such as matchboxes, cigarette packets and tobacco tins.

Okains Bay is about 20 km from Akaroa. The museum is open 10 a.m. to 5 p.m. (closed Christmas Day).

Onawe Peninsula, Akaroa Harbour

Rising to a height of 100 metres, Onawe Peninsula juts out well into the upper harbour and is only linked to the mainland by a narrow strip of land that is virtually underwater at high tide. An ideal position for a fortified pa, Onawe was a Ngai Tahu stronghold and one that was considerably more than able to resist the Ngati Toa chief Te Rauparaha on his raid into rival territory. After the fall of the major pa at Kaiapoi with a great loss of life, Ngai Tahu initially successfully defended Onawe against Te Rauparaha. However, the wily chief used local captives to trick his way into the pa, and after capturing it massacred the inhabitants and followed with a cannibal feast at Barrys Bay. Today, little remains of the pa but it's a great place for a walk, with excellent views of Akaroa Harbour. The easy walk takes around one hour return.

Onawe Peninsula is reached off Barrys Bay, about 12 km from Akaroa.

Quail Island/Otamahua, Lyttelton Harbour

Windswept and exposed in Lyttelton Harbour, this island has fascinating geological, natural and human history. Built up by three distinct volcanic eruptions, the oldest stone of the island dates back to an eruption at the head of the harbour 14 million years ago. A second eruption 11 million years ago added more lava to the island, while yet more was added during the third, six million years ago. The volcanic origins of the island are very clear from the steep cliffs of distinct columnar basalt on the eastern side. Pre-European Maori used the island, known as Otamahua, both for food and as a source of good workable stone.

Otamahua takes its European name from a native quail that appears to have been confined to the island and that quickly became extinct once the land was cleared for farming. Interestingly, Californian quail are common on the island today, so perhaps the name is still appropriate after all. The island is best known as a quarantine station for both people and animals. Once extensive, only a few buildings survive from this period, the oldest being the single men's barracks built in 1874 and occupied from 1875 to 1910. The island was then used as a sanatorium, a hospital during the 1918 influenza epidemic, and for a period from 1907 to 1925 as a leper colony. The grave of the only leper to die on the island occupies a lonely headland overlooking the harbour.

On the western side of the island is a shipwreck graveyard, where eight old vessels are clearly visible, especially at low tide. These ships were dumped here rather than wrecked, the largest being the *Darra*, built in 1865 and wrecked in 1951, and the oldest the steamer *Mullogh*, built in 1855 and scuttled in 1923, still with its boiler intact.

Today the island is virtually devoid of native trees but is slowly being replanted by volunteers, though these plantings are still at an early stage. The exception is the area around the old quarantine station where superb old trees offer both shade and shelter and a large grassy area ideal for a picnic (the beach here is good at high tide). The complete circuit of the island takes around two hours, with a shorter walk taking about 50 minutes.

> Black Cat Cruises runs regular trips to the island through the summer, ph 03 328 9078, www.blackcat.co.nz.

《《 Torpedo Boat Museum

Mad or brilliant? The Torpedo Boat Museum is not easy to find, but this curious slice of naval history is well worth the effort of hunting out. Torpedo boats had their heyday in the late nineteenth century, originating in the American Civil War and further developed for the British Navy in the 1870s. These extraordinary, small, semi-submerged vessels were equipped with a charge that was designed to explode against a ship below the water line. The charge itself was fixed to the end of a 10-metre-long pole that was rammed against the enemy ship while at the same time the torpedo boat rapidly reversed to avoid being overwhelmed by the blast from the explosion.

During the 1880s, the British Empire felt threatened by the rapid expansion of the Russian Empire and in particular the Russian interest in a warm-water port on the Indian Ocean. Colonies such as Australia and New Zealand suddenly realised just how defenceless they were and rushed to arm themselves against any naval invasion (the 1886 Tarawera eruption was initially thought to be a Russian invasion). New Zealand's response, among much fanfare and flag waving, was to acquire four torpedo boats in 1884, each costing £4,000 pounds – one each for Auckland and Port Chalmers and two for Lyttelton, including the *Defender*. But the technology was not a great success. Their low sleek lines, partially to make them hard to see but also to avoid the blast of the explosion, also made them very unstable in rough

water. By 1900 the development of the modern destroyer, that could easily defend itself against the torpedo boat, finally made the semi-submersibles redundant.

Eventually sold off, for many years the *Defender* lay abandoned and ended up buried at Purau Beach on the side of the harbour. Rediscovered and recently rescued, the partially restored boat is housed in the old Powder Magazine Building (built 1874 and itself an interesting building). The museum is small and contains not only the remains of the only surviving torpedo boat, but also a working engine from the Dunedin boat, and some amazing archive film showing the boats in action. There are signs to this museum, although they can be confusing – but persevere, as it is worth seeking out.

Charlotte Jane Quay. Open 1 p.m. to 3 p.m., summer: Saturday, Sunday, Tuesday and Thursday, winter: Saturday and Sunday; entrance fee.

SOUTH CANTERBURY & MACKENZIE COUNTRY

Geraldine

1066: A Medieval Mosaic

If you are a puzzle or a history buff then this re-creation of the Bayeux tapestry is nothing short of irresistible. Created by Michael Linton and his daughter Rachel using the teeth of knitting-machine pattern discs, the mosaic is 42 metres long, took 25 years to complete, and is made up of no fewer than 1,500,000 pieces. While that in itself is impressive, Michael has also extended the story of the Norman Conquest that in the original tapestry ends at the coronation of William the Conqueror.

But wait, there's more! Not content to re-create the tapestry and then some with tiny metal pieces, to make things even more interesting the mosaic contains an alphametric puzzle code, as yet unbroken. This is a puzzle where a letter represents a number and the key to working it out is to find the number for each individual letter. While all this may sound weird, the result is plain fascinating and well worth a visit.

The knitting shop The Giant Jersey, which houses the 1066 Mosaic, is also the home of the largest knitted jersey in the world, measuring over 2 metres high and 5 metres across. Now, how can you drive past all that and not drop in?

> 10 Wilson Street (The Giant Jersey), Geraldine. Open daily Monday
> to Friday 9 a.m. to 5 p.m., Saturday and Sunday 10 a.m. to 4 p.m.,
> ph 03 693 9820, www.1066.co.nz; entrance fee.

The Wilcox Special – Vintage Car and Machinery Museum

Recently expanded, this museum has a very extensive and well-displayed collection of vehicles, with a strong emphasis on tractors and farm implements. My favourite item here is the incredible 'Wilcox Special'. Designed and built by Reid & Gray in Invercargill in 1939, this enormous plough was produced especially to 'plough the unploughable', and it did just that. This huge and tough plough literally turned over swamp and scrubland, ripping its way through manuka and heavy soil and eventually turning marginal land into productive usable farmland. In addition, this museum also has a good range of vintage cars, including an 1877 horse-drawn fire engine, a 1913 Sanderson

& Mills tractor, a 1929 International truck restored and rebuilt by John Britten as a gypsy caravan, plus just one aeroplane – the rare, English-built 1929 Spartan.

178 Talbot Street, Geraldine. Open daily 10 a.m. to 4 p.m. October to June, weekends only July to September, ph 03 693 8756; entrance fee.

Mackenzie and Hakataramea Passes

For those who like a different driving route, these two passes are an interesting and not difficult detour from the usual route through South Canterbury, though it does involve a considerable stretch of gravel road.

◀◀ Mackenzie Pass

The pass through which James McKenzie (so spelt) drove his stolen sheep lies on a rugged stretch of road just to the south of the more frequently travelled Burkes Pass. Born in Ross Shire, Scotland, McKenzie (better known as Jock) emigrated first to Australia and then on to New Zealand, coming to fame in March 1885 when he 'acquired' a flock of 1000 sheep. According to McKenzie, he came by the flock by legitimate means, but not so according to the law, and he was apprehended near a pass leading to a previously unknown high-country basin. McKenzie's dog, Friday, was equally legendary, and apparently capable of moving the entire flock of sheep without command.

McKenzie, whose native tongue was Gaelic, sat silently throughout the trial, was found guilty, and sent to jail. He twice escaped and was last seen in Lyttelton before vanishing from history altogether. Both the pass and the basin now bear his name (though spelt differently), and a plaque at the spot where he was apprehended written in English, Gaelic and Maori commemorates McKenzie's exploits.

◀◀ Hakataramea Pass

After travelling through the Mackenzie Pass the road joins the sealed route from Tekapo. Turn left on this road and after a few kilometres turn left into the Hakataramea Pass. Again, this road is gravel and although it involves a number of shallow fords and closed gates is navigable by the average family

car. This is lost and lonely tussock country of rolling hills and stark beauty – much like Central Otago, but without all the people. At one point the road travels right through the middle of the stockyards and homestead of a high-country station. Eventually the gravel runs out and back on seal the road meanders down the Hakataramea Valley to Kurow on the Waitaki River.

> Coming into the Mackenzie Country from Canterbury, turn off towards Mackenzie Pass at Burkes Pass township; while from the south, cross the Waitaki River at Kurow and then turn left into the Hakataramea Valley.

◀◀ Opihi Vineyard

Located at the enigmatically named Hanging Rock on the slopes above the Opihi River just inland from Timaru, this vineyard is well worth the short diversion for those travelling either SH1 between Christchurch and Dunedin or the road to Mt Cook via Geraldine. Originally one of the 'down-country' homes of high-country run holder Edward Dark, the beautiful restored homestead was built in 1882 of hand-hewn limestone blocks quarried just 500 metres from the house. With its warm timber floors, it is now a superb and not expensive café, while the vineyard itself produces Pinot Gris (Opihi's flagship wine), Pinot Noir, a blend of Müller-Thurgau and Riesling, Oaked and Unoaked Chardonnay and a Late Harvest Riesling. Surrounding the homestead is a broad sweep of lawn, large enough to accommodate a game of cricket or touch rugby, and certainly large enough to occupy energetic children while their parents contentedly eat and drink on the terrace.

Hanging Rock takes its name from a large rock that perched above the river just below the vineyard. It was for a long time very popular with local youngsters to jump off the rock into the river, until one jump proved fatal, and locals blew up the rock to avoid such a tragedy reoccurring. Situated a short distance away on farmland owned by the winery is one of the most spectacular and best-known examples of Maori rock art. Easily accessible either on foot or by vehicle, this huge stylised taniwha adorns a limestone overhang, and will be easily recognised by many as it was featured on a New Zealand postage stamp from the 1960s.

804 Opihi Road, Hanging Rock (off SH8 from Pleasant Point), South
Canterbury. Open Tuesday to Sunday 11 a.m. to 4 p.m., closed June to
August, ph 03 614 7232, www.opihi.co.nz.

Tasman Glacier, Aoraki/Mt Cook National Park

At over 30 km, the Tasman Glacier is the longest glacier in the country and
reaches far into the mountains at the base of Mt Cook and terminates in the
Tasman River. But don't come looking for a spectacle of sparkling white ice.
The glacier has been slowly shrinking over the past 10,000 years, leaving
a thick layer of rocks and gravel covering the ice and looks more like an
abandoned quarry than the spectacular glaciers of the West Coast on the
other side of the Alps. However, beneath the scruffy surface the ice is much
deeper than it appears, going down over 100 metres and still grinding its way
down the valley, through a vast landscape of rock torn apart by the power of
moving ice. Small, slowly melting icebergs drift in the icy green water of the
glacier's terminal lake. The walk to the lookout is relatively easy, apart from a
rocky scramble at the end, and takes around 40 minutes return.

Just before Mt Cook Village, turn right into Tasman Valley Road and continue
8 km to the car park. The road is gravel but in good condition.

Timaru

Aigantighe Art Museum

Housed in a wonderful old Edwardian house, this small but lively art gallery
offers the perfect combination of traditional and contemporary art and
will appeal even to those who rarely set foot in an art gallery. Including a
substantial European collection dating from the sixteenth century, Aigantighe
also has a significant holding of works by New Zealand artists including C.F.
Goldie, Frances Hodgkins, Petrus Van der Velden and Colin McCahon, who
was born in Timaru and whose parents lived in Geraldine. In addition to
the permanent collection, the gallery hosts innovative art from both New
Zealand and around the world, and takes pride in providing each artwork
with an extensive caption, making the art very accessible to the layperson.

A particularly appealing aspect of the gallery exhibitions is the way a wide range of art types and styles is arranged around a particular theme, enabling the viewer to appreciate differing views on that theme.

Housed in an historic 1908 home belonging to the original benefactors, the gallery also has a substantial collection of sculptures from both New Zealand and international artists in the garden surrounding the house, which are open to view at all times. Aigantighe is pronounced 'egg-and-tie' and means 'at home' in Scottish Gaelic.

49 Wai-iti Road, Timaru. Open Tuesday to Friday 10 a.m. to 4 p.m., Saturday and Sunday 12 noon to 4 p.m., ph 03 688 4424; koha/ donation.

◀◀ Timaru Botanic Gardens

Dating from 1864, making them one of the earliest established botanic gardens in New Zealand, these gardens tucked away just south of the city centre have retained a wonderful Victorian and Edwardian flavour. Covering 19 hectares, the surprisingly large grounds contain over 30 different plant collections as well as formal flower beds, an aviary, children's playground, fern house and rose gardens. But it is the older structures that give the gardens a special feel. The very grand war memorial was originally erected to commemorate the First World War, and the Edwardian band rotunda was built in 1911 to celebrate the coronation of King George V and Queen Mary (which, of course, is then not strictly Edwardian). Another gem is the former tea kiosk, a small elegant building delightfully remembered as 'Erected in 1923 by the Floral Fete Committee'.

The gardens are located on the corner of King and Queen Streets, Timaru.

Waimate

Although just a few kilometres off SH1, quaint Waimate is often bypassed by busy tourists rushing between Dunedin and Christchurch, but it is worth the short detour from the main road.

Norman Kirk, New Zealand's second prime minister to die in office (Michael Joseph Savage was the first), was born here in 1923, attended primary school in the town, and is buried in the local cemetery. Dr Margaret Cruickshank, this country's first woman GP, practised medicine in the town until she tragically died tending her patients during the 1918 influenza epidemic, and today a fine statue inscribed with the legend 'The Beloved Physician, Faithful unto Death' stands in the main street.

Waimate boasts two very fine churches, one Catholic and the other Anglican, appropriately at different ends of town. St Augustine's Anglican Church in John Street is an extremely attractive church, built in 1872 of locally milled matai and totara on land donated by settler Michael Studholme. The very handsome lantern tower was added in 1883, giving the church a distinctive and almost oriental roof line. The stand-alone bell tower was added in front of the church in 1903, and a rare stained-glass window features Sir Galahad's vision of the Holy Grail, which in this case is a chalice. St Patricks Church, on the Timaru Road, was built in 1909 and seems far too big for a town the size of Waimate. Tall and grand in style, the design is distinctly the work of F W Petre, who built several other Catholic churches in the South Island. Its three bells were cast in Belgium in 1922, the largest weighing over half a tonne, and the organ was one of the last built by renowned organ builder Arthur Hobday, in 1916. Another handsome historic building is the old courthouse in Shearman Street and now the Waimate Museum. One of the country's most appealing small buildings, the courthouse was constructed in 1879 and still contains the magistrate's bench. Alongside the museum are a cob cottage and a pit-sawn totara cottage and jail, both built around 1880.

In addition to its historic buildings, the town has two very fine public parks. Established in 1881, Victoria Park is appropriately Victorian with formal gardens, playgrounds and an aviary. An unusual feature for a small town is the park's banked cycle track, built in 1891 and still in use. Also within the park is a small enclosure housing Bennett's, or red-necked, wallabies. Imported from Tasmania in 1870 and released into the Hunters Hills west of the town, these wallabies quickly became pests and today are still a fine trophy for local hunters. The other park, Knottingley, established

in 1874, is a combination of sports fields and arboretum and now contains over 3000 trees.

If all that activity works up an appetite, then head off to the Savoy Tearooms and Bakery at 59 Queen Street. Established in 1904, the Savoy still retains its old oak panelling, period furniture, and even an old upright piano if you fancy leading a singsong. More importantly, all food is home-made on the premises, including raspberry buns that are still made to the original recipe and pies also made from recipes handed down through the various owners over the years.

Ted's Bottle, Waihao Forks Hotel

A word of warning before reading this – get your hankie out now. LeTour Mollet D'Auvergne, known by his nickname Ted, grew up and farmed at Waihao Forks, 10 km south of Waimate, and enlisted in the New Zealand Army on 19 September 1939 (his family were originally from Jersey in the Channel Islands, hence the unusual French name). As part of the 27th Machine Gun and Infantry Battalion, Ted was due to leave for overseas on the 27 December 1939, and after spending some time with his family decided on a few beers at this local pub, the Waihao Forks Hotel, before the train left for Waimate and then on to Burnham Military Camp near Christchurch.

Stories vary somewhat, but the most popular version is that Ted had lined up two bottles of his favourite brew, Ballins XXXX ale, but after finishing the first, the train whistle blew and Ted left the second bottle with publican George Provan to keep on the shelf for when he came home. Other versions of the story have Ted drinking in the pub a few days earlier and leaving the extra bottle with the publican, as the train he caught to Waimate would have left just after 7 a.m. in the morning and it was unlikely that the pub would have been open at this time. Whatever the story, Ted never returned for his second bottle, as he died in battle among the vineyards of Crete on 2 June 1941 aged 35.

However, in 1947, Ted's father received a letter from Yakovos Kalionzakis, a Cretan partisan who was only 17 in 1941 and who found Ted wounded by a shot in the chest in the vineyard. Unable to move the badly wounded soldier, who was a big man, Yakovos managed to hide him from the Germans and brought him food for two days before he died. Sadly, the tragedy doesn't end there, as Ted's sister, with the very Kiwi name Rata, served in London during

the war driving fire engines and died there in 1945.

Today, Ted's bottle is an official RSA war memorial, and each Anzac Day locals gather at the pub to ensure that Ted and other men and women like him who never returned are not forgotten.

> The Waihao Forks Hotel is about 10 km south of Waimate on the road
> to Kurow.

◀◀ The White Horse Monument, the Hunters Hills, Waimate

The White Horse Monument high on Mt John (446 m), and dedicated to the work of the humble Clydesdale horse, is best appreciated from a distance. Constructed from rough blocks of concrete in the 1960s, this is a quaint piece of New Zealand folk art which owes more to Kiwi enthusiasm than to any form of high art. It is easy to see that the materials to construct the horse cost only $240. Behind the project was retired farmer Norman Hayman, who while on a visit to the Netherlands was inspired by a statue of a Friesian cow to establish a similar tribute to the stoic Clydesdale.

But the good folk of Waimate also have a sense of humour, and at times the horse has been repainted with black stripes to turn it into a zebra, while at others it has been painted a vivid pink. The views from up here are worth the effort, whether you come by road, via the walkway, or on mountain bike.

NORTH OTAGO

Danseys Pass

If you're looking for a yesteryear driving experience, then a trip over the Danseys Pass is for you. Linking the Waitaki Valley to Central Otago through to Naseby, this was originally a coach road supplying the goldfields of the Maniototo basin – and, quite frankly, the road hasn't changed much since the coaching days. The first section after leaving Duntroon is sealed and winds gently through the handsome limestone farmland along the Maerewhenua River. Once off the seal (after about 15 km), the road is narrow, winding and gravel for the next 45 km, with enough corrugations to shake your brain loose.

But don't let any of that put you off the trip. The countryside is wild, empty and beautiful, and twists and turns through stunning wild tussock country before dropping down into Naseby. The pass itself is just shy of a thousand metres (at 934 m) and was named after William Dansey, who had a run on the Waitaki side of the pass. For a reward on the southern side, near Naseby, call in at the historic Danseys Pass Coach Inn. Built of local stone and beautifully restored, this is a popular stopping point, offering refreshments and accommodation. The inn was built in 1862 (legend has it that the stonework was paid for in beer) and serviced the nearby Kyeburn Diggings, a goldfield that at one stage supported a population of 2000 people. The road is occasionally closed by snow in the winter.

From the Waitaki Valley, the turnoff to the pass is at Duntroon; and from the south, via Naseby.

Katiki Point

There's much more to Moeraki than a quick stop at the famous boulders. This short 45-minute walk is a gem usually bypassed by the busy tourist, but one which has it all – great coastal views, an old pa site, an historic lighthouse, and a great hide for watching wildlife. The walk begins at the elegant wooden lighthouse constructed in 1878. Originally intended for Hokitika, numerous shipwrecks along this wild coast convinced authorities to build it at Moeraki instead. The views are amazing: north to Cape Wanbrow near Oamaru and south to Shag Point, and beyond that, even further south, a glimpse of the Otago Peninsula.

Just below the lighthouse is a large fenced area of coastal vegetation and a short track which leads down to a small sandy cove overlooked by an excellent hide complete with binoculars! Both blue and yellow-eyed penguins nest here and the beach is also home to fur seals as well. A short way south of the lighthouse is a superb pa site located on a narrow spur of land and almost surrounded by sea. Although very little remains, this historic pa – known as Te Raka a Hineatea – was established in the eighteenth century, and owing to its outstanding defensive position resisted many attempts to capture it.

Turn off SH1 at Moeraki and then turn right into Tenby Street, which becomes Lighthouse Road. Drive 3 km to the end of this gravel road.

◀◀ The Kurow Hotel

It's not unusual for a pub to declare its allegiance to a particular brand of beer, but the Kurow Hotel is definitely a case of split (if not triple) personality. Built around 1880, this historic pub clearly aims to keep its customers loyal by painting the entire building in the colours of the favourite local brews. The eastern half of the two-storey hotel is dolled up in Speight's colours, while the western half is decorated in the hues of DB Draught. Not to be outdone – and possibly closer to heaven – the roof is emblazoned with huge red letters that read 'Lion Red'.

It is uncertain whether the devotees of each beer keep to their half of the pub – though where that would leave the Lion Red drinkers is anyone's guess. For sale at the time of writing, let's hope the pub's new owners honour tradition and leave the paint job as is.

The Kurow Hotel, 55 Bledisloe Street, Kurow (SH83).

◀◀ Macraes Gold Mine

Gold was discovered round here in the 1860s and small-scale mining continued through to 1954, when all the operations closed down. Then, in the 1980s, when the price of gold escalated, the area was investigated for a new mining operation, which eventually opened in 1990. Now New Zealand's largest gold mine, Macraes produces on average over 50 per cent of the

country's production, though the number of pits varies from time to time.

The scale of this operation is impressive. The main pit goes down over 200 metres and the huge machinery – the biggest in New Zealand – is reduced to toy dimensions. The largest dump trucks are capable of up to 330-tonne loads when full, and the massive excavators scoop an amazing 40 tonnes in one go. But this equipment doesn't come cheap – the dump-truck tyres cost $35,000 each and the excavators use 250 litres of diesel per hour.

The mine has been active in restoring the local wetlands and heritage sites, and has a rainbow trout hatchery that releases over 15,000 fish per year into local streams. The two-hour tour of the mine includes the heritage mining sites, viewing the giant Frasers open-cast pit, and the maintenance area with its mighty machinery. If time is short and a tour is not an option, Macraes is still worth a detour as there is a marvellous viewing platform that looks deep into the heart of the pit.

> Macraes Flat, 35 km from Palmerston off SH1. Tours most days
> 10 a.m. and 2 p.m. (bookings essential), freephone 0800 465 386,
> www.oceanagoldtours.com.

◀◀ Matanaka

These plain wooden farm buildings set on a bare hill have a surreal quality about them. Minimalist in style and simple and rectangular in structure, all the buildings are painted a uniform deep red colour, with only the faded and lightly rusting iron roofs (which are original) offering any contrast. The long tawny-coloured grass around the buildings is offset by the two-tone blue of sky and sea in the distance. On a still summer's morning this place is magical, with the only sound being the distant surf far below.

Believed to be the oldest surviving farm buildings in New Zealand, they were originally built during the 1840s by Johnny Jones, a Sydney wheeler and dealer involved in whaling at nearby Waikouaiti and who later bought land to the north of the bay on which the buildings stand today. Once more extensive, still standing are the stables (complete with old leather horse harnesses), the granary, a schoolhouse and a barn that houses an old boat, an echo of Johnny's connection to the sea. The stylish old buildings provide a strong contrast with the utilitarian but charmless modern farm sheds nearby.

An extra bonus on this detour is the marvellous views over Waikouaiti

Beach and the verdant country inland. There is an easy 10-minute walk from the car park through farmland to the buildings.

> Matanaka is signposted from SH1 at Waikouaiti. The road is mainly sealed
> but becomes narrow and gravel on the uphill stretch to the farm. (Note: this
> is also an easy trip for anybody heading north from Dunedin.)

◀◀ Nicol's Forge, Duntroon

Anywhere else this building would have been pulled down long ago, but the smart locals of Duntroon know what a little gem they have on their hands in this place. Looking much the same as when it was established in 1898, the corrugated-iron shed that is Nicol's forge looks ready for the smithy to walk straight in and start work. The grimy interior, the tools, and even the tiny front office with its ancient typewriter and narrow fireplace, all look at least a hundred years old, while outside is a collection of old farm machinery. Nicol's Forge is a real peek into New Zealand's pioneering past.

> Nicol's Forge is on SH83 and is open when the Flying Pig Café next door
> is open, usually 10 a.m. to 4 p.m.

Oamaru

◀◀ Criterion Hotel

Standing proud in the heart of Oamaru, this handsome old hotel is a rare survivor of New Zealand's roller-coaster liquor laws. Through the second half of the nineteenth century the temperance movement grew from strength to strength, and in 1893 the government allowed individual electorates to decide whether their area was to go 'dry' (that is, ban the sale of alcohol) or stay 'wet' (or continue the sale of alcohol). The vote needed a two-thirds majority, and no doubt influenced by the strong Presbyterian presence in the south and the fact that women could now vote, Clutha was the first electorate to go dry in 1894. A raft of other electorates followed suit in 1902, 1905 and 1908, accompanied by hotel closures in each of these areas.

Built of Oamaru stone in 1877, the Criterion closed its doors in 1906 after

the area went dry the previous year. For other hotels, that was usually the end, as the old buildings were either pulled down or radically reshaped for other purposes. Not so the Criterion, which extraordinarily not only retained its original facade and fittings, but also reopened in 1998. The other feature of the Criterion that makes it extra special is that it is possibly the only hotel in New Zealand that has a surviving 'Ladies Bar', though of course today anyone can drink there.

In a previous era the pub was never considered a suitable place for respectable women. Consequently, many early hotels had a separate 'Ladies Bar' strictly for women only, and more often than not these small bars had their own entrance from the street, with no internal access to the main bar. As the temperance movement grew increasingly more powerful, women were banned from working as barmaids in 1909 and, incredibly, this ban remained in effect until 1961 – and even when it was repealed there was considerable opposition from the industry and barmaids had to be over the age of 25.

While the outside door to the bar is now closed, the 'Snug', as it is known, is a great place for a quiet drink in a yesteryear atmosphere. Having been lovingly restored, the Criterion is today one of New Zealand's most authentic old watering holes.

3 Tyne Street, Oamaru, ph 03 434 6247, www.criterion.net.nz.

Janet Frame House

This modest dwelling, a short walk from the centre of Oamaru, was the home of Janet Frame, one of New Zealand's best-known authors, who lived here between 1931 and 1943. Janet attended Oamaru North School and Waitaki Girls High School, and her time in Oamaru made a deep impact on the young writer (her three-part autobiography, beginning with *To the Is-land*, is particularly worth reading).

The house has altered very little from the time she lived here, though the weatherboards have since been rough-casted over and the windows altered. Today it is simply furnished in the style of the period as well as containing Frame memorabilia. Incredibly, a collection of childhood writings was recently discovered under the floorboards, hidden away for over 65 years.

56 Eden Street, Oamaru. Open daily November to April 2 p.m. to 4 p.m.

⟨⟨ New Zealand Malt Whisky Company

Despite a heavy Scottish influence, especially in the southern half of the South Island, New Zealand doesn't really have a strong history of distilling good whisky. Located in a handsome old wool and grain store on Oamaru's waterfront, the New Zealand Malt Whisky Company – the country's only whisky specialist – is trying to change all that. Having acquired all the ageing Wilson's stock following the mothballing of that distillery in the 1990s, this has now been rebranded as Milford Whisky, and there are future plans to produce near Queenstown.

Here's an opportunity to taste a range of good New Zealand whiskies (there is a charge), and tour the spacious barrel hall upstairs where the original character of the old building is carefully preserved. Even if whisky is not to your taste, the Whisky Bar and Café is a great place for a good lunch or just a coffee in the sun.

14–16 Harbour Street, Oamaru, ph 03 434 8842,
www.nzmaltwhisky.co.nz.

⟨⟨ Whitestone Cheese

Feeling hungry? Then drop by Whitestone Cheese for a good cup of coffee and a spot of cheese tasting. Established in 1987, and creating cheeses from both goat's and cow's milk, Whitestone won the 2006 Champion of Champions award with its outstanding Windsor Blue, which had already collected 10 trophies and 10 gold medals. Now producing a range of around 18 varieties, this award-winning cheese maker offers tastings with the option of matching their cheeses to Otago wines.

Around the back of the building is a viewing area with large windows offering a great view of the cheeses actually being made. In addition to their cheese, the café at Whitestone has a fabulous baked cheesecake and excellent coffee.

3 Torridge Street, Oamaru. Open daily 9 a.m. to 5 p.m.,
www.whitestonecheese.co.nz.

Yellow-eyed Penguin/Hoiho Colony

While folk flock to Oamaru to see the blue penguins' evening parade, a short distance away is a colony of yellow-eyed penguin, and it doesn't cost a cent.

The hoiho, or yellow-eyed penguin, is much larger than the blue penguin and much less sociable, preferring nesting spots isolated from other penguin neighbours. At Bushy Beach, a small colony of these rare birds has established itself in the low-growing vegetation above the beach and a special hide has been constructed to allow public viewing. These penguins come ashore late in the afternoon (the blue penguin comes ashore at dusk), and the beach is closed after 3 p.m. as the birds will not come ashore if they are disturbed by people positioning themselves on the shore between the sea and their nests.

> To get to Bushy Beach from Oamaru town, follow Tyne Street to Bushy Beach Road to the car park at the end of the road.

Oamaru Dog Grounds, Waianakarua

Dog trialling as a sport had its origins in the sheep-farming boom of the nineteenth century in Australia and New Zealand. Like the dessert pavlova, the sport is claimed by our neighbours from across the ditch, where as the honours really should go to New Zealand. It is widely regarded that the first dog trials were held in Bala, New South Wales, Australia in 1873, but in the 9 July 1869 edition of the *Oamaru Times* it was reported that a third dog trial had been held at Wanaka in June of that year. Clearly, New Zealand has the prior claim to originating the concept.

By 1900 the sport was well established throughout the country with regular trials being held in both islands, though the first national championships were not held until 1936 in Hawera. Today there are 161 New Zealand clubs, and while the rules have been formalised, the sport is still solidly grounded in practical shepherding skills. Internationally, dog trialling is confined to New Zealand, Australia, Scotland, Wales and England, and competitions are divided into four classes – two heading (long head and short head), and two huntaway (zig-zag hunt and straight hunt), though a more recent development has been the running of show and yard trials throughout the year, and the televising of events has ensured great public interest.

The Oamaru dog trial grounds were established at Waianakarua in 1949 and are about as Kiwi as it gets. Consisting of a wide flat paddock leading up to the steeper terrain that is essential for some of the events, the grounds are on the farm of Ross McMillan who also donates the crossbred sheep for the events. Trials are held here annually for two days in the middle of April as part of the North Otago circuit, and attract competitors from all over the South Island. Recognised as one of the stronger dog trialling areas in New Zealand, North Otago has produced some notable triallers, including names such as Jack Warkworth, Andy Gibson, Bert White and Angus Fergusson. The buildings are 'homely' verging on the ramshackle (but not run-down), and include the bar known as 'The Dog Triallers Retreat' where apparently the biggest lies are told. The toilets, created out of water tanks donated by the local council, are a fine testament to Kiwi ingenuity.

Waianakarua Road, 3 km from the Mill House, where SH1 crosses the Waianakarua River. For dates visit www.sheepdogtrials.co.nz.

The Rock Piles of Omarama

Clearly, the trip through the Lindis Pass has a strange effect on people. Along a 10-km stretch of the long lazy road from the pass to Omarama stand numerous rock piles built by passers-by just for the sheer hell of it – much like building sand castles, but more permanently, out of stone. Some are just mere piles, others are created in stylish geometric patterns, while yet others are delicate geological balancing acts, though it is doubtful these last for long in the howling nor'westers that frequently blow through the Mackenzie basin.

Some cairns are clearly little roadside shrines, though the deity to which those topped by a beer bottle or an old broken jandal are dedicated to remains a mystery. The etiquette of pile construction is also unclear. Do you reuse previously collected stones or do you gather fresh ones? While it probably doesn't matter, plainly it would be in really bad form to actually destroy a still-intact pile, but collapsed piles are surely fair game. Happy building!

◀◀ Shag Point

This high bluff to the north of the Shag, or Waihemo, River is rich in both natural and human history. Rich forest, flocks of moa, and a bountiful sea drew early Maori to settle this area, and even after the moa were hunted to extinction the local iwi flourished here. Whalers were the earliest Europeans to settle on this coast in the early 1830s, and it was they who first noticed the dark seams of coal right at sea level. Coal mining began as early as 1863, mostly below sea level, and reached a peak in 1880 when over 170 people were employed in its extraction. Originally, coal was shipped out by sea, but in 1879 the railway line reached Shag Point and followed what is now the road that runs along the north side of the bluff. In 1902 the underwater mining came to an end, but the mines only finally closed in the 1970s.

Surprisingly, considering the relatively recent closure, very little remains of the coal-mining era, though the string of small houses – that at first glance appear to be cribs – are in fact mainly old miner's cottages. The main attractions today are the colonies of fur seals and yellow-eyed penguin that now make Shag Point their home. The small narrow coves, offshore rocks and reefs make the point an ideal playground for seals and a sheltered spot to raise their pups. Walking tracks weave along the windswept bluffs giving several excellent views of the seals lounging on rocky ledges or ducking and diving in the rolling waves below.

Shag Point is 2.5 km off SH1, 9 km north of Palmerston.

◀◀ Waitaki Valley Limestone and Fossil Country

Interested in geology and palaeontology? The area around Duntroon has some of New Zealand's most fascinating rock formations and fossils that are easily accessible from the road. The Vanished World Centre in Duntroon is an excellent starting point, with a collection of impressive fossils up to 30 million years old including ancient penguins, whales and dolphins, some species of which are yet to be classified. Even better, the centre has a kids' table where youngsters (why do *they* have all the fun?) can crack open rocks and find their own fossils to keep.

A brochure available for purchase from the centre, the 'Vanished World Fossil Trail', details a self-guided tour of the most interesting geological sites

in North Otago. And don't forget to check out the mysterious 'rattling rocks'. Three significant areas are a short loop drive from Duntroon and the trip will take around two hours including walking. They are:

Anatini Whale Fossil

A short walk from the road takes you to the fossil of a baleen whale. The fossil is very clear and protected by Perspex from prying fingers and has an interpretative board explaining what parts of the whale are visible.

Elephant Rocks

This wonderland of limestone formations shaped by erosion stands out starkly in the open farmland. Part of the first *Narnia* movie was filmed here.

Earthquakes

Huge rocks have broken away from the cliffs to expose fossils of an ancient seabed. Take care, as rocks still fall and there are crevices in the area.

Vanished World Centre, SH83, Duntroon. Open daily 10 a.m. to 4 p.m. October to June, Saturday and Sunday only 11 a.m. to 3 p.m. July to October, www.vanishedworld.co.nz.

DUNEDIN, OTAGO PENINSULA & ENVIRONS

◀◀ Aramoana Beach and Breakwater

For many New Zealanders the name Aramoana is synonymous with the 1990 massacre of 13 locals by gunman David Gray, but this association does a great disservice to what is a very attractive area. Situated at the entrance to Otago Harbour, opposite Taiaroa Head, Aramoana is a natural sand spit that has built up over millennia to almost enclose the harbour and protect the shallow waters from the open sea.

The beautiful white sandy beach is split by the long breakwater that was primarily constructed to stop the channel silting up. This is a great place for a stroll, especially with a heavy swell rolling in from the east, or to watch ships coming and going from the harbour. Take binoculars and you might spot albatross in flight from the colony just opposite on Taiaroa Head, and fur seals and blue penguins are not uncommon here.

Just inside the breakwater, a track and boardwalk leads through the extensive tidal salt marshes, home to numerous wading birds, including godwits in the summer months. The beaches either side of the breakwater are ideal for that leisurely stroll, and for those in the mood for something more demanding, a three-hour return hike to Heyward Point with fantastic coastal and harbour views is recommended. This track begins to the left when coming into Aramoana.

The settlement itself consists mainly of old-fashioned cribs sheltering behind the dunes, and fortunately plans to build an aluminium smelter here in the 1970s came to nothing, preserving a particularly attractive spot for the enjoyment of future generations.

10 km from Port Chalmers continuing east along the Otago Harbour to the very end of the road.

◀◀ Careys Bay Hotel

The upper harbour at Dunedin is too shallow and the channel too narrow for anything other than small vessels, so from the beginning of European settlement in 1844 Port Chalmers was developed as the port for the city, making it New Zealand's third-oldest town. Like Dunedin, it has many fine stone buildings, most erected between 1874 and 1880, and while these include churches and banks, it is fitting for a port town that there are several great

old pubs including Careys Bay Hotel (1874), Chicks Hotel (1876), and Port Chalmers Hotel (1846). It was from Port Chalmers that New Zealand's first cargo of frozen sheep meat left for Britain on the clipper *Dunedin* in 1882.

While the Careys Bay Hotel is popular with locals, most visitors don't make the short trip out to Port Chalmers and miss one of this region's most pleasant spots. Constructed of local bluestone, this pub was built in 1874 at Careys Bay, just out of Port Chalmers itself, and today looks out over the local fishing fleet. Immaculately restored, walking into the hotel is like stepping back in time to the nineteenth century (or at least the very best of the nineteenth century). Warm wood panelling, original sash windows, a timber staircase and beautiful stonework over 125 years old meld together to create one of New Zealand's best pub experiences. But the hotel is not all about history. Careys Bay Hotel also has an impressive collection of Ralph Hotere paintings, who is without doubt one of New Zealand's leading contemporary artists. The pub also serves very good food in the dining room and the attractive courtyard.

◀◀ Duke of Wellington Tavern

At first glance the Duke of Wellington looks like a handsome old Victorian pub, and to a certain point it is exactly that. Warm and welcoming, this opulent tavern has ornate plaster ceilings intricately picked out in green, gold and red, old wooden floors and a unique goods lift, built in 1873 and said to be the oldest in New Zealand. On tap are up to 18 British beers (plus cider), and overlooking Queen's Gardens is a small terrace, ideal on warm summer days. Downstairs is a smaller bar, mainly used for functions, with walls of handsome bluestone block that also forms the building's foundations.

Appearances, however, are deceiving, and this pub was only established in 2002. The building itself, though, has a history associated with one of New Zealand's best-known stores. It was here in 1875 that Bendix Hallenstein set up his first clothing factory, establishing the iconic menswear business known today as just plain old Hallensteins. Born in Germany in 1835, Bendix immigrated with his two brothers initially to Australia and then on to New Zealand, setting up his first general store in Invercargill. The business was not a success and the family moved on to Central Otago, setting up stores in Lawrence, Queenstown, Cromwell and Arrowtown (the land for the Queenstown Gardens was donated by Bendix).

In response to difficulties in sourcing good clothing, Bendix established a factory in Dunedin, and the part of the building now housing the Duke of Wellington was the company's retail shop. In 1883 Hallensteins moved from Rattray Street to Dowling Street and the building then became the head office of the National Fire and Insurance Company, later to become Royal Insurance. In more recent years, Mooneys, the furriers, had their showroom here, but despite all the changes the essential Victorian character of the premises remains unaltered. Michael McCarrigan saw the building's potential for becoming the most perfect small pub and today the Duke has all the ambience of a cosy 'local', with a relaxed and friendly atmosphere quite different from the more rowdy student pubs north of the Octagon.

1 Queen's Gardens (corner Rattray Street), Dunedin, ph 03 479 2870.

◀◀ Dunedin Botanic Gardens

Established in 1863, the oldest botanic gardens in New Zealand fall naturally into two parts. The original lower gardens are flat and laid out in a formal fashion, while the upper section, across the Water of Leith, is quite different with steep terrain and the planting, containing the larger tree and shrub collections, far less formal. There are three highlights within the gardens worth seeking out.

The first highlight is the stunning perennial herbaceous borders. Much loved in traditional English gardening, herbaceous borders do not thrive in the generally warmer New Zealand climate. Here in Dunedin, however, with its cool winter and mild summer temperatures, the herbaceous border walk is the best in the country. One side of the walk is a long perennial border, while the other side is a series of short borders arranged in blue, red, white and yellow. The borders are at their peak between December and February.

Number two on the list is the ornate Wolfe Haven Fountain. Built in 1898, the fountain originally stood in the Queen's Gardens by the railway station. During the New Zealand and South Seas Exhibition held in Dunedin in 1925, the fountain graced the foyer of the Grand Court, after which it was moved yet again, this time to the Botanic Gardens where it has finally stayed put. The cast-iron fountain comprises three tiers, with the traditional theme of cherubs and fish and topped by a heron spouting water. The setting is further enhanced by a formal garden of box hedging and topiary.

Number three is the parrot aviaries. Located uphill and well worth the short hike, the aviaries house a collection of New Zealand parrots that includes the yellow-fronted, red-crowned and the rare Antipodes Island kakariki, as well as kea and kaka. In addition to showing these birds to the public, the aviaries do a great job with a breeding programme for endangered native birds.

Cumberland Street, Dunedin.

Dunedin Gasworks Museum

Opened in 1863, these gasworks were the first in New Zealand to produce coal gas. Located in South Dunedin, this was also a rapidly growing industrial area at the time, supplying goods to the goldfields in Central Otago and the boom town of Dunedin. After 124 years of production, the gasworks finally closed in 1987. Most of the remaining buildings are largely Edwardian, though the 24-metre-high boiler-house chimney is believed to date back to the 1880s. One of only three such museums in the world, the highlight is the working stationary steam engine that at one time pumped coal gas to Dunedin households and even now is driven by steam.

20 Braemar Street, South Dunedin. Open 12 noon to 4 p.m. on the first and second Sunday of each month; entrance fee.

Huriawa Pa, Karitane Beach

Volcanic in origin, with steep cliffs and sea on three sides, Huriawa Peninsula is located between two beautiful beaches and was the perfect location for a fortified pa. Defenders had uninterrupted views both north and south along the coast and over the estuarine marshes to the east. A Ngai Tahu stronghold, in the eighteenth century, the pa resisted a protracted siege of over six months.

The entrance to the pa is through a beautifully carved gateway and the track meanders gently to the end of the peninsula, with great views along the coast in both directions (the walk takes around 45 minutes). Hooker's sea lions and fur seals are common along the shore, and there are several blowholes on the south side of the pa that are dramatic when a swell is

running. Oddly, what must be one of the most spectacular spots along this Otago coast is not signposted, possibly because the locals are not keen to share this gem and want to keep it to themselves!

> From SH1, turn off towards Karitane and take the road right to the beach. At the beach, turn left along Sulisker Street and continue 500 metres uphill to the pa entrance.

◀◀ New Zealand Marine Studies Aquarium

While aquariums are not so unusual, what makes this small establishment appealing is that it is part of the University of Otago's marine research facility rather than just the usual tourist trap. With a focus on southern sea life, the aquarium promotes education rather than entertainment, and here you can see pigfish, sea horses, and an octopus with a 1-metre arm spread, as well as dabble in the popular Touch Pool. The aquarium also has a great view of the harbour and Quarantine Island/St Martins Island just offshore. For those especially interested in marine life, the personalised tour at 10.30 a.m. is highly recommended.

> Turn left opposite the Portobello Hotel and drive for 1.5 km – don't be put off by the road. Open daily 12 noon to 4.30 p.m., closed Christmas Day, www.marine.ac.nz.

◀◀ New Zealand's Tallest Tree

For those who take the Australia/New Zealand rivalry to heart, this is going to be hard to take. Not only do they trash us at sport, but also the tallest tree in New Zealand is a blimmin' Aussie! This gum tree, *Eucalpytus regans*, towers 30 metres higher than the revered kauri Tane Mahuta and 10 metres taller than our tallest tree, the kahikatea. Reaching 70 metres, the tree is part of a large grove of gums that were self-sown after a fire in 1900, with the ash from the fire providing a fertile base to give the seedlings a good start in life. The grove is surrounded by native bush and the area has recently been given protection as a 'mainland island', that in the near future will see a proliferation of native bird life. The walk to the tree takes around one hour return.

Turn off SH1 at Waitati and continue on the road towards Port Chalmers for 1 km, then turn left into Orokonui Road and travel for another 11 km. The car park for the walk is on the left just 50 metres before Orokonui Park. (Note: this park is private property.)

◀◀ Olveston

Often overlooked by visitors to Dunedin interested in a trip to the more dramatic Larnach Castle, Olveston is without a doubt one of the best 'old house' experiences in the country. In most old homes, the furniture has long since disappeared, but what makes Olveston so special is that it is crammed full of the original furniture and ornaments with almost nothing changed since the house was first built.

Completed in 1906, the house was commissioned by David Theomin, a Jewish immigrant who developed a very successful music business in Dunedin in the latter half of the nineteenth century. Designed by London architect Sir Ernest George, no expense was spared in the construction, and the house included every modern convenience, from a central heating system and telephone through to a shower and heated towel rail in the bathroom. Unfortunately for the family, the only son, Edward, died at an early age and the only daughter, Dorothy, died childless in 1966. She left the house to Dunedin City, which, at the time, was not particularly thrilled to receive such a gift, although today it is recognised as a great asset.

So little has been altered in the house over the last 100 years that it appears the Theomins have just gone out for the day and are due back any moment. The kitchen contains complete dinner sets (all ready for serving), personal ornaments still sit on the bedroom dressing tables, while the only thing missing from the billiard room is the cigar smoke. All tours of the house are guided, which adds immensely to the experience, so if your time in Dunedin is short put a visit to this magnificent house at the top of your list.

42 Royal Terrace, Dunedin. Open daily, tour times 9.30, 10.45, 12 noon, 1.30, 2.45, 4.00, ph 03 477 3320, www.olverston.co.nz; entrance fee.

⟨⟨ Otakau Marae

The name Otago is a European corruption of the Maori word Otakau, meaning 'the place of red ochre'. This peninsula suited the needs of early Maori, and the pre-European population was estimated to be well over 3000 people, though overall the Maori population in the cooler southern climate was relatively small. The warm, north-facing bay favoured the growing of crops, the sheltered harbour was ideal for safe fishing, the forests were home to numerous birds, and the large tidal estuaries offered easy access to shellfish beds. Early relationships between Maori and Pakeha were mainly mutually beneficial and intermarriage was common, but as the number of settlers increased, Maori were gradually marginalised and disadvantaged.

Otakau, always a major settlement, is today one of the few surviving marae in Otago. The existing complex was built in 1940 and opened by the then Prime Minister, Peter Fraser. Set on a small rise and consisting of the wharenui *Tamatea* and a small Maori church, the buildings at first glance appear fairly typical of any marae in the country, though the wharenui has an unusually high gable and very shallow porch. But take a closer look. At a distance, the buildings appear to be constructed of stucco with traditional wooden carvings, but on closer inspection all the 'carvings' – and in fact the whole building – is made entirely of concrete. Maori were adept at adapting European technology for marae buildings while at the same time retaining key traditional elements. One of the most enduring arts has been carving, and the use of concrete at Otakau instead of wood is very radical if not totally unique.

Harrington Point Road. Koha/donation.

⟨⟨ Ross Creek Reservoir

Tucked away off the Leith Valley, Ross Creek Reservoir is recognised as an outstanding engineering achievement by IPENZ (Institute of Professional Engineers New Zealand). The earth dam was built in 1867 to provide water to a town rapidly expanding with the influx of wealth from the gold rushes further inland, and today the reservoir is the oldest still in existence in New Zealand and is still part of the city's water system.

A short walk from the road through a mixture of introduced and native

trees (including some very large native tree fuchsias), the original bluestone walls still line the dam, though it is the old valve tower that is the highlight. The tower was built at the same time as the dam in 1867 and the simple, elegant structure with its curved roof is distinctively Victorian.

Access to the reservoir is by a track that starts just over the bridge on Rockside Road near the intersection with Malvern Road, North Dunedin.

◀◀ St Clair Hot Saltwater Pool

Saltwater pools were once common in coastal cities and towns as they were an economical way to provide a swimming facility by merely building a simple concrete pool that was filled by the high tide. Today only two saltwater pools survive, Parnell in Auckland and St Clair in Dunedin. St Clair and St Kilda are two magnificent sandy beaches on the south coast of Dunedin and have been a popular swimming spot for locals for many years. With nothing between them and the Antarctic, the beaches are often exposed to dramatic seas, and at the rocky southern end of St Clair beach the saltwater pool cops its share of wild water. The site is spectacular and that is what makes this pool so special. Located on a rocky shelf, the pool is open to the ocean on two sides. To the east is the long sweep of shoreline, popular with surfers who zip past the pool just metres away. To the south is the southern ocean, pounded by high seas that break over the protecting walls, occasionally even closing the pool.

A pool was first built in 1884 and has gradually developed over the years, at one stage in the 1940s even including a hydrotherapy clinic. Thankfully, heated since the early 1960s, St Clair was thoroughly renovated in 2003. St Clair Pool today is a modern swimming facility particularly popular with those of mature years keeping fit, and it is claimed that some older local folk walk down to the pool early in the morning still clad in their pjs and dressing gown. A small café, part of the pool complex, offers good coffee, wraps, cake and the ubiquitous cheese rolls. Adding to the charm are the nearby renovated Hydro Hotel and several good cafés and bars.

The Esplanade, St Clair. Open Labour Weekend until March, Monday to Friday 6 a.m. to 7 p.m., weekends 8 a.m. to 7 p.m.; entrance fee.

◀◀ The Pyramids and Victory Beach – Okia Reserve

In the third century BC Egyptian colonists arrived on the ship the *Victory* and established a settlement on the Otago Peninsula, and while the colony died out, they left behind two pyramids marking the graves of the 'Pacific Pharaohs' . . . Okay, so imagination is not such a bad thing, and the walk from the road to Victory Beach passes between two pyramids that will spark plenty of flights of fancy.

The two small hills called 'the Pyramids' are actually volcanic in origin – a testament to the peninsula's fiery birth. Take a careful look at the seaward side of the smaller pyramid, and the volcanic basalt columns, precise in their geometric structure, are very obvious (similar to the Organ Pipes on Mt Cargill, south of Dunedin City). There is also a short scramble to the top of the smaller pyramid for a view over the dune country.

The Pyramids are located in the Okia Reserve, a mixture of wetland and dune country that lies behind Victory Beach, itself a beautiful, isolated sweep of white sand and home to sea lions, fur seals and blue and yellow-eyed penguins. Take care in the scrub-covered dunes behind the beach, as Hooker's sea lions, easily camouflaged, that rest there can be quite aggressive if disturbed. Penguins also nest in the dunes, so respect their space.

The beach takes its name from the ship *Victory* that foundered on its shores while under the command of a proverbial drunken sailor, though very little remains of the wreck. The beach is totally undeveloped, open to the Southern Ocean, and is about as close as you can possibly get to pristine on the peninsula.

> Just beyond Portobello village, turn right into Weir Road and follow it to the end. It is a gravel road but in reasonable condition.

◀◀ The Savoy Tearooms/Etrusco

In their day, the Savoy Tearooms were the epitome of the great English tearooms. Located on the first floor of the Haynes Building in Princes Street, the Savoy was the place for high teas, lunchtime dinners, and those special occasions. Closed in 1989, the tearooms stood empty for some time before being resurrected as a restaurant.

Fortunately, all the features that made the Savoy so attractive and elegant

have not only survived, but are also loving valued by the current owners. The magnificent plaster ceilings are all original, along with the oak panelling, the faux marble pillars and even most of the furniture. In particular, all the fabulous Edwardian leadlight windows, each with three-coloured heraldic shields, have survived intact; and recently the original wooden floors have been restored, complete with thousands of tiny indentations made by generations of elegant high heels clicking across the surface. In winter the old fireplace blazes with both real and remembered warmth.

A real bonus is that the Savoy is presently run by an Italian family, moderately priced, and an ideal place for dinner out when you are in Dunedin.

8A Moray Place, Dunedin, ph 03 477 3737, www.etrusco.co.nz.

◀◀ Tunnel Beach

The Otago coast is not short of dramatic scenery, but Tunnel Beach is a standout. Accessed by a short walk of around one hour return over farmland, Tunnel Beach is a magnificent seascape of dramatic cliffs, a boulder beach cove and natural sea arch. From the top of the arch there are marvellous views south along the coast and in wild weather waves pound the rocks beneath – the greater the swell, the more impressive the wave action. From the top of the arch a low tunnel with shallow steps leads down to a small boulder-strewn cove.

This tunnel was constructed by John Cargill, son of the prominent settler William Cargill, as private access to the beach so his daughters could swim away from prying eyes at the public St Clair beach. The tunnel turned out to be a big mistake for Mr Cargill, as unfortunately one of the girls drowned here. Needless to say, the sea here is not safe for swimming.

It is a bit of a mission to find Tunnel Beach as it is not clearly signposted, but follow the 'Southern Scenic' route south of Dunedin, and from Blackhead Road turn left into Tunnel Beach Road.

CENTRAL OTAGO

◀◀ Bendigo Goldfields

In 1873, Thomas Logan discovered gold in this area and, like so many others, promptly named a town after himself. Logantown is just one of the many old townships, mineshafts, water races and ruined stamper batteries that spread among the rocks and tussock of the Bendigo goldfields. What makes this area particularly appealing is that the dry climate has preserved many of the mining relics and the high altitude provides a magnificent backdrop to the picturesque ruins.

Not too much remains of Bendigo at the foot of the hill that climbs to Logantown, which today consists of just a ruined cottage and a surprisingly well-preserved wooden cart. Just beyond Logantown are Welshtown and the Matilda Battery that are considerably more substantial. Opened in 1878, the shaft at Matilda went down 178 metres and the 16-stamper battery, powered by steam, crushed the ore hauled up from the depths. The mine closed in 1884, and in 1908 ten of the stampers were relocated to the nearby Come In Time Battery where they remain today.

Welshtown has some of the best-preserved miner's huts in Central Otago (several of which are only missing the roof), as well as old rock walls and the remains of the Matilda Battery itself. Just across the valley is the incredibly tiny Pengelly's Hotel, with rooms so small it is hard to imagine how the patrons actually squeezed in.

> To get there from Cromwell, take SH8 towards Tarras, and after 14 km turn right into Bendigo Loop Road. Continue down this road for 2 km then turn right at Bendigo township to Welshtown. The road beyond Bendigo is pretty rough, especially between Logantown and Welshtown, and you might prefer to park at Logantown (recognisable by the wooden wagon) and walk the short distance uphill to Welshtown.

◀◀ Chatto Creek, New Zealand's Smallest Post Office

Hang on to all your postcards and then mail them at New Zealand's smallest post office at Chatto Creek, just north of Alexandra. Opened in 1892, this post office was originally little more than a canvas tent a few metres square with just one window. Later, the building went very upmarket and had corrugated iron nailed over the canvas – and in fact the original cloth material is still

visible on a section of the inside wall. In keeping with the style of the period, the internal walls are lined with both old wallpaper and magazine spreads, and today you can still read the news from the *Otago Witness* on 23 July 1919.

The post was the domain of the legendary Miss Kinney, who ran the post office for over 40 years and knew everyone and everything in the district. Using only a butter box for a chair, Miss Kinney was a woman of strong opinion and biked the 4 km from her home daily. Often, when the weather wasn't so great, she was offered a ride by local motorists, but being a woman of firm principle only accepted a lift from Catholics and never from Anglicans, Methodists, Presbyterians or any other denomination.

The post office was closed in 1975, but with the support of locals reopened in 2004 complete with old typewriter, wooden telephone and the old post boxes. It is administered by the Chatto Creek Tavern, built in 1886, which is right next door and worth a visit on its own.

Chatto Creek is 14 km north of Alexandra on SH85.

⟨⟨ Cromwell Chafer Beetle Reserve

Those travelling from Cromwell en route to the Bannockburn wineries may not consider this actually worth a detour at all – but let's face it, even beetles have a right to a home too, and good on the people with the foresight to protect this rare and helpless insect from total annihilation.

The Cromwell chafer beetle is a small flightless beetle that is the rarest and most endangered of 18 such beetles, and this 81-hectare reserve is virtually the chafer beetle's entire habitat, with a population of between one to two thousand of the little creatures. You can walk over the reserve if you really want to, but as the beetles spend most of their time underground you are unlikely to ever see them.

Consisting of tough dry vegetation just a few centimetres high, this little reserve also protects a small fragment of the original and unusual inland sand-dune country and offers a rare glimpse into what the area around Cromwell once looked like.

The reserve is 2 km south of Cromwell on the road to Bannockburn.

‹‹ Earnscleugh Historic Tailings, Alexandra

There isn't actually that much to see here other than a ruined landscape, but the tailings are a most bizarre attraction in their own right and a testament to human ingenuity and determination. Covering hectare after hectare, these piles of shingle and stone are the remains of an industry that boomed in the early twentieth century.

Gold was discovered here in 1862, and once the easily worked ore was exhausted, dredges moved into the riverbed with varying degrees of success. In 1895 the invention of the tailings elevator that allowed dredges to stack the tailings behind them – and therefore work into the riverbank rather than just the bed – radically changed things. At its height, 20 dredges worked the riverbed between Alexandra and Clyde, leaving behind a moonscape of debris. The tailings are part of the Otago 50th Anniversary Walkway that runs from Alexandra to Clyde.

> From Alexandra, cross over the Clutha River Bridge and turn right into Earnscleugh Road, and then after 3 km turn right into Marshall Road.

‹‹ Hayes Engineering Works

The modest mud-brick and corrugated-iron buildings that form Hayes Engineering are representative of the Kiwi knack of being able to make everything from anything. From this remote workshop, established by Ernest Hayes in 1895, issued forth a wide range of simple but effective agricultural innovations, that by his death in 1933 had gained a worldwide reputation. In particular, the Hayes Wire Strainer invented in 1905 was widely exported internationally. The company moved to Christchurch in 1952 (and is still in operation and owned by the Hayes family), and today this unique collection of buildings is much the same as when they were fully operational in the 1930s.

What is so appealing about the engineering works is that not only does much of the equipment still work, but so many of the original tools still remain. Everywhere are lathes and drills, while the benches and walls are covered in tools that in most places would have long since disappeared. For those aficionados of the home workshop, this place is the home mechanic's heaven.

Ida Valley/Omakau Road, Oturehua. Open Saturday and Sunday 11 a.m.
to 4 p.m. August to May, other times by arrangement, ph 03 444 5810,
03 444 5817.

◀◀ Lake Onslow

The drive to Lake Onslow, east of Roxburgh, is as appealing as the lake
itself. Although the idea of travelling 40 km on a winding gravel road may
not sound like a lot of fun, the trip passes through wonderful open, high
tussock country slashed by deep gullies and looking every bit like a Grahame
Sydney painting.

The man-made lake was originally known by the very unattractive name
'The Dismal Swamp', no doubt due to the open and windswept nature of the
area. Flooded in 1888 to provide water for mining operations, the dam was
later raised several times, and from 1924 provided water for irrigation and
power. Now covering an area of over 800 hectares, the lake has excellent
fishing (brown trout) and boating facilities. A handful of small cribs nestle
amongst the tussock, along with the attendant 'dunnies' that are firmly wired
down to stop them being blown away in the relentless wind.

> Initially the lake is not so easy to find as it is not signposted from Roxburgh.
> From the main street of Roxburgh (SH8), turn down Jedburgh Street
> (signposted Roxburgh East) and cross the Clutha River. At the T junction
> turn right, and after 1 km turn left into Wright Road. From this point on it is
> reasonably signposted.

◀◀ Maniototo Curling International, Naseby

No doubt most people have seen curling on television at some time or other.
You know, those half-frozen individuals in woolly tam-o'-shanters sliding
great chunks of stone along the ice while their team-mates furiously sweep
a path with witch-like brooms. Originating in Scotland, the game found a
natural home in Central Otago, with winters cold enough to freeze over
small lakes and ponds. Traditionally, a bonspiel (or curling) tournament
was held outdoors in winter on frozen lakes and ponds throughout
Central, but here at Naseby, summer or winter, you can try your hand at
this ancient sport.

Maniototo Curling International has both an outdoor rink for winter and a brand-spanking-new indoor rink for all-year-round sport. If you have never tried the game, no worries, the friendly people at Naseby provide not only all the equipment but full tuition as well. You will need to bring flat-soled shoes and warm clothing, as the indoor rink is maintained at a chilly 4°C (ideal on one of those scorching-hot Central afternoons!). Curling also holds a unique New Zealand record, in that the Baxter Cup was first contested in 1884 and is the country's oldest national sporting trophy.

Maniototo Curling International, 1057 Channel Road, Naseby,
ph 03 444 9878, www.curling.co.nz.

◀◀ Mitchells Cottage

While there are plenty of stone cottages scattered throughout Central Otago, Mitchells Cottage stands out from the crowd. For a start, it has the most impressive location, set among rocky tors and facing north high above the Clutha Valley with marvellous views and exposed to the elements. The cottage itself is perfectly built into the landscape it occupies, and it is doubtful whether any other New Zealand building has been constructed so sympathetically with the surrounding environment.

A natural rock slab forms the foundation of the house, the front step, and at the same time acts as a stone terrace in front of the small building. The cottage, the outhouses and the fence are constructed of local split schist rock, carefully shaped and crafted and then fitted together with a precision that even today is impressive. Experienced with building in stone in their native Shetland Islands, the Mitchell brothers John and Andrew built numerous cottages in the district before completing this house in 1904, which became the home of John and his wife Jessie who raised 10 children in the two-bedroom cottage. The interior of the house is lined with tongue-and-groove wood and is currently unfurnished with just a lovely old photo of John and Jessie hanging on the kitchen wall.

Just below the cottage is a sundial cut into solid stone and a number of hardy trees planted by the Mitchells around the turn of the nineteenth century. Just below that again and built into the rock wall is a small forge, while behind the house are a number of small outbuildings including a stone chook house. It's a wonderful place, often bypassed, and when I was there in

early March only one other visitor had signed the visitor's book in the past three days, so there is a good chance you will have the place to yourself.

> End of Symes Road, 1 km off SH8, 8 km north of Roxburgh. There is just a small sign from the main road so it is easy to miss. There is no charge for entry.

◀◀ Museum of Fashion and the Jim Beam Decanter Collection

What do fashion and Jim Beam have in common? Well, nothing really, apart from the fact that these two very different collections are both housed at the Museum of Fashion just out of Naseby. If that coincidence is not extraordinary enough, the story of how they both came to be here most certainly is.

The museum is located on the farm of the late Eden Hore, a sheep farmer who, let's say, had a larger-than-life personality. His fascination with fashion developed initially out of his interest in the uses of wool, one of which was in contemporary women's fashion. Eden began by collecting a few 100 per cent woollen garments in the late 1960s, but during the 1970s his interest expanded to include the very best of women's couture. From 1964 through to 1995, the cigarette manufacturer Benson & Hedges sponsored the annual fashion awards and many of the garments Eden collected were finalists in this competition. The result is a collection of seventies chic that any museum would give their eye teeth for.

The clothes are a wonderful and eclectic snapshot of the vibrant 1970s, ranging from smart evening wear through to some weird and wonderful costumes in amazing seventies colours, such as the vinyl cat suit. Along with the 220 frocks are shoes and hats, marvellous period photos of models wearing the actual clothes, a collection of 1960s Miss New Zealand photos, and a replica of Princess Anne's wedding dress. At the time, Eden regularly held fashion shows on the lawn in front of the house, but eventually converted the tractor shed into a showroom to hold his burgeoning collection. They are now protected in glass cases.

As if that isn't enough, there is also an amazing collection of over 500 Jim Beam ceramic decanters that come in every conceivable style. Themes include Christmas, American cars, birds, telephones, operatic characters, and cowboys, and there is even a train set comprised of individual decanter carriages. Home-grown personalities 'make it with Jim Beam' too, with

decanters of Richard Hadlee and Colin Meads. And just so you don't have to ask, they are not all empty!

Still want more? Well, there is also a stuffed yak – but that's another story, so just go and see for yourself.

Glenshee Park, Danseys Pass Road, Naseby. Open 7 days 10 a.m. to
5 p.m. except Tuesday and Friday mornings and Christmas Day,
ph 03 444 9624, email: mas.glenshee.park@xtra.co.nz; entrance fee.

◀◀ Naseby

If you have ever wondered what Arrowtown was like before all the tourists arrived, then Naseby is the place for you. Situated in the northern Maniototo under the Kakanui Mountains, gold was discovered in the Hogburn in May 1863, and by the end of the year the diggings were home to over 5000 men. Four years later the rush was over, but gold could still be extracted by hydraulic sluicing – effective, but with a ruinous impact on the landscape. Fortunately, conifers were later planted over the old tailings and today Naseby is an attractive forested township.

Originally the area was known as 'Parkers', after two brothers involved in the initial gold discovery, and later changed to Mt Ida, and finally to Naseby. The small cosy town has a number of historic buildings including two of Central Otago's oldest pubs, both of which were built in 1863. The elder by just three months is the Ancient Briton, an atmospheric old stone building, while just around the corner is the fine wooden Royal Hotel.

Naseby is 10 km north of Ranfurly off SH8.

◀◀ Rippon Vineyard and Winery

One of the country's most photographed wineries, Rippon Vineyard is located on a broad slope just above Lake Wanaka. Famous for its vistas of rows of grapes leading down to the lake, Rippon is especially attractive in autumn when the yellowing leaves of the vines contrast with the bright blue of the lake. The vineyard is an easy walk along the lake from central Wanaka, and while it doesn't have a café it is a great place to bring a picnic.

One of the earliest vineyards in Central Otago, the DSIR first started

experimental plantings here in 1975, and by 1981 the vineyard was already extensively planted. Pinot Noir is the signature wine, but varietals include Chardonnay, Riesling, Merlot, Shiraz, Osteiner and Gewürztraminer. The vineyard is home to the Rippon Music Festival, held every two years (even numbers) and focusing on contemporary music, from hip-hop and dance to reggae and rock.

> 5 km west of Wanaka on the Mt Aspiring Road. Cellar door open 11 a.m.
> to 5 p.m. December to April, 1.30 p.m. to 4 p.m. July to November,
> closed May and June, ph 03 443 8084, www.rippon.co.nz.

◀◀ Ranfurly Art Deco

Today the little Maniototo town of Ranfurly is best known for its small collection of art deco buildings. What makes Ranfurly so unique is that the architecture came in response to a number of suspicious fires in the early 1930s and just one builder, JM Mitchell and Sons, constructed all of the buildings and continued building in the art deco style long after its popularity had waned elsewhere.

While there are only about 10 art deco buildings in total, the pick of them are the Ranfurly Lion Hotel and the very stylish Centennial Milk Bar. The milk bar was the refreshment room for the rail passengers and today houses a great collection of 1930s and 1940s crockery, period clothing, furniture and memorabilia. The town also hosts a lively art deco festival in February each year.

But one burning question remains unanswered – just who was playing with matches in Ranfurly around 1930? The town wasn't that big, but the fires were, destroying, among other structures, the town hall and a hotel. No one was ever charged, and nor does there seem to be much speculation about the culprit – but surely in a town the size of Ranfurly someone must have had some idea. And why did the fires stop? Possibly, as is typical in a small town, the local coppers had a good idea just who this bad egg was, but did not have enough hard evidence to take it further. Perhaps they either kept a close eye on the pyromaniac or 'suggested' the evildoer leave town. Either way, the legacy of the fire-happy ratbag is a small town with a big art deco heart!

The Road to Skippers

This is the place to test your nerves, and it's definitely not a drive for the less confident motorist. One of New Zealand's legendary roads, the road to Skippers has hardly changed since it was built in the 1860s to service the gold-mining settlements along the Shotover River.

Unsealed and very narrow, the road is more suited to four-wheel drive or at least vehicles with a reasonably high wheelbase. Not for the faint-hearted, there are huge drops into the Shotover River and the road also requires considerable backing skills if another vehicle happens to be coming the other way, as long stretches are only one-way. The scenery, though, is well worth it. Winding high above the dry rocky landscape, the road more or less follows the Shotover River, and with very few trees the views are endless.

All that remains of the Long Gully Pub built in 1863 and burnt down in 1951 is the fireplace and chimneys, while at the end of the road are a camping ground, the restored nineteenth-century stone schoolhouse and the Mt Aurum homestead. The historic Skippers suspension bridge was built in 1901, while an even older bridge over the Shotover was built in 1864 and is now used for bungy jumps. If you don't want to drive, several operators run 4WD tours along the road.

The road to Skippers is north of Queenstown and is a continuation of the road to the Coronet Peak ski field.

The Sluicings and Stewart Town

The Sluicings is an amazing area of cliffs, gulches, pinnacles, tunnels and old ruins set amid a barren landscape and all man-made. In the late nineteenth century, technology enabled gravelly soils to be worked with high-pressure sluicing hoses that resulted in a drastic revision of the landscape. Blasted by water, the flat terrain near Bannockburn has been altered beyond recognition and has a strange appeal all of its own.

After traversing a deep gully, the track reaches a plateau and the remains of Stewart Town, which today consists only of a cottage and old apple and pear trees that still bear fruit. The tiny cottage, minus its roof, was the home of David Stewart and John Menzies, who made a small fortune by providing the water critical to the sluicing operations (the sign makes a point that both

men were bachelors, so you can read into that what you will). As well as the remains of Stewart Town there are the ruins of numerous miners' huts, a blacksmith's forge and old water channels.

Felton Road, Bannockburn, 5 km north of Cromwell.

Somebody's Darling

The legend of 'Somebody's Darling' is a good deal more appealing than the truth, but as the old saying goes, 'Don't let truth get in the way of a good story'. According to the popular tale, in February 1865 the unidentified body of a young man was found washed up on the riverbank by local man William Rigney. Rigney then buried the drowned man not far from the riverbank and provided a headboard for the grave inscribed 'Somebody's Darling Lies Buried Here'. When Rigney died in 1912 he was buried next to Somebody's Darling, with his inscription reading: 'Here Lies the Body of William Rigney The Man Who Buried Somebody's Darling.'

In fact, William Rigney never claimed to have either found the body or to have buried it, but merely provided the gravestone. As for being unidentified, it is reasonably certain that the dead man was Charles Alms, a butcher from the Nevis Valley who drowned in the Clutha on 25 January and was subsequently washed downstream. While the truth is less endearing than the legend, isn't it still rather odd to want to be buried next to someone you never knew?

From SH8, turn over the Clutha at Millers Flat then turn right and follow the river for 9 km. The last section down Beaumont Station Road is unsealed.

SOUTH OTAGO & THE CATLINS

◀◀ Benhar Pottery

Once known as 'the Staffordshire of the South', the area around Milton was once the centre of a major pottery industry rather than a prison. Using local clay, most kilns produced brick, pipes and practical pottery such as toilets and hand basins, but some also produced domestic ware of varying quality. Located south of Milton, and almost at Balclutha, Benhar was one of New Zealand's earliest and most important commercial potteries. During its long history from the 1890s until the 1970s, the pottery produced bricks, pipes, ceramic toilets and in the 1920s and 1930s tableware, which is now very rare and very collectable. Unfortunately today the pottery at Benhar is derelict, but intact, with its beautifully built brick kilns and towering chimney still dominating the landscape. The small village still retains the brick workers' cottages and 'Lesmahagow' the grand Edwardian home of the McSkimming family who owned the pottery (now a bed and breakfast).

Benhar is 1 km off SH1, 4 km north of Balclutha.

◀◀ Bull Creek

Lying east of Milton on the South Otago coast, Bull Creek is a small settlement of cribs huddled near the mouth of a substantial stream. The stream cuts deeply through the rolling coastal hills and a significant stretch of the creek near the sea is flanked by attractive native bush, home to native birds and in particular the bellbird. A walkway along the creek through the bush is an easy stroll and there are several popular swimming holes sheltered from the coastal wind and with warmer and safer water than the sea. Unlike the long stretches of sandy beach north and south, the coast around Bull Creek is rocky with small sandy coves suitable for swimming if you can brave the water temperature. These picturesque coves are further enhanced by unusual sand which consists of coarse golden sand overlying finer white sand creating a beachscape that is especially appealing. The cluster of seaside cribs are mostly of the older homebuilt variety that together with the bush and the coves create a bucolic seaside settlement rarely found on the New Zealand coast.

Bull Creek is 26 km east of Milton off SH1.

Catlins

Cannibal Bay

For years the south-eastern corner of the South Island was very much a remote destination, but in recent years it has become one of the more popular driving trips in the country, though fortunately it does not yet attract bus tourist trade. A short distance off SH92 is Cannibal Bay, a magnificent sweep of deserted beach and just one of several beautiful beaches in the Catlins area, though unfortunately the water is pretty cold even in summer. The cool water does not deter the hardy band of board riders that make the pilgrimage to one of New Zealand's best surf beaches. Cannibal Bay, like other Catlins beaches, is home to sea lions, which are fairly common along this coast. While they may appear awkward sea lions can be very aggressive and move surprisingly fast, so it is best to keep a good distance. If surfing is not for you, then a 30-minute walk south along the beach will take you to False Islet and Surat Bay on Catlins River estuary. Surat Bay takes its name from the ship *Surat* wrecked here in 1974 on New Year's Day. Talk about a New Year's Eve hangover!

> The turnoff to Cannibal Bay is about 5 km north of Owaka on SH92.

The Dolphin at Pounawea

No, this is not a southern version of Opo or Moko, but a device to assist ships navigate narrow rivers. In the middle of the estuary of the Catlins River at Pounawea is a simple wooden structure built in 1882 costing just 25 pounds that in reality is a very fancy and very strong post. All boats had to do was to tie up to the dolphin and then allow the force of the turning tide to swing the boat around in the confines of the narrow estuary channel using the force of the tide. While once very commonplace, the fact that they were usually cheaply constructed out of wood has meant that very few dolphins survive today.

> Pounawea is 3 km east of Owaka and the dolphin is located just off shore on the waterfront at Pounawea just by the camping ground.

◀◀ Traills Tractor

The original 'push me, pull you', the Traills tractor is a hybrid beast that is both train and tractor. A Fordson tractor has been adapted to run on rails and could either push or pull log-laden carriages from the bush to the mill. The tractor is a survivor from the heyday of timber milling in the Catlins area that continued well into the twentieth century, though fortunately large stretches of native bush still remain. Located on the site of the old Cook's Sawmill, the tractor is now restored and protected from the weather.

> The tractor is a 5-minute walk from SH92 just south of the Fleming River Bridge, south of Papatowai.

◀◀ Clutha Punt, Tuapeka Mouth

Tuapeka Mouth was the closest point on the Clutha River to the lucrative goldfields just to the north. The river at this point was too wide and swift flowing to quickly build a bridge so ferries and punts were used to move both people and vehicles across. Punts and ferries were a regular feature on New Zealand rivers, but today few ferries remain and the Clutha punt is said to be the only one left in the Southern Hemisphere (though just how reliable this information is is anyone's guess). Operating since 1896, this unique craft uses the prow of the punt and large rudders to direct the flow of the current to self propel the punt across the river on overhead wires. The punt was part of a network of transport that offers a regular shipping service between Tuapeka Mouth and Balclutha. (Clutha is the ancient Gaelic name of the Clyde River in Scotland). Today the punt only operates 8 a.m. to 10 a.m. and 4 p.m. to 6 p.m. on weekdays so time your trip accordingly.

> Tuapeka Mouth is 20 km north-west of Balclutha.

◀◀ Sinclair Wetlands, Taieri Plains

While we no longer have any doubt as to the importance of wetlands to the environment, more often than not they are not exactly the most exciting places to visit. By their very nature they are damp, muddy and flat; it is often hard to see anything; in winter they flood; and in summer they dry out and

smell bad. The Sinclair Wetlands, however, are fortunate in having two small islands, linked by a high causeway that not only allow the visitor to walk deep into the wetland itself but also have excellent views over the entire reserve. These wetlands are also the testament to the vision of one man, Horrie Sinclair. Horrie (Horace) purchased land in 1960 and allowed it to revert back to its original state, thus saving one of the country's most important wetlands. Now covering 315 hectares, and together with the adjoining lakes Waihola and Waipori, these wetlands are all that remains of the huge swamp that covered most of the Taieri Plain, that has long since been drained for farmland. In addition to 40 bird species known to breed here, another 45 species have been recorded in the wetland. There is camping and backpacker accommodation on site.

> 854 Berwick Claredon Road, South Taieri. This road runs west of Lakes
> Waihola and Waipori just off SH1 south of Mosgiel, ph 03 486 2654;
> donation.

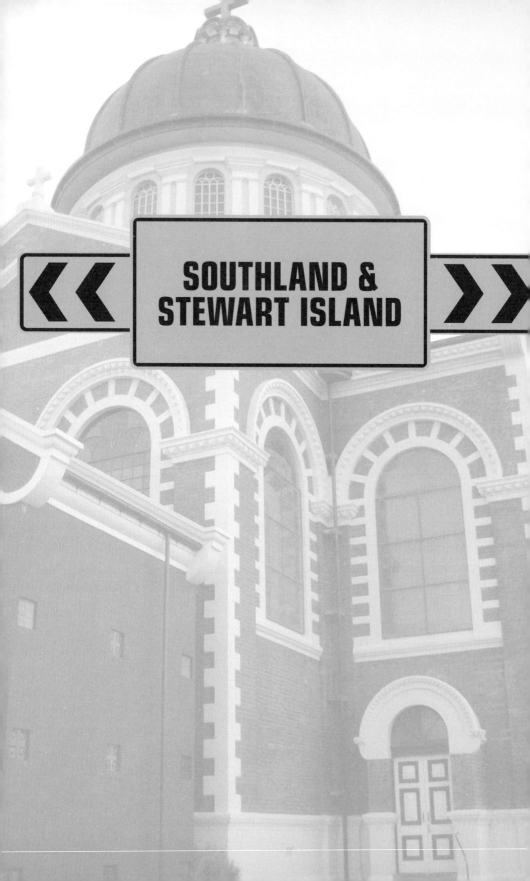

SOUTHLAND & STEWART ISLAND

Bluff

Even though the famed Paua House is no more, Bluff is still a good place to visit. Claimed to be the oldest town in New Zealand, Bluff has seen its fortunes wax and wane over the years. However, Bluff is what it is, an old port town – a bit rough around the edges, a bit windblown, but with a charm all of its own in a battered sort of way. Most people stopping here are either travelling to Stewart Island or just standing for the shortest time possible in the cold wind to take a quick snapshot of the famous signpost at Stirling Point, before jumping in their cars and heading off (it is not even the southernmost point of the South Island, but it is the end of SH1).

That said, Bluff has one of the best small museums in the country, with a strong emphasis on local maritime history. There are displays on whaling, the oyster industry and shipwrecks, an extensive collection of historical photographs, a working steam engine from the *TST Awarua*, and, outside, a real oyster boat – the *Monica II* – which you can go inside.

On the coast, starting from Stirling Point, is a great walk, the Foveaux Walkway. Sure, it's a bit exposed, but a brisk walk in the fresh air will do you the world of good, so wrap up warm and off you go. This superb coastal walk on an excellent flat track winds around the rocky shore of Bluff Hill through tough, salt-resistant flax and hebes to a lookout point with views both far to the west and to the offshore islands. Just off the coast on Dog Island is New Zealand's oldest and tallest lighthouse. At 36 metres, the light was essential to guide shipping through these dangerous waters and first began operating in 1865.

From the Foveaux Walkway, a track leads up to the top of Bluff Hill (265 m), or you can return via the Glory Track, which is much more sheltered. This track takes it name from the English ship *Glory*, which was wrecked on the rocks below – ironically, while taking on board the local pilot. Despite the proximity to constant salt-laden winds and spray, the even temperature and consistent rainfall have created a forest landscape that is verdant and lush. Containing many fine old trees including kamahi, kahikatea, rimu and rata, the track passes a substantial WWII gun emplacement and a low concrete lookout pit, both built in 1942.

◀◀ Clifden Suspension Bridge

When built in 1899, this was the longest span of any bridge in New Zealand at 115 metres, and replaced a punt across the Waiau River. Like most suspension bridges, Clifden has a grace that derives from a combination of good engineering and good design. The bridge remained in use until 1978, and is now open to pedestrians. Add to that an attractive limestone gorge, a pleasant picnic spot and a fast-flowing river, and the Clifden Suspension Bridge is well worth the stop.

12 km north of Tuatapere, Western Southland.

◀◀ Cosy Nook/Mullet Bay

Yes, it is a nook, but it's far from cosy! Mullet Bay, more popularly known as Cosy Nook, is a tiny rocky haven on this wild coastline, and until recently was home to a small fishing fleet. Huddled around the cove were numerous little huts, built out of cast-off materials that were temporarily occupied by fishermen. While the fishing fleet and most of the old huts have gone, a handful of small cottages still cling to the rocky shore, of which the 'Polyfilla Villa' is a classic.

Signposted 5 km east of Orepuki and 5 km from SH99, west of Riverton.

Gore

◀◀ Croydon Aircraft Company

Kiwi ingenuity is a constant source of surprise. At Mandeville, just west of Gore, the Croydon Aircraft Company has successfully based an international business restoring biplanes, in particular the de Havilland Tiger Moth. Now fancy that! It is an appropriate home for such an enterprise as an airfield has existed here since the 1920s. It's a very friendly place, too, and they allow visitors to see a range of projects in various stages of restoration, or you can take a flight in a Tiger Moth.

Right alongside the grass runway is an adjoining restaurant appropriately

named 'The Moth'. Now decorated with an aviation theme, the restaurant was originally the Old Railway Hotel and was the closest pub to Gore when that town was 'dry' in the early years of the twentieth century.

SH94, Mandeville, www.croydonaircraft.com, ph 03 208 9755; donation.

Eastern Southland Gallery

What do you call a moron from Gore? A Goron! Okay, a bad joke, but it accurately reflects the opinion held by many about Gore – albeit clearly an opinion held by those who haven't been to Gore lately. Apart from trout fishing, the Hokonui Moonshine Festival, Hokonui Fashion Awards, Croydon Aircraft Company – and not to mention good coffee and food – Gore has one of the finest art galleries in the country. Nicknamed the 'Goreggenheim', the gallery received a major boost with the gift of a collection from John Money, an ex-New Zealander now living in Baltimore. Along with the art collection, money was also made available to redevelop the 1910 historic Carnegie Library into a modern art gallery.

The Eastern Southland Gallery now holds fine collections by New Zealand artists such as Ralph Hotere, Rita Angus and Theo Schoon. In fact it holds over 50 pieces by Hotere, making this the largest collection of his works in New Zealand. However, what takes the visitor totally by surprise is the amazing collection of African art, the likes of which you are unlikely to see elsewhere in New Zealand. Mainly from the Bambarra, Dogon and Baga regions of West Africa, these carvings feel surprisingly contemporary and their size alone makes them impressive.

Hokonui Drive, opposite the information centre. Open Monday to Friday 10 a.m. to 4.30 p.m., weekends and public holidays 1 p.m. to 4 p.m., closed Christmas Day, Boxing Day, New Year's Day and Good Friday, ph 03 208 9907; donation.

Fleming's Creamoata Mill

You either hated or loved 'Sergeant Dan, the Creamoata Man'. You hated him if you HAD to eat your Creamoata porridge, or loved him if your idea of the perfect breakfast was rolled oats with brown sugar and cream. Dominating

the centre of Gore is the old Creamoata Mill, complete with a huge 'Sergeant Dan' painted down the side of the building.

The iconic 'Creamoata Man' was an advertising device from the 1920s designed to promote Creamoata porridge made from locally grown oats. The main building was constructed in 1892, while the 30-metre chimney dates from 1912, and is classified Category 1 by the Historic Places Trust.

Gorton Street, Gore, in the middle of Gore – and if you can't find it you need glasses!

Hokonui Moonshine Museum

With the advent of prohibition in 1900, locals set up illegal stills in the nearby bush-cloaked Hokonui Hills, and for over 50 years (and 30 arrests) produced what was regarded as the best bush whisky in the country. In particular, the McRae family, originally a clan from the Scottish Highlands who settled in the district in the 1870s, managed to dodge the law, producing a fine dram for over 80 years. The Hokonui Moonshine Museum tells this story, among others, but what makes this place hugely appealing is that it is both informative and entertaining in a way most museums seldom achieve.

Here you will find a recreation of an illegal bush still, as well as the story of the people behind the stills and the law enforcers who set out to catch them. The history of the temperance movement is also outlined, and its strong connection with the early politicisation of women. At one point in the museum, visitors have to choose between the Bar and Temperance Hall – although those who choose the Bar eventually find themselves back in the Temperance Hall. Whisky from the original McRae recipe is now produced legally and for sale at the information centre, along with Hokonui whisky chocolates. While on the last weekend in February, Gore is packed as locals turn out for the Hokonui Moonshine Festival, a celebration of food, music, and of course the famous Hokonui whisky. You can even hire out the pre-prohibition bar for a private function. Miss Gore and you will miss one of the best museum experiences in the country.

16 Hokonui Drive, SH98. The Moonshine Museum, Gore Heritage Centre and Information Office are all in the same building. Open Monday to Friday 8.30 a.m. to 4.30 p.m., weekends and public holidays 9.30 a.m. to

3.30 p.m. (summer) and 1 p.m. to 3.30 p.m. (winter), closed Christmas Day, New Year's Day and Good Friday, ph 03 203 9288; entrance fee to Moonshine Museum.

Forest Hill and Tussock Creek Reserves, Central Southland

Heddon Bush, Ryal Bush, Gummies Bush, Centre Bush, Spar Bush, Mabel Bush, Grove Bush, Wreys Bush, Otaitai Bush, Wrights Bush and Myross Bush are all Southland names that refer to the vast forests that once covered the Central Southland plain. Today there is hardly a stick of native bush left standing.

These two adjoining reserves, just southwest of Winton, contain the only native bush left in Central Southland, and even this was milled for the larger trees. The contrast between the dense bush, the open farmland of the plains, and the stark grassy hills could not be greater. However, this bush contains a surprising number of native birds, a cave complete with cave wetas, a giant rata tree, huge native tree fuchsias, and a good lookout point over the plain.

The track from the Tussock Hill end of the reserve is one of the most beautifully graded bush tracks in the country and can only have been built by someone with roading experience rather than the local scouts on the weekend! It is so gradual and so well graded that you hardly know you are walking uphill. If you're looking for a bush walk to stretch your legs, this is a pretty good option in Southland.

There are two entrances to the reserve off SH6, 5 km south of Winton.

Niagara Falls and Waikawa

It's good to have a sense of humour, and these falls are so tiny that an early surveyor named them after the more impressive Niagara Falls in North America that he had not long visited. No more than half a metre high if that, the Niagara Falls are located on the Waikawa River on the way to Curio Bay and just north of the township of Waikawa.

This town, originally a whaling station, is almost as tiny as the falls themselves and has a small local museum in the old school packed with historic photographs, old Maori adzes, moa bones and local memorabilia. One curious exhibit is an embroidery made by local man Herbert Campbell

while a POW during World War I. Whatever your thoughts on this as an appropriate pastime for a soldier, to his credit he made a very good job of it with incredibly neat and precise stitching.

7 km north of Waikawa in Eastern Southland (Catlins Road).

⟨⟨ Otautau War Memorial

Otautau is a pretty small town on the banks of the Aparima River, at the foot of the Longwood Range, and not being on the way to anywhere it doesn't attract a lot of visitors. The town, however, has an unusual war memorial; two World War I field guns, one Turkish and one German. Apparently they were presented to the town in 1921, but how exactly they were acquired is open to speculation.

I like to think that a few of the local Otautau lads said, 'Hey, let's take a couple of these guns home', and somehow managed to sneak them on board a ship and haul them back to Godzone. Who knows, but imagine trying to slip a couple of field guns past customs these days! Strangely enough, the war memorial guns were in fact borrowed during World War II to train gunners, but were thankfully returned to their rightful place in Otautau where today they form the town's local war memorial.

Main Street, Otautau.

⟨⟨ Saint Mary's Basilica, Invercargill

In strongly Presbyterian Invercargill, it comes as a surprise that the most imposing church is not Protestant but Catholic. Designed by renowned church architect F W Petre and built in 1905, the dome of St Mary's dominates the city's skyline. Perhaps the local Catholics felt they needed to make a bold statement about their presence in the town, as the building, while tall, has a very modest ground-floor plan reflecting more accurately the true size of the Catholic congregation.

Tyne Street, Invercargill.

◀◀ Slope Point

Standing on Slope Point you really do wonder why you came. Bleak, and so windswept that even the grass can't stand up straight, Slope Point's sole claim to fame is that, at 46.4 degrees south, it is the most southerly point of the South Island – just a tad further south than Bluff. Just before you get there, check out the macrocarpa trees on the right – it's so windy that they have no greenery on their south side and only grow to the height of a hedge (at least the wind saves on hedge trimming).

The point is a cold 20-minute walk from the end of a gravel road and is marked by a post pointing to various distant spots around the world. The trick is to walk as fast as possible, dressed as warmly as possible, spend the least time possible, take a photo as quickly as possible, and then hurry back to your car, laughing like a drain at how idiotic you were to come all this way to see bugger all and freeze your bum off at the same time! But let's face it, a good laugh is worth the trip – though remember that it's closed for lambing from 1 September to 1 November.

6 km south of Haldane, Eastern Southland.

Stewart Island

◀◀ Cook's Globe, Rakiura Museum, Stewart Island

When Captain James Cook sailed around the South Island early in 1770 mapping the coast as he went, he made one of his few rare mistakes and assumed that Stewart Island was a peninsula. The Rakiura Museum holds a most remarkable globe in that it is only one of two such globes in the world with a map of New Zealand showing Stewart Island as a peninsula linked to the mainland. The other mistake Cook made was exactly the opposite, in that he thought the Banks Peninsula was an island, and this too is shown on the globe.

The strait was, of course, well known to Maori, but the first European to discover the passage was an American sealer, O F Smith in 1804, who not surprisingly marked it on his chart as Smith's Strait. On his return to Sydney in 1806 he reported his discovery to the Governor of New South

Wales. Eventually, and no one is quite sure how, the strait became known as Foveaux Strait, named after Major Joseph Foveaux, the Lieutenant-Governor of New South Wales, who never actually set foot in New Zealand.

Ayr Street, Oban. Open 10 a.m. to 12 noon Monday to Saturday, 12 noon to 2 p.m. Sunday; entrance fee.

Kiwi Watching

Most New Zealanders have never seen our national bird the kiwi in the wild, though in certain places it is not hard to hear them at night in the bush. Here on Stewart Island the kiwi has developed strange and unusual habits. The island has a substantial brown kiwi population of around 20,000 birds (40 times the human population), and while usually a solitary bird, on Stewart Island kiwi sometimes form family groups and are often active during the day as well as nocturnally.

At Mason Bay, kiwi come out of their usual bush habitat and scuttle down to the beach at night to feed on sand hoppers. While there is still no guarantee of seeing the bird *au naturel*, Stewart Island will probably be your best chance. There are several operators on the island who organise kiwi viewing trips. Visit: www.stewartisland.co.nz.

Waipapa Point

First of all, if you are driving 5 km south of Otara in Auckland you are way off track, as *this* Otara is well and truly in Eastern Southland. This surprisingly attractive spot on a rather inhospitable coastline is dominated by the historic lighthouse built in 1884 – the last wooden lighthouse to be built in the country.

The light was erected in response to New Zealand's worst shipping disaster, which occurred in the early hours of 29 April 1881 when the *Tararua*, sailing from Dunedin to Bluff, struck the Otara Reef just to the north of Waipapa Point. Although the weather was fair, the seas became rough on the incoming tide and several lifeboats were swamped as soon as they were

launched. Eventually the ship broke in two, and despite being clearly visible from shore, few survived the wild surf. Many of the 131 who perished are buried in the 'Tararua Acre' just to the east of the point. The beach below the lighthouse is often frequented by sea lions.

5 km south of Otara, Eastern Southland.

FIORDLAND

Fiordland is a huge national park with an area in excess of 1,252,000 hectares, but much of its terrain is very wild and difficult to access unless you come well equipped for serious tramping. The road to Milford, while no doubt spectacular, is packed with visitors during the summer months, and during the peak of the season up to 100 buses make the trip to Milford Sound each day. But it's still possible to get away from the crowds even in the middle of summer.

Gunn's Camp

In 1926, David Gunn purchased land in the Hollyford Valley, farming cattle and guiding tourists until his death in 1955. His son Murray returned intending only to tidy up his father's affairs – a visit that continued for another 50 years until, at the age of 81, Murray retired to Te Anau. A larger-than-life personality, it was Murray who created the camp that today is still one of a kind.

Located on the banks of a glacial stream, the camp has no cellphone coverage, no electricity (generators provide power in the evening until 10 p.m.), and no phone lines, although they do now have a satellite internet connection. This is truly the place to get away from it all. In addition to camping and campervan sites, there is accommodation in old 1930s Public Works huts, the largest of which originally housed families and come complete with a range for cooking and heating.

A small museum (part of the store) houses Murray's collection of Hollyford memorabilia, though sadly an earlier museum burnt down. While you're at the store, don't miss checking out 'Murray's Fridge'. With no refrigeration on site, drinks are kept cool across the road in a stream, and when you buy a drink you take the warm bottle of drink across the road and swap it with the cold one already in the water. The store also has for sale the rare bowenite greenstone, a variation of pounamu only found in the Hollyford Valley.

Gunn's Camp is located 5 km down the Lower Hollyford Road from the junction with the Milford Road. Email: gunnscamp@ruralinzone.net.

⟨⟨ **Hollyford Airstrip**

If you're not keen on flying, this airstrip will send your head into a spin – so don't even go and look if you are scared of flying! At first glance it just looks like a narrow strip of road, and if there wasn't a sign indicating that this is a landing strip you would never know.

The ultimate bush airstrip, the 'runway' is narrow and very short with the bushes on each side trimmed back just enough to clear the wings. The strip is used to ferry trampers, mountaineers and hunters in and out of the valley, and if you want to see planes land and take off, check with the friendly people at Gunn's Camp store who might know when arrivals are due at this 'airport'.

Hollyford Airstrip is located 6 km down the Lower Hollyford Road from the junction with the Milford Road. Email: gunnscamp@ruralinzone.net.

⟨⟨ **Humboldt Falls**

The total height of these falls is 275 metres (the Sky Tower in Auckland is 328 metres), though they fall in three stages, of which the tallest single drop is 134 metres. The walk is an easy 30 minutes return through bush, but the view of the falls is quite a distance across the Humboldt Creek and naturally they are more impressive after heavy rain.

Humboldt Falls are located 8 km down the Lower Hollyford Road from the junction with the Milford Road.

⟨⟨ **Lake Hauroko and the 1000-year-old Totara**

Located in the southern part of the park, this lake attracts few visitors partly due to the location away from the tourist trail and the fact that it's a 32-km drive into the lake, of which 20 km is pretty rough gravel.

At 462 metres, Lake Hauroko is New Zealand's deepest lake, and one of the 10 deepest lakes in the world. Mind you, 460-odd metres starts to look pretty ordinary against the deepest lake in the world, Baikal, in southeast Siberia, at an incredible 1637 metres. Beautiful, wild and undeveloped, Hauroko stretches deep into the mountains, and while there is a boat launching ramp, the lake is subject to very high winds and can quickly turn extremely rough.

In 1968 the remains of a highborn Maori woman were discovered in a cave on Mary Island, in the middle of the lake. Believed to have been placed there around 1600, she was found buried in a sitting position.

There is a three-hour walk through beech forest on the northern side of the lake to a great lookout point, and for the more hardy the Dusky Track begins from the head of the lake and can be accessed by boat (prearranged) or by guided walk.

Just 5 km down the road to Lake Hauroko is the Lillburn–Monowai Road, an 18-km gravel no-exit road with a grove of truly majestic trees at the very end that includes an ancient totara. Worn and weary, massive and magnificent, the 1000-year-old Hall's totara looks every bit its age among the surrounding totara, rimu, beech and kahikatea. The trees are thickly hung with mosses, the ground is totally covered in lush crown ferns, and the forest is alive with the sound of the bellbird. The walk to the trees is easy and takes around 20 minutes, and while it's a long drive down a gravel road for such a short walk, the trees here are especially impressive.

> From Tuatapere, drive 13 km north to Clifden on SH99 and then turn into the Lake Hauroko Road. Lake Hauroko is 32 km down this road and the totara grove is 23 km.

⟨⟨ Lake Marian and the Marian Falls

Just 1 km down the Hollyford Road from the junction with the Milford Road is a short walk that will take you through deep bush to a spectacular mountain basin above the snow line. The walk begins across a swing bridge (always a good start) and then follows a rushing mountain stream through lush beech forest steadily uphill. Only 10 minutes into the walk are the Marian Falls, where a gantry above the stream looks down over the falls – which to be honest are more a cascade than your typical waterfall, but attractive nonetheless.

From there is a steady uphill climb to Lake Marian situated in a magnificent hanging valley at 695 metres above sea level and surrounded by the towering Darran Mountains, snow-capped even in the warmest months. Apart from the area around the Milford Tunnel, this walk is the easiest way for the casual visitor to experience the grandeur of a true alpine landscape away from the tour buses and bustling crowds.

The track begins on the left, 1 km down the Lower Hollyford Valley Road from Marian Corner, the junction of the Milford and Hollyford Roads.

Lake Monowai

Lake Monowai has had a really bad rap. Usually used as an example of poor environmental planning, it is in reality a really lovely lake and every time I have been here I've had the place to myself. The lake's less fortunate reputation comes from the water level being raised two and a half metres in 1926 to increase the lake's capacity for hydroelectric power generation. The result was an ugly shoreline of dead trees that are still visible (though only in a minor way) over 80 years later.

The distinct U shape disguises the size of the lake, which is relatively large at over 30 square km, and its shape is reflected in the Maori name that means 'channel full of water'. Stretching deep into the mountains, Monowai was formed by glacial action with only one small river – the exotically named Electric River – flowing into the head of the lake. From the road end there are two good walking tracks to huts that both take around six hours one way, but a short walk to the lookout point will take around 30 minutes return.

The turnoff to Lake Monowai is 10 km off SH99 near Blackmount School.

INDEX

253